# UNIFORMS
## OF
# WORLD WAR II

CHARTWELL
BOOKS, INC.

Published by
**CHARTWELL BOOKS, INC.**
A Division of
**BOOK SALES, INC.**
114 Northfield Avenue
Edison, New Jersey 08837

Artworks created by Malcolm McGregor and Pierre Turner

ISBN: 0 7858 0939 2

Editorial and design by
Brown Packaging Books Ltd
Bradley's Close
74-77 White Lion Street
London N1 9PF

Editor: Anne Cree
Design: Colin Hawes

Printed in Singapore

# CONTENTS

# Introduction

This book presents a comprehensive study of the uniforms worn by participants in World War II. With the aid of superb full-colour artworks it has been possible to talk about not only the actual uniform, its manufacture, materials and distinctive features, but also about the different-coloured piping, breast, arm and collar insignia, and the various awards displayed on military attire.

The text accompanying each uniform artwork necessarily concentrates on the clothing itself, but where space has permitted there are also details of the composition of units, on land, sea and in the air, and the weapons used by fighting men and women during the greatest conflict the world has ever seen. Where the uniform of a particular unit in a specific theatre is featured, information is also provided on the actions in which the unit participated. There are two reasons for this. First, to give the maximum amount of information to help build a more complete picture of the individual fighting man illustrated. Second, the battle casualties stated in this book remind the reader that armies are raised to fight and, if necessary, die.

To those who took part in these chaotic and terrible engagements, any deficiencies in their clothing soon became apparent, for let it not be forgotten that most nations began the war with uniforms designed for World War I or even earlier conflicts. In addition, as the weather and the stresses of combat took their toll, the state of the uniforms portrayed in this book deteriorated rapidly: the men of the German 6th Army who surrendered at Stalingrad in February 1943 resembled a horde of beggars, their uniforms in rags.

As the war progressed, the armies of the major belligerents developed uniforms that were more suitable for the modern battlefield, and by 1945 the American and Russian armies in particular were wearing utilitarian clothing. Even the German Army, which by 1944 was suffering from shortages in all things, managed to clothe its men in modern-looking disruptive-pattern uniforms. However, whatever the uniform, the reader should not forget that hundreds of thousands of servicemen were to lose their lives.

**Peter Darman**

# Germany

*The German soldier was one of the most professional and tenacious combatants of World War II. Despite the myth of the German Army being fully motorised, in reality the bulk of the army was made up of infantry divisions whose battalions relied on road or rail transport for strategic movement, and their feet for tactical movement.*

# *Corporal Infantry Regiment*

This *Unteroffizier* (corporal) of a line infantry regiment wears a field-grey blouse with dark blue collar and stone-grey trousers, which were later discontinued and replaced by a field-grey type. This combat uniform was typical of the early period of the war, and was a development of a uniform originally worn in World War I. Indeed, it included many traditional Prussian features which dated back to the Napoleonic Wars, though these were subsequently updated and modified to make them more suitable for wear on a modern uniform.

The aluminium lace around the collar and on the shoulder straps indicates that this soldier is a commissioned officer (all insignia were made from machine-embroidered grey artificial silk thread), while his MP 38 submachine gun shows he is a *Gruppenführer*, a section leader in charge of 10 men.

During the first campaign of the war German infantry were well equipped, even down to shiny helmets complete with the Nazi eagle and national colours. The basic German individual field kit was made up of an integrated system of items designed to complement each other in their wear and practical use. This field equipment at the beginning of the war consisted of a leather belt (to which two carbine pouches were attached), belt support straps, bags and pouches. It was a well thought-out system.

| | |
|---|---|
| *Date:* | *September 1939* |
| *Unit:* | *infantry regiment* |
| *Rank:* | *Corporal* |
| *Theatre:* | *eastern Europe* |
| *Location:* | *Poland* |

# Corporal
# 1st Panzer
# Regiment

In 1935 the Nazis introduced a special black uniform for crews of enclosed panzer (armoured) vehicles. A notable feature of this uniform was the black padded beret which served as a crash helmet. This, together with the short double-breasted jacket and long baggy trousers, made it very practical and thus popular with tank crews. Originally only to be worn when on duty with the vehicle, the uniform's distinctive black collar and silver death's head badge contributed in no small way to the *esprit de corps* of the panzer arm.

This corporal of the 1940 French campaign wears the special armoured units' black collar patches with a 'skull and crossbones' badge with pink piping. Tank crews normally wore only a waistbelt and pistol holster on their person, all other kit being stowed away in the vehicle.

During the Polish and French campaigns a panzer division consisted of two tank regiments of two battalions each, a battalion having four companies with 32 tanks in each. In reality, however, this strength of 561 tanks (including reserves and staff vehicles) was rarely achieved, an average of about 320 being the norm. The tanks were a mixture of Mk I and Mk II light tanks and a few of the heavier Mk III and Mk IV panzers.

Note the Iron Cross and Tank Battle Badge, both worn on the left breast pocket. The latter was instituted on 20 December 1939 and was awarded in silver to tank crews and in bronze to support troops.

| | |
|---|---|
| **Date:** | *May 1940* |
| **Unit:** | *1st Panzer Regiment* |
| **Rank:** | *Corporal* |
| **Theatre:** | *western Europe* |
| **Location:** | *France* |

# *Lieutenant*
# Jagdgeschwader 26 III Gruppe

**Luftwaffe Lieutenant Joachim Müncheburg of *Jagdgeschwader 26* (JG 26), a Luftwaffe fighter unit. The unit was formed in 1937 under the designation JG 234, and was equipped with Messerschmitt Bf 109 fighters by the time World War II broke out in 1939. JG 26 was organised in three *Gruppen*, each having a strength of 30 aircraft.**

Members of the German Air Sport Association started to wear a blue-grey uniform in 1933. It was this organisation which provided the bulk of the cadre for the new Luftwaffe, so naturally the uniform its members wore formed the basis for the air force uniform, which was displayed in public for the first time in March 1935. The Luftwaffe uniform consisted of headgear of peaked cap with artificial mohair band, tunic (worn open with shirt and tie), and either matching long trousers and black shoes or breeches with high boots. The uniform bore a close resemblance to the blue-grey attire of the British Royal Air Force.

Lieutenant Müncheburg is seen here sporting the Knight's Cross, Iron Cross 1st and 2nd Class, and pilot and wound badges. JG 26 was deployed during the Battle of Britain to give fighter cover to bombers and to destroy RAF Spitfires and Hurricanes in the air. The unit was first committed in mid-August 1940. A month later Müncheburg had scored his twentieth victory and was awarded the Knight's Cross. By the time of his death in action on 23 March 1943 he had gained 135 victories.

| | |
|---|---|
| *Date:* | *September 1940* |
| *Unit:* | *Jagdgeschwader 26* |
| *Rank:* | *Lieutenant* |
| *Theatre:* | *northwest Europe* |
| *Location:* | *Pas de Calais* |

# Lance-Corporal Infantry Regiment

**A German lance-corporal during the early stages of Operation 'Barbarossa', the German invasion of Russia, which began on 22 June 1941. At this time his uniform was basically the same as the uniform which was worn at the beginning of the war. However, economy measures were starting to filter down to front-line units.**

The most important of these economy measures was that the army uniform began to lose the dark bluish-green badge cloth that had appeared on the greatcoat collar, shoulder straps, field blouse and on the rank badges worn on the sleeve. In its place field-grey was used, a colour which was also rapidly replacing the grey trousers. In addition, a colour termed 'mouse-grey' was replacing the white or silver of the thread used in the manufacture of insignia and rank distinction.

In the German Army NCOs wore the basic soldier's uniform – a practice which differed from many other European armies, where NCOs wore officers' uniform – but with silver lace on the tunic collar and shoulder straps, and rank badges on the left upper sleeves.

This soldier has attached camouflage material to his helmet by means of a piece of rubber cut from an inner tube. His main weapon is the Bergmann MP 34 submachine gun, while his secondary armament consists of a 9mm Luger pistol stuffed into his left boot. Hanging from his belt on the left can be seen a bayonet and an entrenching tool.

| | |
|---|---|
| **Date:** | *June 1941* |
| **Unit:** | *infantry regiment* |
| **Rank:** | *Lance-Corporal* |
| **Theatre:** | *Eastern Front* |
| **Location:** | *western USSR* |

# Colonel-General Third Panzer Group

*Generaloberst* (Colonel-General) Hermann Hoth, commander of the Third Panzer Group, in Russia in 1941. (A panzer group consisted of approximately three panzer corps made up of five panzer and four motorised divisions.) Hoth is wearing the new pattern field cap for officers, which was introduced in 1938. He sports the Knight's Cross of the Iron Cross at his collar.

Like other ranks of the German Army, he wears two badges on his head-dress: the Nazi eagle and the black and red cockade of Germany. He wears gold piping and a gold embroidered eagle to denote his rank of general. The collar patches are of traditional design: gold on scarlet.

Hoth, like other German Army officers, displays his rank on his shoulder straps, with three cords (two gold and one silver) interlaced to denote the rank of general. His gold buttons and silver 'pips' indicate his rank. The cords were made of bright gold and silver thread, or of frosted yellow or grey thread for field uniforms to give a matt appearance.

He wears an obsolete *Reichswehr*-pattern tunic with slash side pockets and breeches with red stripes. Like most German soldiers at this time, Hoth also sports a pair of marching boots, though these began to disappear from 1943, to be replaced by British-type anklets and ankle boots. Hoth was one of Germany's leading tank commanders. He fought valiantly, but was unable to relieve Stalingrad in 1942 or to achieve victory at Kursk in 1943.

| | |
|---|---|
| *Date:* | *June 1941* |
| *Unit:* | *Third Panzer Group* |
| *Rank:* | *Colonel-General* |
| *Theatre:* | *Eastern Front* |
| *Location:* | *western USSR* |

# Lieutenant Panzer Regiment

**This German Army lieutenant is wearing the special black clothing for crews of enclosed armoured vehicles. He is also a veteran of the Spanish Civil War. In his button hole he wears the ribbon of the Iron Cross, 2nd Class, and next to it sports the Condor Legion Tank Badge, Iron Cross 1st Class and Wound Badge. The latter award was worn on the left breast pocket of the tunic or just below the pocket. It was issued in three classes: gilt, silver and black.**

The first Wound Badge was instituted before World War II, on 22 May 1939, for German military personnel wounded in the Spanish Civil War. Its design was essentially the same as that used in World War I, but with a swastika added in the centre.

By the time of this artwork, 1941, a German panzer division consisted of about 15,600 men and up to 200 armoured vehicles: one tank regiment of two or three battalions (each made up of three companies), a panzergrenadier brigade of two (sometimes three) regiments, an artillery regiment and the divisional support units, such as anti-tank battalions of anti-tank and reconnaissance troops.

Note the special black collar patches with a 'skull and crossbones' badge with pink piping. This piping, the 'arm and service' colours the Germans called *Waffenfarbe*, denoted the service of which the wearer was a member. The pink piping sported here by this lieutenant indicates armoured troops and anti-tank units.

| | |
|---|---|
| **Date:** | *July 1941* |
| **Unit:** | *panzer regiment* |
| **Rank:** | *Lieutenant* |
| **Theatre:** | *Eastern Front* |
| **Location:** | *western USSR* |

13

# *Lance-Corporal Panzer* Lehr *Regiment*

**Lance-Corporal Friedhelm Ollenschäger is kitted out in wartime walking-out dress. As mentioned on page 9, the black uniform was only worn when on duty with the vehicle, while for walking out the field-grey uniform was worn. NCOs were allowed to wear gloves only on duty.**

Lance-Corporal Ollenschäger's belt, like that worn by millions of other German Army troops, consisted of a simple black·smooth leather design 45mm (1.8in) in width. The buckle was fixed to a leather tongue on the right end which allowed it to be adjusted to fit, and the left end was fitted with a metal catch. The belt was worn with all classes of soldiers' and NCOs' uniforms, including parade, field service and walking out, and was also worn with the greatcoat on garrison duty. In general, leather items were either black, darker shades of brown or, in rarer cases, natural brown or tan.

The *koppelschloss* (belt buckle) was adopted in January 1936 to replace the similar *Reichswehr* model. Made of stamped aluminium and painted field- or matt-grey, it was 64mm (2.5in) wide and 49mm (1.9in) deep.

The general distribution and modification of German equipment was governed by Army Service Instructions and Army Order Books. Unit War Strength Authorisations, War Equipment Authorisations and their Annexes were very specific as to the allocation of particular equipment items to individuals and to types of units.

| | |
|---|---|
| **Date:** | *July 1941* |
| **Unit:** | *Panzer* Lehr *Regiment* |
| **Rank:** | *Lance-Corporal* |
| **Theatre:** | *Eastern Front* |
| **Location:** | *western USSR* |

# Corporal 15th Panzer Division

**This NCO of the 15th Panzer Division is wearing the standard uniform of the Africa Corps. That said, however, in the North African theatre dress regulations were very relaxed in comparison with those of other theatres. This corporal is wearing a *Bergmütze* (peaked field cap), as well as a lightweight tropical field service jacket with the 'death's head' insignia on his lapels and a pair of flared 'riding breeches'.**

The lower half of the uniform is totally impractical for desert wear. The breeches, for example, narrow below the knee to button tightly around the calves and are tucked into lace-up boots. It is doubtful whether this corporal would have persevered with such clothing. Instead he may have opted for something more comfortable and practical for desert conditions.

This NCO is a member of the 15th Panzer Division, which contained two armoured battalions in the 8th Panzer Regiment. Each battalion was made up of three companies, with 20 tanks (initially Panzer IIIs but later Panzer IVs) per company, each divided between four troops. In addition to the artillery regiment, the 15th Infantry Brigade (Motorised) comprised support for the tanks. The brigade's two infantry regiments, the 115th and 200th, each had three battalions of three rifle companies, plus a machine-gun company, an engineer platoon and a signals section. The division also had a reconnaissance battalion, motorcycle battalion and an anti-tank and anti-aircraft battalion.

| | |
|---|---|
| ***Date:*** | *July 1941* |
| ***Unit:*** | *15th Panzer Division* |
| ***Rank:*** | *Corporal* |
| ***Theatre:*** | *Mediterranean* |
| ***Location:*** | *North Africa* |

# Sergeant Assault Artillery Regiment

**This sergeant of an assault artillery unit wears a field-grey version of the special panzer uniform introduced in 1940 for crews of self-propelled guns (later in the war it was also worn by newly formed and equipped *panzergrenadier* divisions). It was worn with a variety of different types of collar patch depending on the unit. The patches on this sergeant's collar are woven in matt silver or grey yarn on a dark green or field-grey background. The red piping around the collar patches indicates artillery, and the shoulder straps are edged with silver braid, which shows his NCO rank.**

This uniform was worn circa 1942, by which time the German Army had experienced the realities of a Russian winter. It is no exaggeration to state that the winter of 1941-42 was a disaster for the *Wehrmacht*: troops were exposed to sub-zero temperatures wearing little more than their totally inadequate field uniforms. With no special winter clothing troops resorted to stuffing newspapers into their tunics and filling their boots with straw in an effort to fend off the bitter cold. The first Russian winter was the beginning of the end for German dress regulations – the result of extreme temperatures, lack of facilities for cleaning and repairing uniforms, and problems in transporting replacement clothing to the front.

Note the wearer's decorations: Knight's Cross at neck, Iron Cross 1st and 2nd Class, General Assault Badge and Wound Badge.

| | |
|---|---|
| *Date:* | *April 1942* |
| *Unit:* | *assault artillery regiment* |
| *Rank:* | *Sergeant* |
| *Theatre:* | *Eastern Front* |
| *Location:* | *Smolensk* |

# Officer
# 90th Light Division
# Africa Corps

**This German Army officer of the Africa Corps (commanded by Erwin Rommel, the famed 'Desert Fox'), is wearing the tropical field cap, which has been bleached white by the sun. Dust was a particular hazard in the desert for both men and vehicles, and so an essential item of clothing was goggles. The greatcoat was a standard-issue pattern, and the wearer usually had shoulder straps to identify his rank. His web belt was the special pattern for officers, complete with round buckle.**

The German Army arrived in North Africa, at Tripoli, in mid-February 1941, in what was to become the famed Africa Corps. However, the campaign in the desert presented immediate problems with the issue of uniforms, forcing Germany to produce a complete range of tropical clothing and equipment in a short space of time. The first efforts – sun helmets, well-tailored tunics and breeches, and laced field boots – proved impractical and were replaced by comfortable clothing. The archetypal German desert uniform soon appeared: field cap with large peak to shield the eyes from the sun, shirt, long trousers gathered at the ankles, or shorts, woollen socks, and leather and canvas boots. The Italian field blouse, the *sahariana*, was more comfortable than its German equivalent, and so many Africa Corps members 'obtained' them for themselves.

The troops had to contend with scorching temperatures during the day, but at night it got very cold and so a greatcoat was essential.

| | |
|---|---|
| *Date:* | *January 1942* |
| *Unit:* | *90th Light Division* |
| *Rank:* | *Officer* |
| *Theatre:* | *Mediterranean* |
| *Location:* | *Tripoli* |

17

# *Officer 15th Panzer Division Africa Corps*

**This Africa Corps lieutenant is wearing the tropical version of the side cap, which was issued to crews of armoured fighting vehicles because it was more convenient than the field cap (its large peak being an encumbrance when worn inside a tank). The lieutenant also wears the insignia from his Continental uniform on his tropical blouse (note the 'death's head' badges on the lapels which he has transferred from his black panzer jacket). This lieutenant also proudly wears the Iron Cross 2nd Class ribbon and badge on the left breast pocket, plus the Silver Tank Assault Badge underneath.**

High-laced tropical field boots and shorts formed part of the basic tropical uniform, as did the field flask. The basic M1931 field flask and drinking cup was an unpainted 794g (28oz) aluminium bottle, in which a metal screw cap was retained by an extension of the vertical leather securing strap. The brown felt insulating cover served both to prevent freezing and also to cool the water when wet. The cover could be removed for cleaning or for replacement via the slit secured by three snaps on the left upper edge. Leather loops were sewn on the front and back for the black leather securing strap, which was also attached via a stud riveted to the bottom of the cover. The securing strap served to retain the cup, and also to attach the canteen to the wearer's bread bag. It was not unusual for two canteens to be issued to each individual in North Africa.

| | |
|---|---|
| *Date:* | *March 1942* |
| *Unit:* | *15th Panzer Division* |
| *Rank:* | *Officer* |
| *Theatre:* | *Mediterranean* |
| *Location:* | *North Africa* |

# 2nd Lieutenant Infantry Regiment

**This infantry 2nd lieutenant in Russia is wearing the standard attire for an officer at the front (note the white piping on his shoulder straps, indicating his membership of the infantry arm). His headgear is the M1938 officers' side cap and his decoration the German Cross in Gold, instituted for distinguished leadership in battle, and forming an intermediate award between the Iron Cross 1st Class and the Knight's Cross.**

Because of the many variants of pistols used by the German Army during the war, there were a large number of different holsters. The most commonly used pistols were the 9mm Luger P08 and Walther P38, 7.65mm Mauser Hsc, Walther PP and PPK, and Sauer M38. Though enlisted men who needed pistols – mortar crewmen, machine gunners, tank and other armoured fighting vehicle crewmen, and those requiring unrestricted movement – were issued pistols, officers had to purchase their own. Generally, officers in combat favoured 9mm calibre, while senior officers and those in support units carried 7.65mm models.

Holsters were made of smooth or pebbled black leather, though some were made of canvas and artificial leather. A typical holster was closed by a large flap to retain and protect the weapon inside. The latter was secured by a strap and stud, either with the strap attached to the holster's body and the stud to the flap, or the other way round. Most had an integral magazine pocket on the side or edge covered by the pistol's protecting flap.

| | |
|---|---|
| *Date:* | *April 1942* |
| *Unit:* | *infantry regiment* |
| *Rank:* | *2nd Lieutenant* |
| *Theatre:* | *Eastern Front* |
| *Location:* | *Orel* |

# *Sergeant* Grossdeutschland *Division*

**The** *Grossdeutschland Panzergrenadier* **Division was made up of two infantry regiments, a heavy weapons battalion, and armoured and artillery support. It was an excellent unit and its members wore a distinctive shoulder strap, which had the letters 'GD', interlaced, embroidered on the straps in white, this being the colour of the infantry.**

The figure illustrated here is an NCO of the *Grossdeutschland* Division's assault-gun detachment. He is wearing the field-grey version of the special panzer uniform. He has distinctive shoulder straps: piped red to indicate the artillery arm, though they retain the 'GD' lettering.

This sergeant is obviously a veteran, as is indicated by the General Assault Badge on his left breast and the just-visible Wound Badge. His other decorations are clearly visible, namely, the Knight's Cross worn around the neck, and the Iron Cross 1st and 2nd Class. The badges on his right arm indicate that he has single-handedly succeeded in destroying two enemy tanks.

Tank destruction badges were awarded in two classes. The 1st class depicted a gilt tank on a gilt band edged with black, while the 2nd depicted a black tank or aircraft on a silver cord edged with black. Four consecutive silver badges could be worn on the sleeve, but with the winning of the fifth the gilt badge was awarded.

This NCO wears the standard German helmet and a pair of marching boots.

| | |
|---|---|
| *Date:* | *July 1943* |
| *Unit:* | Grossdeutschland *Division* |
| *Rank:* | *Sergeant* |
| *Theatre:* | *Eastern Front* |
| *Location:* | *Kursk* |

# Sergeant-Major Military Police

**This figure is a sergeant-major in the Military Police (*Feld-gendarmerie*) in the Africa Corps. He** sports a typical Africa Corps uniform, a distinctive feature of which is the metal gorget and cuff-band – the badges of the German Military Police (MP). German Army regulations stated that all MPs had to wear the gorget on their chest when on duty. The gorget itself had a luminous national emblem and chain, which led to its wearers being nicknamed *Kettenhunde* ('chained dogs').

The Military Police arm and service colour was orange (also the colour for engineer officers), and it appeared as a chevron on the field cap and on the shoulder straps.

Cuff titles, also known as armbands, were issued by the German Army to its soldiers to commemorate outstanding battles or campaigns. They were intended to be worn around the left sleeve cuff of all uniforms, including greatcoats. Africa Corps members were granted two cuff titles. The first, worn on the right sleeve, was adopted on 18 July 1941. The second, which had the same status as a campaign award, was adopted on 15 January 1943. The cuff title was embroidered in silver thread on sandy khaki cloth. By early 1943, the Africa Corps had undergone a number of expansions, and was renamed, in succession, Africa Corps, Panzer Group Africa, then Panzer Army Africa in January 1942, and finally Army Group Africa in February 1943.

| | |
|---|---|
| *Date:* | *1942* |
| *Unit:* | *Military Police, Africa Corps* |
| *Rank:* | *Sergeant-Major* |
| *Theatre:* | *Mediterranean* |
| *Location:* | *North Africa* |

# Private 389th Infantry Division 6th Army

**This rather sorry-looking figure is a German prisoner-of-war taken by the Russians following the fall of Stalingrad. He has stuffed old newspapers and straw under his greatcoat to improve insulation against the bitter cold of the Russian winter, and over his leather boots he wears a pair of straw overboots. The latter were usually issued to soldiers who had to remain stationary when on duty, such as sentries, as it was very difficult to move quickly when wearing them.**

He carries blankets over his right shoulder and a clothing bag in his left hand. In the German Army each soldier in a combat unit issued with a pack received a single M1931 clothing bag (those in rear-area units who did not get a pack were issued with two clothing bags). Originally the bags were field-grey canvas, but from 1941/42 they were manufactured in olive green. The clothing bag was very straightforward: it was a simple single-compartment satchel-like bag which was closed by a flap secured by two buckled leather straps. A leather carrying handle was also fitted to the top edge. For the line infantryman, the contents of the bag included spare clothing items which were needed only on a limited basis in the field: underwear, socks, tunic collar linen and drill uniform.

Despite this soldier's ragged appearance, it should be remembered that by the time of the second winter in Russia the German Army had produced cold-weather clothing for its men, such as special under-clothing and weather-resistant attire.

| | |
|---|---|
| *Date:* | *2 February 1943* |
| *Unit:* | *389th Infantry Division* |
| *Rank:* | *Private* |
| *Theatre:* | *Eastern Front* |
| *Location:* | *Stalingrad* |

# Private Infantry Regiment

**This private in the German Army is wearing the typical uniform of troops serving on the so-called Adriatic Coast Line, an area which stretched from Trieste in Italy to the Greek Isles in the Mediterranean. This particular German soldier is a machine gunner wearing tropical uniform.**

Slung over his right shoulder, this private carries an MG 42, a 7.92mm-calibre weapon, one of which was issued to each rifle squad in the infantry, *Panzergrenadier*, mountain and cavalry regiments. Each gunner carried a replacement parts pouch on the right front of his belt, while a pistol was carried on the left front. The pouch was a rigid black leather box, complete with reinforcing rivets. A leather strap was attached to the lid which fastened to a stud on the pouch's bottom. Inside the pouch was an oil canteen, cleaning brush, two bolt assemblies, a small wrench, bolt carrier, firing pin, firing pin lock and a firing pin retainer. In addition, an asbestos pad for use when handling hot barrels was usually carried under the securing strap. Each machine gunner was also issued with a metal tool kit, which contained a ruptured cartridge extractor, plastic sulphur container, oil can, chamber brush and an anti-aircraft ring sight.

Spare barrels for the weapon were carried in barrel protectors. These lengthwise-hinged steel housings were fitted with a canvas or web sling, and they were carried slung behind the back, two for light machine guns and three for heavy machine guns.

| | |
|---|---|
| *Date:* | *February 1943* |
| *Unit:* | *infantry regiment* |
| *Rank:* | *Private* |
| *Theatre:* | *Mediterranean* |
| *Location:* | *Adriatic* |

# *Private*
# **Panzergrenadier**
# *Division*

This *Panzergrenadier* private, circa 1944, wears a field-grey uniform. This is because all *Panzergrenadier* were, in theory at least, mounted in armoured or semi-armoured vehicles. In reality, by 1944 all field units were experiencing difficulties with equipment and vehicle supplies. Unusually, this soldier carries two 98K rifles and a metal container for a spare MG 42 barrel.

The KAR 98K was the standard infantry rifle of the German Army in World War II. It fired the powerful 7.92mm round and an integral box magazine held five rounds, which were fed into the chamber by working a long bolt above the trigger. The bolt pushed the top round into the breech, then locked it in place by twisting the operating handle downwards.

Ammunition for the rifle was carried in the M1911 cartridge pouch, made from black pebbled leather with three pockets (sometimes with a pocket divider), fastened to a curved leather backing. The pocket lids were secured via a strap which fastened to a stud on the bottom of each pocket. Two leather belt loops and a 'D' or rectangular ring for attachment to the support straps were on the back. Each pouch contained 30 rounds of ammunition; each pocket two five-round loading clips.

| | |
|---|---|
| *Date:* | *April 1944* |
| *Unit:* | panzergrenadier *division* |
| *Rank:* | *private* |
| *Theatre:* | *Eastern Front* |
| *Location:* | *Poland* |

# Senior Sergeant 916th Regiment

*Feldwebel* (Senior Sergeant) Mayer of the 916th Regiment, 352nd Grenadier Division, wears a reed-green denim combat jacket over field-grey trousers. The crude wire mesh over his steel helmet is for the attachment of camouflage foliage. By the time of this artwork, D-Day, 6 June 1944, the German Army field uniform was becoming increasingly grey and baggy as the quality of the material deteriorated. Most insignia were now made in mouse-grey yarn, and arm-of-service colours appeared only on the shoulder straps. The marching boot had been replaced largely by ankle boots and canvas anklets, nicknamed 'retreat gaiters' due to Germany's strategic situation at this time.

On his back Mayer carries a cylindrical gas mask container, green canvas bread bag, water bottle and folded tent quarter. The German Army had three models of carrying case for the gas mask. They were made of fluted steel with a hinged lid, which contained a hinged compartment for spare eyepiece lenses. The lid was held closed by a spring-loaded latch fitted with a web pull strap. Underneath the lid were two small brackets to which an adjustable web-carrying sling was fastened. At the canister's bottom edge, in line with the two small brackets, was a third bracket with a short web support tab and belt hook.

The M1913 tent quarter was a triangular, water-repellent cotton gabardine twill multi-purpose shelter, ground cloth and poncho.

| Date: | 6 June 1944 |
|---|---|
| Unit: | 916th Regiment |
| Rank: | Senior Sergeant |
| Theatre: | northwest Europe |
| Location: | Normandy |

# *1st Lieutenant* Jagdgeschwader 52 *S. Ukraine Army Group*

An *Oberleutnant* (1st Lieutenant) of *Jagdgeschwader 52* on the Eastern Front in 1944. He wears a fur-lined windcheater, a Luftwaffe field cap, service breeches and black leather and suede flying boots (note the altimeter attached to his belt). On his left upper sleeve he wears his rank badge. Special rank badges were worn by Luftwaffe personnel on the upper sleeves of flying uniforms and overalls. The background of these badges matched the colour of the material of the uniform on which they were worn, hence grey blue, sandy brown and other colours were sported by officers and NCOs.

Field-marshal and colonel-general ranks were denoted by oval badges with a yellow embroidered eagle on an oak wreath, with field-marshal having additional white crossed batons at the base of the wreath. The rank badges of all the others were indicated by a combination of wings and bars, in white for officers and NCOs and in yellow for generals.

In the severe cold of the Russian winter, Luftwaffe air crew were fortunate to be able to fly, sleep and eat in their warm, fur-lined clothing. The ground crews were not as fortunate, and so various kinds of underclothing and fur-lined waistcoats for wear underneath uniforms were issued, together with a sheepskin cap with peak and earflaps.

This lieutenant wears the Luftwaffe eagle on his field cap. This differed from the army eagle, denoting an eagle in flight holding a swastika.

| | |
|---|---|
| *Date:* | *April 1944* |
| *Unit:* | Jagdgeschwader 52 |
| *Rank:* | *1st Lieutenant* |
| *Theatre:* | *Eastern Front* |
| *Location:* | *southern Russia* |

# *Major* Stukageschwader 2 *Army Group Centre*

German air ace Major Hans-Ulrich Rudel wears a two-piece flying suit, which was nick-named the 'Invasion Suit'. The outfit had large pockets in which to put maps and survival equipment. Both officers and NCOs wore their rank badges on collar patches and shoulder straps, on the upper sleeves of their flying suits and jackets and on their paratroop smocks.

The shoulder straps and collar patches had a dual function: they served to identify the rank and also the branch of service of the wearer. The rank was shown by the pips on the shoulder straps and by the wings on the collar patches. In addition, the background colour of both the pips and the wings identified the wearer's branch of service. Major Rudel sports a background colour of golden yellow, which indicates his status as that of flying personnel. The shoulder straps consisted of silver double cords: these were plain in the case of junior officers and interlaced, as in Rudel's case, for senior officers.

Rudel wears the Luftwaffe emblem on his right breast. There were several variations on the badge itself; some were embroidered on grey-blue, white or khaki, while others were made in white metal with a brooch pin for the white summer uniform. Major Rudel wears a silver badge for officers; generals wore gold badges, while other ranks wore grey woven badges.

At his neck is the Knight's Cross with Swords and Oakleaves for outstanding military service.

| Date: | *August 1944* |
|---|---|
| Unit: | *Stukageschwader 2* |
| Rank: | *Major* |
| Theatre: | *Eastern Front* |
| Location: | *western USSR* |

# *Private* **Das Reich** *Division*

**This is a Waffen-SS private dressed in typical attire in Russia, early 1942. He is a member of the crack *Das Reich* Division, which, together with the *Leibstandarte*, *Totenkopf* and *Wiking* divisions, were withdrawn from the front in Russia in mid-1942 so that they could be rested and refitted to become *Panzergrenadier* divisions.**

Pre-war the uniform of the Waffen-SS was black in colour, but from 1935 onwards a grey uniform began to be worn on active service. Gradually the soldiers of the SS (the term Waffen-SS – armed SS – was first used in 1940) adopted the field-grey army uniform, though they retained their SS cap badges (a national emblem over a death's head), their SS rank badges on the left collar and their army rank badges on the shoulder straps. Unit emblems were worn on the right collar patch and on the left cuff was worn a narrow black band with silver edging, on which was embroidered the name of the unit. A distinctive feature of the Waffen-SS uniform was the wearing of the field blouse open at the neck with field-grey shirt and black tie.

Before the war the SS had already developed lightweight equipment and camouflage clothing, and soon camouflage smocks and helmet covers were issued to its troops. These features became a distinctive part of Waffen-SS troops' uniform during the war. This soldier wears an M1940 side cap and the fur-lined anorak and overalls which had been designed and manufactured by the SS.

| | |
|---|---|
| ***Date:*** | *February 1942* |
| ***Unit:*** | Das Reich *Division* |
| ***Rank:*** | *Private* |
| ***Theatre:*** | *Eastern Front* |
| ***Location:*** | *western USSR* |

# *Major* Leibstandarte *Division*

**SS-Sturmbannführer (Major) Joachim Peiper of the Waffen-SS *Leibstandarte Adolf Hitler* (LAF), an elite division whose role was to act as Hitler's bodyguard. Peiper wears one of the many winter caps and special one-piece reversible winter tank overalls which were issued in January 1943.**

Waffen-SS officers were required to wear white piping on their head-dress, including their side caps, while general officers had grey lapels on their great-coats.

Waffen-SS officers and NCOs were termed *Führer* (leader) and had rank titles that were entirely different from those worn in the German Army. Officers wore silver aluminium-edged collar patches, while *Waffenfarbe* was worn in the form of piping on the shoulder straps. The collar patches of high-ranking officers, from colonel upwards, were made of black velvet, while cloth was used for all other ranks. Both generals and officers sported an edging 1.5mm (0.06in) wide made of silver aluminium twisted cords around both collar patches, though some officer ranks initially wore edgings made from black and silver aluminium cords.

Initially the first elite SS regiments to be formed – *Leibstandarte Adolf Hitler* (LAH), *Deutschland*, *Germania* and *Der Führer* – wore a regimental device embroidered on the shoulder straps in white silk. Here, Major Peiper wears the LAH cypher in bronzed metal on his shoulder straps and the Knight's Cross at his neck.

| | |
|---|---|
| *Date:* | *March 1943* |
| *Unit:* | Leibstandarte *Division* |
| *Rank:* | *Major* |
| *Theatre:* | *Eastern Front* |
| *Location:* | *Ukraine* |

# *Corporal*
# **Das Reich**
# *Division*

**A typical Waffen-SS corporal of a** *panzer-grenadier* **regiment. This corporal is wearing a peaked service dress cap which differed from the officers' model in that it had a leather chin strap. He also wears a field-grey tunic and trousers, though the blouse is a late war model with plain patch pockets without the pleats.**

The four large pockets were designed to allow the wearer to carry personal effects or extra rounds of ammunition. The triangular embroidered SS eagle on his right upper arm indicates his membership of the Waffen-SS. Rank badges are on the shoulder straps and the left collar patch, and the two lace rings around the cuffs show him to be a *Spiess* or *Stabsscharführer-diensttuer* (acting sergeant-major).

This corporal wears the Waffen-SS rectangular plate belt buckle at his waist, which is manufactured from white metal and is stamped with the motto of the Waffen-SS: *Mein Ehre heist Treue* (Loyalty is my Honour).

The eagle and swastika worn by the SS was different from that which was worn in the German Army. In the 1930s it was smaller, with pointed wings, and the eagle itself was smaller in proportion to the wreath that it clutched. A new eagle was eventually introduced, as in the one illustrated in this artwork, which was larger than the earlier eagle and which also had open wings. The distinctive feature of the newer eagle was that the middle section of each wing was longer than the others.

| | |
|---|---|
| *Date:* | *June 1943* |
| *Unit:* | Das Reich *Division* |
| *Rank:* | *Corporal* |
| *Theatre:* | *Eastern Front* |
| *Location:* | *Kharkov* |

# Private Leibstandarte Division

This private of a tank crew in the *Leibstandarte* Division is wearing a two-piece drill uniform. This version was issued from 1944 onwards to replace the one-piece overall that was brought into service in 1941 in SS camouflage material. Waffen-SS units were among the first to make use of disruptive pattern clothing. The patterns were carefully designed to break up the wearer's outline, with small hard-edged splodges of colour outlined in contrasting colours. The four basic patterns used were 'palm tree', 'pea', 'oakleaf' and 'plane tree'.

The Waffen-SS began designing a new uniform for its troops in 1942, beginning with the M43 drill camouflage uniform: a single-breasted jacket and trousers in a rayon mixture. The follow-on M44 was made of coarse herringbone twill, which was not as warm or as waterproof as the M43. However, by 1944 shortages had forced the Germans to make economies.

On his head this private wears the Waffen-SS black *Feldmütze* (field service side cap), which was similar in style to that worn in other armies during the war. His shoulder straps are piped pink – the panzer arm of service – and carry the *Leibstandarte Adolf Hitler* cypher.

At the beginning of the Russian campaign the Waffen-SS wore the standard German calf-length leather marching boots. However, experience led to the introduction of the more practical *Schnürschuhe* (lace-up ankle boot), which gave greater support to the ankle and thus aided mobility.

| | |
|---|---|
| *Date:* | *April 1944* |
| *Unit:* | Leibstandarte *Division* |
| *Rank:* | *Private* |
| *Theatre:* | *Eastern Front* |
| *Location:* | *Poland* |

# Lieutenant-Colonel Prinz Eugen *Division*

**SS-*Obersturmbannführer* (Lieutenant-Colonel) Schmidhuber of the 7th SS *Freiwilligen-Gebirgs* Division *Prinz Eugen*, one of the five Waffen-SS mountain divisions, the other divisions being *Handschar*, *Nord*, *Skanderbeg* and *Karstjäger*. Schmidhuber wears the standard Waffen-SS mountain troop uniform complete with ski cap, field blouse, mountain trousers, mountain boots and short elasticated puttees.**

The ski cap was soon replaced by the M1943 standard field cap, which was a more practical form of headgear for the environment and which was based on the mountain trooper's cap, which had a shorter visor. It came in several variations with either one or two frontal buttons. The national eagle was sewn either above the frontal 'death's head' badge or on the left-hand side.

Schmidhuber's badges of rank appear on his shoulder straps and left collar patch. Because he is an SS member serving in a unit not entitled to wear the SS runes on his right collar patch, he sports them on his left breast pocket (*Prinz Eugen* was composed of foreign recruits, mainly Romanian and Yugoslav volunteers). In general, foreign detachments wore their own devices on the right collar patch, and *Totenkopf* units wore the 'skull and crossbones' on their right collars. The various branches of the Waffen-SS were, like the army, distinguished by the different colours that were worn on the uniform under the shoulder cords. The piping here is the light green of mountain troops.

| | |
|---|---|
| *Date:* | *April 1944* |
| *Unit:* | Prinz Eugen *Division* |
| *Rank:* | *Lieutenant-Colonel* |
| *Theatre:* | *Eastern Front* |
| *Location:* | *Yugoslavia* |

# Pilot Condor Legion

**This Luftwaffe pilot of the Condor Legion in Spain wears a German uniform re-tailored for the Condor Legion, together with officers' boots. The latter were made of black leather and suede and were lined with lambswool. On his right breast pocket he sports the German 'Spanish' Cross, while above this he wears a Spanish Air Force pilot's brevet.**

In November 1936 Hitler had sent the Condor Legion to Spain to aid the Nationalists in their fight against the Communists. The Legion numbered around 50 bombers, 50 fighters and an auxiliary squadron, plus anti-tank and anti-aircraft units and two tank companies. Its strength was maintained at around 6500, which meant that 16,000 Germans were able to gain valuable military experience in Spain.

The Spanish Civil War provided a highly effective training ground for German Luftwaffe pilots in that it allowed aerial tactics to be perfected. For example, the four-aircraft *Schwarme* tactic was to give many advantages to the Luftwaffe during the early campaigns of World War II. Another aerial tactic, the 'finger four' formation, was found to provide the best compromise between a concentration of fighter firepower on the one hand, and freedom of action in the air on the other. Finally, the dive-bombing tactics which were perfected by the German Air Force during the Spanish Civil War were to be put to devastating use during the *Blitzkrieg* campaigns in Europe in 1939–41.

| | |
|---|---|
| **Date:** | *May 1939* |
| **Unit:** | *Condor Legion* |
| **Rank:** | *Pilot* |
| **Theatre:** | *Spain* |
| **Location:** | *Madrid* |

# Senior Sergeant Anti-Aircraft Artillery Unit

A senior sergeant of an anti-aircraft artillery unit. His blue-grey tunic identifies him as a member of the air force, but his head gear and trousers are unusual. In fact, between 1 April and 30 September – the summer months – before the war, officers and NCOs were allowed to wear a cap with white top and white trousers and shoes, and officers could also wear a white tunic. The latter was identical in cut to the blue-grey tunic shown here. When war broke out, the white-topped cap continued to be worn in Italy, the Mediterranean, southern Russia and sometimes in Germany.

Air force NCOs wore their rank badges on the collar, while senior NCOs wore rank badges additionally on their shoulder straps. Rank was shown on the collar by wings attached to patches of the same colour as those of the officers. Collar patches which were worn on the greatcoat had a strip of lace attached to the patch itself, while collar patches worn on tunics had silver lace stitched all around the collar instead. In addition, white metal pips were worn on the shoulder straps. The red arm of service colour identifies this soldier as being a member of the anti-aircraft artillery.

Note the badge on his left cuff, which shows him to be a qualified armourer. The device is embroidered in matt silver or grey thread on a grey-blue backing (some NCOs' badges had an additional edging of silver twisted cords).

| | |
|---|---|
| *Date:* | *August 1939* |
| *Unit:* | *anti-aircraft artillery unit* |
| *Rank:* | *Senior Sergeant* |
| *Theatre:* | *Germany* |
| *Location:* | *Berlin* |

34

# NCO *Luftwaffe* Staffeln

**The Luftwaffe working dress was either the natural-coloured cotton dress uniform or, as can be seen here, black working overalls. This NCO is wearing a black twill side cap and the overalls, which were made from cotton. This man's rank group is indicated by the grey lace on his overall collar. All Luftwaffe NCOs wore their rank badges on the upper sleeve of their tunic, greatcoat and overalls. This comprised aluminium lace on the shoulder straps, tunic and blouse collar, greatcoat collar patches, and grey lace on the ends of the overall collar.**

This NCO is a member of the Luftwaffe ground crew, who performed essential duties in maintaining aircraft in flying order. By the time war broke out on 1 September 1939, there were 80,000 men in Luftwaffe maintenance and supply units out of a total air force strength of 1,500,000 men (900,000 in anti-aircraft artillery, 25,000 headquarters and administration staff, 50,000 aircrew and other flying personnel, 100,000 in air signals, 60,000 construction personnel and others undergoing training).

The close relationship between the ground crews and aircrews resulted in well-maintained flying machines which were able to perform at optimum efficiency. The result was a staggering victory in Poland: only 285 aircraft lost out of a total strength of 1250 and the loss of only 734 airmen killed.

The Poles, on the other hand, lost 398 aircraft during the campaign most destroyed on the ground.

| | |
|---|---|
| *Date:* | *March 1940* |
| *Unit:* | *Luftwaffe* Staffeln *(Squadron)* |
| *Rank:* | *NCO* |
| *Theatre:* | *northwest Europe* |
| *Location:* | *western Germany* |

# *Major* *Heinkel He 111* Luftflotte 2

**A Luftwaffe major dressed in the one-piece beige canvas flying suit which was issued for summer use. This officer wears a yellow life jacket over the suit, the bright colour being essential for air-sea rescue purposes. His rank of major is denoted by the special uniform badge worn on the upper sleeve of his flying uniform. This particular officer is a bomber commander taking part in the Battle of Britain.**

For the air campaign against Britain in the summer of 1940, Reichsmarschall Göring mustered 2800 aircraft. Against this force, Britain's Fighter Command could only put 650 operational fighters in 52 squadrons into the air. The German strategy was to lure the British into combat by strafing seaports and fighter bases, and then shoot the British fighters out of the sky. However, newly developed radar allowed Britain's Fighter Command to concentrate superior force at vital spots. Nevertheless, sheer weight of numbers meant the Germans were still able to inflict great damage on British airfields and communications and control centres.

Luftwaffe flight clothing usually included a beige linen flight helmet, although this officer has chosen to wear the air force peaked cap, with its chin strap cords in silver to denote officer status. The cockade, oak wreath and side wings were all in one piece and were embroidered on a black cloth backing, which matched the colour of the cap band. The eagle was embroidered on the cloth of the blue-grey uniform.

| | |
|---|---|
| *Date:* | *July 1940* |
| *Unit:* | Luftflotte 2 |
| *Rank:* | *Major* |
| *Theatre:* | *northwest Europe* |
| *Location:* | *France* |

# NCO
# 1st Parachute
# Regiment

**This air force paratrooper NCO wears the uni-
form which was designed within the German
Army for the airborne forces (the army had
organised the first unit of paratroopers). The
overall, or 'bone sack', as it was known, is
made of cotton duck material and is worn
over the field equipment.**

The grey-green combat trousers were full-length
and were worn gathered in at the ankles and tied with
tapes. The ends were tucked into the tops of the jump
boots, and at knee level the outer seam of each leg
there was a concealed opening, which was fastened by
three press-studs. These slits allowed the paratrooper
to reach into his trouser legs and unfasten his knee
protectors. Immediately behind the opening on the
right leg was a pocket designed to carry a gravity
blade knife.

The *Fallschirmjäger* steel helmet was especially
designed to meet the needs of the German paratrooper in action. The helmet provided him with protection
against shrapnel but also against injury from the hard
blows to the head that sometimes occurred during an
airborne landing. The helmet was also shaped to prevent any part of it becoming fouled with rigging or
with parachute harness lines. Inside was a dome-
shaped piece of leather which was held in position by
a band of strong yet flexible aluminium. The latter
was backed with rubber padding and fixed to the helmet shell by four special screws. These screws also
anchored the chin straps to the helmet at the rear and
at the sides.

| | |
|---|---|
| *Date:* | *August 1940* |
| *Unit:* | *1st Parachute Regiment* |
| *Rank:* | *NCO* |
| *Theatre:* | *northwest Europe* |
| *Location:* | *Belgium* |

# Senior Sergeant Messerschmitt Bf 109 Luftflotte 5

**A senior sergeant of flying troops wears the Luftwaffe NCO side cap, which has a white woven Luftwaffe eagle and swastika badge above the black-white-red national cockade on the front of the cap. His tunic is the *Fliegerbluse* (flying blouse), a garment originally intended to be worn under flying suits. The first pattern carried no national emblem or pockets but did have twisted cord, in the arm-of-service colour, around the collar. Originally issued to flying personnel only, it eventually became popular throughout the whole Luftwaffe.**

This version of the blouse is a short, shaped garment with a fly front, which was similar to British battle dress in function. The standard air force eagle badge is sewn onto the right breast. The NCO rank badges are sported on the collar, the rank being indicated by wings attached to patches of the same colour as those of the officers. Senior NCOs were denoted by collar patches containing three wings.

The Luftwaffe introduced two new systems of badges for wear on collar patches and on the flying suit. Air force general officers were further distinguished by white lapels on the undress jacket and greatcoat, with white stripes, called *Lampassen*, on the breeches and trousers.

A Luftflotte did not have a fixed number of aircraft, and it was common for it to contain a variety of aircraft types, such as fighters, fighter-bombers, dive-bombers, ground-attack aircraft and bombers.

| | |
|---|---|
| *Date:* | *September 1940* |
| *Unit:* | Luftflotte 5 |
| *Rank:* | *Senior Sergeant* |
| *Theatre:* | *northwest Europe* |
| *Location:* | *Norway* |

# Private
# 7th Air
# Division

A *Jäger* (rifleman) during the invasion of Crete in May 1941. He wears the Luftwaffe parachute jump smock manufactured in pale green and grey cotton. The smock was of the step-in variety, which entailed the wearer stepping into the short legs of the garment, pulling the smock up over his body, pushing his arms into the sleeves and shrugging the jacket onto his shoulders. The smock was then buttoned up in the front from the crotch to the collar.

Like the para helmet, the smock was designed to avoid all possibility of the wearer's kit or clothing becoming entangled in his parachute harness or being caught up on any projecting part of an aircraft's interior. Ironically, a major disadvantage of the whole arrangement occurred when the soldier wished to relieve himself. To do so he had to let down his smock, which meant he had to remove all his equipment. In battle this proved to be time-consuming and somewhat dangerous.

This private's trousers are paratroop issue, which are coloured field-grey and have fastenings on the outside leg for the knee bandages to be removed once the soldier lands on the ground. The trousers have two side pockets, two hip pockets plus a small fob pocket, which was located near the waistband on the right side of the trouser front.

Note his side lace-up leather boots, the soles of which were of moulded rubber with a large chevron pattern.

| Date: | 20 May 1941 |
|---|---|
| Unit: | 7th Air Division |
| Rank: | Private |
| Theatre: | Mediterranean |
| Location: | Crete |

# *Major* Jagdgeschwader 51 *Army Group Centre*

**Major Werner Mölders, one of Germany's leading air aces, who by September 1940 had already won the Oakleaves to his Knight's Cross of the Iron Cross. Here, Mölders is shown in his role as commander of** *Jagdgeschwader 51***, a fighter unit, on the Eastern Front. Major Mölders wears a side cap and a non-regulation black leather flying jacket. Over this he wears a self-inflating life jacket, which was issued to all crews of single-engined aircraft.**

Though the Luftwaffe had suffered a setback during the Battle of Britain, Operation 'Barbarossa' seemed to confirm German aerial tactical doctrines, with the *Schwarm* of two pairs (*Rotten*), each of a leader and wingman, forming the standard Luftwaffe fighting unit. Major Mölders and his fellow pilots quickly gained air superiority over their Russian foes at the start of the campaign. But the war in Russia continued into the winter, and in the bitter cold personnel were in desperate need of warm clothing. The Luftwaffe therefore issued the winter clothing mentioned on page 26.

By the end of 1941 the Luftwaffe began to run into serious difficulties: the Soviets were still fighting, there was a shortage of airworthy aircraft and essential supplies of spare parts had become erratic. By December 1941, the Luftwaffe had lost a total of 2092 aircraft, plus another 1361 damaged. For a force which began with 2800 aircraft, these losses were devastating.

| | |
|---|---|
| *Date:* | *December 1941* |
| *Unit:* | Jagdgeschwader 51 |
| *Rank:* | *Major* |
| *Theatre:* | *Eastern Front* |
| *Location:* | *west of Moscow* |

# Captain
# Luftwaffe
# Army Group Centre

**This is Captain (*Hauptmann*) Hans Phillipp, who was awarded the Swords to the Knight's Cross of the Iron Cross with Oakleaves on 12 March 1942, having chalked up 82 victories in that time. Phillipp wears the side cap and flying blouse, together with breeches and boots, to which he has strapped extra flare pistol cartridges.**

His rank is indicated by the two yellow pips on the shoulder straps and the three wings on the collar patch. His officer's collar patches are 40–80mm (1.6–3.2in) wide and 60mm (2.4in) high and contain six leaves with two acorns, plus three small silver wings to indicate his rank of captain (re-enlisted captains had two wings). The arm of service is yellow, indicating he is a flyer, while his flying badge is worn on the left breast. The first air force badges were introduced in January 1935, for pilots and observers, and new badges followed in March 1936 for pilots, observers, pilots/observers and wireless operators/air gunners.

Captain Phillipp wears a pair of leather gloves which have an extended gauntlet-type wrist that is elasticated on the back to give a tight fit to his wrists and lower forearms. His brown leather belt holds a stiff leather holster for his Luger pistol, plus two magazines.

The Knight's Cross was Germany's highest iron cross award for valour, of which Knight's Cross with Diamonds was the very highest award. It was comparable to Britain's Victoria Cross.

| | |
|---|---|
| *Date:* | *March 1942* |
| *Unit:* | *Luftwaffe* |
| *Rank:* | *Captain* |
| *Theatre:* | *Eastern Front* |
| *Location:* | *Ukraine* |

# Lieutenant-General X Fliergerkorps *Africa Corps*

**Like the German Army, the Luftwaffe was committed to the war in North Africa in support of Rommel's Africa Corps. The first deployment occurred when *X Fliergerkorps* flew from Norway in December 1940, thus achieving the twin aims of supporting ground units and of cutting British supply routes in the Mediterranean.**

The Luftwaffe deployment to Africa necessitated the development of special tropical dress. The figure seen here is a lieutenant-general wearing the standard Luftwaffe tropical uniform with the peaked service cap which was worn with the temperate uniform. The jacket was manufactured from a lightweight tan-coloured material and had four pockets. The pocket flaps were straight edged and were each secured by a single tan-coloured metal button. There were five similar metal buttons down the front of the jacket.

The tropical trousers matched the jacket in terms of both colour and quality, and they were cut full to allow the ends to be worn gathered at the ankles. As can be seen here, there was a large map pocket with a large flap on the front of the left leg at thigh level. In addition, there were two side pockets and two hip pockets with flaps which usually fastened with concealed buttons.

This soldier's senior rank is indicated by the gold badge, piping and cords on his hat, while on his jacket he wears the 1939 Bar to the Iron Cross 1st Class, Iron Cross 1st Class 1914, Pilot's Badge and a Wound Badge.

| | |
|---|---|
| **Date:** | *June 1942* |
| **Unit:** | X Fliergerkorps |
| **Rank:** | *Lieutenant-General* |
| **Theatre:** | *Mediterranean* |
| **Location:** | *Tripoli* |

# Sergeant-Major 1st Airborne Division Air Force

**This member of a parachute unit is wearing a special helmet with German camouflage net, a smock in geometric pattern and the special assault rifle for paratroopers, the *Fallschirmgewehr*, slung over his shoulder. His cloth bandolier holds spare magazines for his rifle, while the four white cloth wings on his sleeve identify him as a sergeant-major.**

Under his smock can be seen the distinctive Luftwaffe tropical trousers. These matched the tropical jacket both in quality and colour, were cut full in the leg so that the ends could be worn gathered in at the ankles. Aluminium buckles and cloth straps meant the trousers could be fastened around the wearer's ankles just over the tops of the boots, thus giving the trousers their baggy appearance. A prominent map pocket with a large flap was positioned on the front of the left leg at thigh level. There were also two side pockets and two hip pockets with flaps, which could usually be fastened with concealed buttons.

Just visible is the tan-coloured cotton shirt, which opened down the full length of its front, with four small brown buttons positioned from the collar down. Flaps to the two patch-breast pockets were fastened by buttons identical to those on the shirt front. Also, there were two small brown buttons on each cuff.

His FG42 weapon was designed as a combination of rifle and light machine gun, capable of being used as either. It was never intended that it should be used by soldiers while parachuting as there were no arrangements for folding the butt or taking it to pieces.

| | |
|---|---|
| **Date:** | *June 1943* |
| **Unit:** | *1st Airborne Division* |
| **Rank:** | *Sergeant-Major* |
| **Theatre:** | *Mediterranean* |
| **Location:** | *Italy* |

# Lieutenant-Colonel X Fliegerkorps *Africa Corps*

**This Lieutenant-Colonel wears the Luftwaffe tropical uniform with the unique air force tropical peaked cap, which also came with a neck flap. The tropical uniform was used not only in the desert, but also in Sicily, Italy, the Balkans and in southern Russia during the summer months. The light tan colour of the uniform quickly washed out and bleached into an off-white shade.**

No collar insignia was worn with the tropical uniform, though the shoulder straps, which served to indicate the wearer's rank and arm of service, were looped and buttoned to the tunic. There was no specific tropical Luftwaffe greatcoat, so air force members continued to wear the blue-grey temperate model. Altogether, the air force tropical uniform was much more comfortable than the uniform worn by army personnel.

Above his left breast jacket pocket this Lieutenant-Colonel wears a Front Flight Bar with pendant, which bears the number of the missions he has flown. Luftwaffe qualification clasps were instituted on 30 January 1941 to be worn over the left breast and above any service ribbons. These clasps were awards given for a number of specific operational flights. The badge itself consisted of a central device surrounded by a wreath, with a spray of oak leaves on either side (both cloth and metal versions were worn). The class of the clasp was indicated by its colour: gold, silver or bronze. This officer also proudly wears the Iron Cross 1st Class, Pilot's Badge and Wound Badge.

| | |
|---|---|
| *Date:* | *January 1942* |
| *Unit:* | X Fliegerkorps |
| *Rank:* | *Lieutenant-Colonel* |
| *Theatre:* | *Mediterranean* |
| *Location:* | *Tunis* |

# Corporal Hermann Göring *Panzer Division*

**A corporal of the *Hermann Göring* Panzer Division, an air force unit which was shipped to Tunisia in early 1943 to take part in the German Army's desperate attempts to hold back the Allied advance. This corporal wears a camouflage shelter quarter as a poncho over his Luftwaffe tropical uniform, while on his belt he has two pouches for submachine gun magazines.**

The shoulder straps and piping of this formation are interesting. Originally the collar patches had a white backing and a red piping edge (rank devices were applied in the normal way). The enlargement of the unit to include both *Jäger* and grenadier regiments led to the adoption of green-edged patches (because green was the colour of rifle regiments). After February 1943 all branches within the division wore shoulder straps with the appropriate *Waffenfarbe*. Officer wore white patches with the traditional silver rank devices and silver cord edging, with shoulder straps displaying the relevant underlying arm of service colour.

Members of the *Hermann Göring* Panzer Division wore a blue cuffband on their right cuffs which bore in white letters the name Hermann Göring (the idea was to name special Luftwaffe units after a World War I ace or Nazi Party 'hero'). The lettering was usually on a dark blue background, with the exception of the titles of the Parachute Division and Parachute Rifle Regiments, the backgrounds of which were dark and light green respectively.

| | |
|---|---|
| *Date:* | *March 1943* |
| *Unit:* | Hermann Göring *Panzer Divsion* |
| *Rank:* | *Corporal* |
| *Theatre:* | *Mediterranean* |
| *Location:* | *Mareth* |

# *Private Luftwaffe Field Division*

**A Private of a Luftwaffe field division. In late 1942, in response to army requests for additional manpower, the decision was taken to transfer surplus personnel from the air force into the army. However, Göring insisted that these personnel be organised as Luftwaffe field divisions under air force control, a move which ensured they suffered on the battlefield as the officers and other ranks had no experience of combat.**

A standard Luftwaffe field division comprised two regiments, each, in turn, of three battalions. They had a strength of around 9800 men. All in all some 20 field divisions were formed, but they suffered badly during combat, and the divisions that were most heavily mauled were subsequently absorbed into the army.

The uniform worn by the field divisions was the same as in other Luftwaffe branches, though collar patches were often omitted from tunics and flying jackets. The most distinctive item of the uniform was the camouflage jacket. The smock featured a camouflage pattern of angular segments or splinters in three colours, and was identical to that used by the army for camouflaged shelter quarters, helmet covers and smocks. The original air force camouflage pattern was rather short-lived. It consisted of rounded splodges and elongated streaks. Used during the invasion of Crete in 1941, it was eventually replaced by a slate-green pattern, which, in turn, was replaced by the segment camouflage design mentioned above.

| | |
|---|---|
| *Date:* | *March 1944* |
| *Unit:* | *Luftwaffe Field Division* |
| *Rank:* | *Private* |
| *Theatre:* | *Eastern Front* |
| *Location:* | *Lvov* |

# 1st Lieutenant Jagdgeschwader 52
## *Army Group Centre*

**By the early summer of 1944 the Luftwaffe was able to deploy 2085 aircraft along the whole of the Eastern Front. However, the Soviets still had numerical superiority in the East, and by early 1945 the German Air Force, being desperately short of fuel, was able to offer only token resistance. Many German pilots, such as Lieutenant Erich Hartmann of *Jagdgeschwader 52* illustrated here, fought with great skill and bravery, but were only able to delay the inevitable.**

In particular, the Luftwaffe could not stop the Soviets deploying ground-support aircraft, which, during the early battles on the Eastern Front, acted as mobile air artillery.

The uniform worn by Luftwaffe personnel basically remained the same throughout the course of the war , and any changes that did occur were small. From 1943, for example, some officers began to wear their tunic and flying blouse closed at the collar, as opposed to open with shirt and tie. In addition, the side cap was swapped for the standard peaked field cap. Lieutenant Hartmann is wearing the peaked cap with *Jagdfliegerknicke* (literally, 'pilot's nick'), an effect achieved by removing the wire stiffener from the cap and squashing it flat. His other items are the Luftwaffe leather flying jacket with Luftwaffe silver eagle emblem on the right breast and rank badges on the shoulder, blue-grey trousers and Luftwaffe black leather and suede flying boots. Note the altimeter fastened to his brown leather belt.

| | |
|---|---|
| *Date:* | *June 1944* |
| *Unit:* | Jagdgeschwader 52 |
| *Rank:* | *1st Lieutenant* |
| *Theatre:* | *Eastern Front* |
| *Location:* | *East Prussia* |

# *Auxiliary Flak Unit Luftwaffe*

**When the Germans overran the Baltic states in 1941 they discovered large numbers of the population were sympathetic to their cause. They therefore recruited personnel from these regions to serve them (these were quite separate from the foreign personnel recruited by the Waffen-SS). More than one million men were recruited from the Soviet Union in total.**

In September 1943 the Luftwaffe began to establish Latvian formations, which were amalgamated in August 1944 to form the Latvian Aviation Legion. This formation was composed of three night bomber squadrons, an aviation school, an anti-aircraft battalion and various support units. It had a total strength of 628 men.

In August 1944, Latvian conscripts unsuitable for frontline duty were transferred to the Luftwaffe as war auxiliaries. Such an auxiliary is shown here. This *Flakhelfer* is wearing the uniform originally introduced for the members of the Hitler Youth. However, instead of the Hitler Youth insignia he wears the Latvian national emblem on his cap and left arm. The auxiliaries were taken to Germany and distributed among the various air force units. As an anti-aircraft artillery crew member this auxiliary would be badly needed to serve the air defences of the Third Reich, which was being hard hit by Allied bomber raids, both day and night.

At the end of the war all flak auxiliaries were taken over by the SS and renamed SS-*Zoglinge*, though they did not always wear SS insignia.

| | |
|---|---|
| *Date:* | *September 1944* |
| *Unit:* | *Flak unit* |
| *Rank:* | *Auxiliary* |
| *Theatre:* | *Germany* |
| *Location:* | *Leipzig* |

# *Petty Officer* Panzerschiff Deutschland

**This Petty Officer of the *Kriegsmarine* is wearing the pre-war walking-out dress, which was discarded after 1941. The cap tally advertising the name of his ship – *Panzerschiff Deutschland* – was soon to be replaced by a standardised model bearing the title *Kriegsmarine*.**

Essentially, the German naval uniform worn in World War II was the same as that introduced in 1848 for the Prussian Navy. The navy began life as a tiny force: by the time of the 1870 Franco-Prussian War, the North German Federation had only 37 warships. But less than 30 years later, under Emperor Wilhelm II, the German Navy had become one of the strongest in the world. There were three types of uniform: navy blue, white for tropical and summer wear and field-grey for land-based personnel.

Petty officer rank is shown by the gilt metal badge on the left upper sleeve and the rank distinction lace on the cuff. All petty officers wore a departmental badge combined with an anchor on the left upper sleeve, except for those sailors of the Line who wore the anchor alone. In addition, the Boatswain had a badge of crossed anchors. Senior petty officers had a small chevron below the badge and the Candidate Officer had two chevrons of differing sizes. The badges themselves were embroidered in yellow silk on a dark blue background for use on blue backgrounds, or in medium blue silk or wool on white for the summer uniforms. Brass badges were worn on the short overcoat and on the parade jacket, complete with two rows of buttons at the front and buttons on the cuff tabs.

| | |
|---|---|
| ***Date:*** | *September 1939* |
| ***Unit:*** | Panzerschiff Deutschland |
| ***Rank:*** | *Petty Officer* |
| ***Theatre:*** | *Germany* |
| ***Location:*** | *Kiel* |

# Seaman German Navy

A seaman wearing the pre-war summer parade dress, which was worn between 30 April and 30 September 1939. He also wears a white cap cover, white shirt and cap tally sporting the name of his ship, those these items were not officially worn during the war. German Navy ratings wore the cap with either a white or blue top, the former being discontinued at the beginning of the war. The cap itself fell into disuse during the war and eventually was only worn either with the walking-out dress or as full-dress headgear.

On his cap this German seaman wears the standard cap badge for ratings, which consists of machine-embroidered Nazi eagle above a plain black, white and red national cockade. All ranks in the German Navy wore the national insignia on their right breasts, though there were many variations of style and manufacture. Essentially officers wore gold embroidered eagles on blue uniforms and gilded eagles with a pin at the back on white uniforms, while ratings' badges were either machine embroidered or made from woven silk embroidered in yellow cotton on a navy blue background.

When the summer uniform was worn, all insignia appeared in cornflower blue, apart from the red specialist training badges. In addition, as shown here, tropical white sports vests had a cornflower blue national emblem on the right breast.

For security reasons the tally with the ship's name was not worn during the war.

| | |
|---|---|
| *Date:* | *September 1939* |
| *Unit:* | *German Navy* |
| *Rank:* | *Seaman* |
| *Theatre:* | *Germany* |
| *Location:* | *Baltic Sea* |

# *Admiral Baltic Sea Fleet*

**Admiral Rolf Carls, Commanding Admiral of the Baltic Sea Fleet. He wears a peaked cap with embroidered oak leaves. Officers, warrant officers and midshipmen wore the same cap badges, together with eagle and cockade with wreath on a peaked cap.**

The wreath consisted of twelve oak leaves and four acorns and was embroidered in gold; the national cockade was also trimmed with gold wire. Officers' cap visors were covered with blue cloth and bound with black leather, on which were displayed rows of gold oak leaves (two for flag officers and one for senior naval officers; junior officers wore a gold waved rim). The peaked cap itself was blue with a black mohair band, while petty officers had a cap with a chin strap.

Admiral Carls wears the naval greatcoat, which was double-breasted with two rows of six gilt or silver buttons, turn-back cuffs and slanting side pockets with rounded flaps. The half-belt fastened in the centre with one button, while the false pocket flaps had three buttons each. Because Admiral Carls is a flag officer, he wears cornflower blue lapels. On his shoulders are straps indicating his rank: two gold and one silver interwoven braid straps on a dark blue background with two large four-pointed stars. Admiral Carls carries an M1938 dagger made of gilt metal with a white ivory grip, which was worn suspended from two black straps with gilt metal fittings.

Carls was awarded the Knight's Cross of the Iron Cross on 14 June 1940.

| | |
|---|---|
| ***Date:*** | *April 1940* |
| ***Unit:*** | *Baltic Sea Fleet* |
| ***Rank:*** | *Admiral* |
| ***Theatre:*** | *Baltic* |
| ***Location:*** | *Norway* |

# Lieutenant-Commander Kriegsmarine

**This *Korvettenkapitän* wears the standard German Navy uniform for officers, petty officers and cadets: a peaked cap with a single row of embroidered oak leaves on the peak and a reefer jacket with rank distinction lace on the cuffs.**

In the German Navy, executive officers or officers of the line sported cuff stripes with a five-pointed star above and no device on the shoulder cords. German officers wore their stripes higher on the sleeve than their American or British counterparts. Flag officers sported a single large gold lace stripe, together with from one to four medium stripes above it. Those personnel serving in other branches wore embroidered badges on the cuffs, which replaced the star, and metal badges on the shoulder cords. These shoulder cords for senior and junior officers were made of silver braid (plaited for the former and straight for the latter), while pips, badges and buttons were made of gilded brass.

The German Navy was organised into three basic arms, each one being under the command of a flag officer, or *Führer*. The capital ships came under the control of the *Oberkommando der Kriegsmarine* (OKM); the naval security section controlled the minesweepers, patrol boats, coastal defence ships and auxiliary vessels; while the third arm comprised the submarine command. The latter was to pose the greatest threat to the Allies at sea. At the outbreak of war in September 1939, the navy had 59 U-boats compared to 58 surface vessels of all types.

| | |
|---|---|
| **Date:** | *September 1940* |
| **Unit:** | Kriegsmarine |
| **Rank:** | *Lieutenant-Commander* |
| **Theatre:** | *Atlantic* |
| **Location:** | *North Sea* |

# *Petty Officer* Kriegsmarine *Baltic Fleet*

**The German naval effort in the Baltic consisted mainly of laying minefields, protecting German convoys and harassing Russian supply routes. After the war had turned irrevocably against Germany in the East in 1944, the navy also assisted in the evacuation of German forces in the Baltic.**

The basic uniform worn by naval personnel in the Baltic was the standard German Navy issue. In winter the typical naval foul-weather attire was as illustrated here, though personnel could also wear a black leather cap with fur ear flaps, a heavy lined watch coat with leather shoulder pads, plus special sea boots and waterproof mittens. The foul-weather suit, pea-coat and sou'wester were essential items in the unforgiving winter months at sea.

Rank was indicated on the coat, as here, by the lace on the collar and the anchor badge on the left sleeve. German Naval petty officers wore departmental badges combined with an anchor on their left upper sleeves. Chief petty officers wore officers' uniform while petty officers wore the same uniform as sailors. Medium blue collar patches were adopted to be worn on the overcoat on 1 December 1939. One stripe denoted petty officer rank.

In the summer months, sailors in the Baltic wore summer white vests and shorts, though in 1943 a sand-coloured tropical uniform was also introduced. The tunic was a standard four-pocket pattern which could be worn over either a long or short-sleeved shirt.

| | |
|---|---|
| **Date:** | *August 1944* |
| **Unit:** | Kriegsmarine |
| **Rank:** | *Petty Officer* |
| **Theatre:** | *Baltic* |
| **Location:** | *Kiel* |

# Chief Petty Officer
# **Kriegsmarine**

This chief petty officer is wearing the khaki battle-dress that was reportedly made from stocks of captured British clothing. It was undoubtedly very similar to the British model, being a single-breasted blouse with stand-and-fall collar, pleated patch breast pockets with pointed flaps and buttons, shoulder straps, a waistband fastened on the right hip with a flat metal belt buckle, and sleeves gathered into cuffs which were each secured with a small button. The three pips on the shoulder straps indicate his rank (shoulder straps were made of blue cloth, edged by gold lace of a special naval pattern and sported silver pips according to rate).

This petty officer is a U-boat crewman. By 1944 the Battle of the Atlantic had turned against Germany. In total, more than 39,000 officers and men served in German submarines during World War II, and 32,000 of them were killed in action. Despite these appalling losses, however, morale remained high in the U-boat arm. This was due in no small part to the relaxed attitude and dress code aboard individual ships. In fact, dress codes were so informal that appearances could be decidedly unmilitary. Officers wore a peaked cap with a white cover or a side cap, and different types of shirt worn open at the neck with shoulder straps. Ratings wore white sports vests, which sometimes had the blue national emblem on the breast. Other items of clothing included shorts or swimming trunks, and canvas shoes or sandals.

| | |
|---|---|
| *Date:* | *October 1944* |
| *Unit:* | *Kriegsmarine* |
| *Rank:* | *Chief Petty Officer* |
| *Theatre:* | *Atlantic* |
| *Location:* | *Kiel* |

# United States of America

*In terms of hardware, the American effort was crucial in securing an Allied victory in World War II and the average American serviceman was, in the main, superbly equipped with clothing, weapons and supplies. The United States mobilised 16,354,000 men and women during the war, of whom 11,260,000 were in the army and air forces.*

# Lieutenant-Colonel 1st Cavalry Division US Army

**It is a curious fact that by the end of World War II the US Army was able to equip its soldiers with uniforms which were the most advanced in the world, but back in 1941 the uniforms worn by its personnel had appeared outdated. But then, before the war the Regular Army had numbered just 243,095 men – of which only 1400 were officers – and the army itself was scattered in 130 camps, posts and stations.**

This lieutenant-colonel is wearing the older-style uniform. This includes the campaign hat with yellow cords for cavalry, 'chino' or khaki drill, worsted or gabardine shirt, cord breeches and russet field boots. The latter were already scarce by the time the United States entered the war in December 1941.

At this time the US Army had three classes of uniform. First was the winter dress uniform, Class A; second came the intermediate season uniform with shirt, Class B; while third came the uniform worn in hot climates, Class C, which is shown here. It was made of khaki drill, or 'chino' as it was known in America. This diversity of uniform type was a reflection of the temperature extremes experienced on the American continent itself. The uniform shown here is from November 1942, the date of the first great involvement of American troops in the Mediterranean theatre. Combat experience soon led to changes in the uniform, and the American soldier began to look less like a participant in World War I and more like a modern combatant.

| | |
|---|---|
| *Date:* | *November 1942* |
| *Unit:* | *1st Cavalry Division* |
| *Rank:* | *Lieutenant-Colonel* |
| *Theatre:* | *Mediterranean* |
| *Location:* | *Morocco* |

# Corporal
# Tank Battalion
# Armoured Division

Just as in other armies, the US Army had to design a uniform for crews of armoured fighting vehicles. This uniform consisted of a one-piece herringbone twill overall with patch pockets on the thighs and breasts and matching cloth belt. Other items included a short jacket with zip fastener in front, knitted woollen collar, cuffs, waistband and vertical slash breast pockets (although the earlier style of pockets is shown here). The lined field jacket was so popular that most soldiers tried to get their hands on one.

Head protection when inside the armoured fighting vehicle has always presented problems for uniform designers because of the need to combine ease of mobility, protection and compactness. The US solution in World War II was the fibre helmet, which had ventilation holes and was very lightweight.

Around his waist this NCO wears a woven pistol belt, suspended from which is a russet leather holster for his .45 Model 1911 pistol, a small pouch on the right containing a field dressing and a pouch on the left for pistol ammunition.

A US armoured division consisted of a reconnaissance battalion and four battalions of tanks. In 1942 — when the uniform pictured here was first worn — a division translated into 159 medium and 68 light tanks. In addition, there were three battalions of mounted infantry, three battalions of 105mm self-propelled howitzers and a host of service troops. The division numbered more than 10,000 men.

| | |
|---|---|
| *Date:* | *November 1942* |
| *Unit:* | *tank battalion* |
| *Rank:* | *Corporal* |
| *Theatre:* | *Mediterranean* |
| *Location:* | *Morocco* |

# Corporal US Army Military Police

**The US Army first wore khaki in 1903, for tropical dress. The standard soldier's uniform in 1941 was made up of an olive-drab (khaki) single-breasted tunic with open collar, matching shoulder straps, four gilt buttons in front, breast and side patch pockets with flaps and buttons, and matching cloth belt. An example of this type of uniform is illustrated here worn by an NCO in the US Military Police.**

Up to February 1942 a black tie was worn with the khaki shirt, but was then replaced by an olive-drab tie. Trousers were manufactured from the same material as the tunic, and were worn with brown shoes or with ankle boots and canvas leggings.

As shown here, NCOs in the US Army wore chevrons on both upper sleeves. At first there were only two ranks – sergeant and corporal – but the sergeant's rank was progressively developed into five classes. The chevrons originally pointed downwards and were twice as wide as those worn in World War I. During the war NCOs were divided into Line NCOs and Technicians, and the latter had a small 'T' within the chevrons. The chevrons themselves were 80mm (3.2in) wide and were machine embroidered in light khaki silk or woven in light yellow on a dark blue gabardine material.

This figure is typical of the American MPs who worked in Britain during the war. They were nick-named 'snow drops' on account of their white helmets, belts, gloves and anklets.

| | |
|---|---|
| *Date:* | *December 1942* |
| *Unit:* | *US Army Military Police* |
| *Rank:* | *Corporal* |
| *Theatre:* | *northwest Europe* |
| *Location:* | *London* |

# Private 29th Infantry Division

**This US Army private is wearing the Class A uniform underneath his olive-drab overcoat. His trousers, of the same material, are tucked into canvas leggings and worn with russet leather ankle boots, over which are worn rubber overboots. His headgear comprises overseas cap with light blue piping.**

This attire is typical of the American servicemen who poured into Britain from 1942 onwards in preparation for the Allied invasion of German-occupied Europe. The gas mask, carried in a large sack under the left arm, was often the first item of equipment to be dumped by troops when they got to the front – it was too bulky and cumbersome. In addition, the knapsack and blanket roll were often left in the transport when units reached the front. All infantrymen were issued with a first-aid pack, which at first was worn on the left rear hip, but later moved to the right front of the belt for ease of reach.

The soldier here is a member of an infantry division, which was the basic formation in the US Army. This comprised 15,500 men divided into three artillery regiments and an artillery regiment, plus support units of engineers, signals and supply. The division was further streamlined in 1942 and its overall mobility increased with the addition of trucks, jeeps and trailers – some 1440 vehicles. This reduced manpower levels to an average of 14,253 men. Firepower, though, was vastly increased, with the introduction of the 57mm anti-tank gun and the replacement of the 75mm howitzer with the 105mm-calibre model.

| | |
|---|---|
| *Date:* | *December 1942* |
| *Unit:* | *29th Infantry Division* |
| *Rank:* | *Private* |
| *Theatre:* | *northwest Europe* |
| *Location:* | *East Anglia* |

# Staff-Sergeant 1st Infantry Division

**This US Army NCO wears the standard army combat uniform and kit. Over his olive-drab wool shirt he wears a lightweight field jacket, together with olive-drab trousers, canvas leggings and russet ankle boots. (Originally US infantrymen were issued with a one-piece twill suit in light olive-drab, but this was soon replaced with a wool shirt and trousers of the same material.) The sand-coloured weatherproof field jacket had a zip fastener and six or seven (depending on its length) buttons in front and diagonal slash side pockets.**

This GI (government issue) is wearing the new American Mk 1 steel helmet, which has a rough sandy finish. It replaced the British pattern steel helmet in the winter of 1941, which comprised a lightweight fibre liner and a steel shell for wear in combat. This design was to continue in US Army use until the 1980s.

Because the US landings in Algeria were amphibious, this GI is wearing a life jacket under his woven equipment. In addition, he carries cloth bandoliers slung round his neck which contain extra ammunition for his .30 M1 Garand semi-automatic rifle. (This weapon, which was reliable and able to take a lot of punishment, remained in US service until 1958.) His sleeve insignia comprises rank badge and US flag (the Americans were anxious that the French in North Africa should not mistake them for British soldiers because of poor Anglo-French relations).

| | |
|---|---|
| **Date:** | *November 1942* |
| **Unit:** | *1st Infantry Division* |
| **Rank:** | *Staff-Sergeant* |
| **Theatre:** | *Mediterranean* |
| **Location:** | *Oran* |

# Major-General 1st Cavalry Division

**Major-General Innis P. Swift at Los Negros in the Admiralty Islands in 1944. He wears the typical light khaki trousers and shirt commonly worn in the Pacific theatre, together with canvas leggings and russet-brown leather boots.**

At the beginning of the war in the Pacific the Americans wore Class C uniforms or 'chinos': khaki drill uniforms. Enlisted men wore a sun helmet, a side cap, a long-sleeved shirt either worn open or with matching tie, and long marching trousers with black shoes and socks. Officers sported the same uniform but also wore a khaki drill service dress tunic (officers and men also had a drill version of the peaked cap with brown leather peak and chin strap).

In combat troops also wore the Class C uniform, with the addition of either the old pattern British helmet or the new Mk 1 model, plus canvas leggings and brown laced ankle boots. This was both impractical and uncomfortable for jungle fighting. Its replacement was the M1942 one-piece olive-drab overall, but that too was found wanting.

Swift sports two stars on his helmet denoting his rank of major-general. Marking helmets in this way was common practice for US Army officers in all theatres throughout the war.

Though the US Army had two cavalry divisions in the Pacific, only the 1st Cavalry Division saw action, as part of the 6th Army. It was composed of two cavalry brigades, each of two regiments, plus two field artillery battalions and support.

| | |
|---|---|
| *Date:* | *January 1944* |
| *Unit:* | *1st Cavalry Division* |
| *Rank:* | *Major-General* |
| *Theatre:* | *Pacific* |
| *Location:* | *Los Negros* |

# *Private 3rd Infantry Division*

**This private is a member of the US 5th Army serving in Italy. This particular formation was a multi-national force comprising British, French, Indian and Brazilian troops in addition to Americans, though the majority of its divisions were American. It provided troops for the Anzio landings, and after the fall of Rome seven of its divisions were withdrawn to take part in the invasion of France.**

The private illustrated here wears the standard M1 helmet, M1941 olive-drab field jacket, olive-drab trousers, canvas leggings and leather boots. His equipment consists of a haversack with entrenching tool, M1942 bayonet and a canteen suspended from his cartridge belt. His weapon is the ubiquitous M1 Garand rifle.

On his left upper sleeve this private wears the divisional insignia. Coloured patches had been used for identification purposes during the American Civil War, but it was only in 1918 that shoulder patches were officially introduced. During World War I the US Army had a plethora of shoulder patches, but in the interwar years these patches were simplified and changed. They were worn either on the left upper sleeve or on the right upper sleeve by personnel temporarily attached to a higher formation. The 3rd Infantry Division shoulder sleeve insignia shown here had three white bars to denote the division's number on a blue background.

This private is a member of the smallest unit in an American division – the 14–16 man squad.

| | |
|---|---|
| *Date:* | *January 1944* |
| *Unit:* | *3rd Infantry Division* |
| *Rank:* | *Private* |
| *Theatre:* | *Mediterranean* |
| *Location:* | *Anzio* |

# Private Indian Army Group

In response to complaints concerning the M1942 one-piece olive-drab overall worn by American troops in the Pacific theatre, the Office of the Quarter-Master General (OQMG) began modifying the overall and developing other items for jungle wear. This development had to be speeded up when General Douglas MacArthur suddenly made a request for 150,000 sets of special jungle equipment.

The result was the one-piece camouflage jungle uniform, which was adequate for the jungles of Panama but found to be wanting in New Guinea, where it was too heavy (and became even heavier in the humid jungle atmosphere), too uncomfortable and too hot. It was back to the drawing board. The new suit, the two-piece jungle suit shown here, did not get so heavy when wet, and became standard issue in May 1943.

There had been additional problems regarding uniform colour. Experience showed that stationary troops were well hidden, but when on the move the uniform was easy to spot. Therefore, in early 1944 sets of a new jungle uniform in both cotton drill and poplin were field tested. The comments of those who wore them resulted in a new two-piece jungle uniform made from 142g (5oz) olive-green poplin.

This sniper is loaded down with water bottle, ammunition pouches, wire cutters attached to his belt, rucksack and M1 helmet. His weapon is the M1903 sniper rifle fitted with the M73 B1 (Weaver 330c) telescopic sight.

| | |
|---|---|
| **Date:** | *March 1944* |
| **Unit:** | *Indian Army Group* |
| **Rank:** | *Private* |
| **Theatre:** | *Pacific* |
| **Location:** | *Burma* |

# *Sergeant Grade 4 101st Army Airborne Forces*

This NCO presents a rather ragged appearance, but in fact the special two-piece combat uniform he is wearing, together with the M1 steel helmet and high lace-up boots, were all developed for wear by airborne soldiers. American paratroopers differed from their German and British counterparts in that they did not wear smocks over their equipment. Instead, American paratroopers strapped everything which might become entangled in their rigging lines to their body with lengths of webbing strap.

On his upper right sleeve this sergeant wears an American flag as a means of identification for the benefit of the local population, who in June 1944 were French. On his other sleeve he carries the badge of his unit, the 101st Airborne Division. The 'Screaming Eagle' is Old Abe, the mascot of a regiment of the Iron Brigade during the American Civil War. The black shield commemorates the Iron Brigade itself. His weapon is the folding-stock US .30-calibre M1A1 carbine.

The 101st took part in the D-Day landings, dropping behind the lines to cause maximum disruption, and although the division became scattered during the pre-dawn landings — at first light the division mustered only 1100 men out of 6600 — and it had lost vast amounts of equipment and all its glider-borne artillery, the presence of its men among the enemy served to prevent a counterattack against the invasion beaches.

| | |
|---|---|
| *Date:* | *June 1944* |
| *Unit:* | *101st Airborne Division* |
| *Rank:* | *Sergeant Grade 4* |
| *Theatre:* | *northwest Europe* |
| *Location:* | *Normandy* |

# Major-General 82nd Airborne Division

This major-general of the 82nd Airborne Division is wearing an overseas cap with gold piping. In the US Army, arm of service was indicated by metal badges worn on both lapels by officers, or on the left side of the collar by other ranks. The latter also wore their arm of service badges on the left front of the overseas cap. In addition, all ranks wore cords on their campaign hats and coloured piping on the overseas cap. The gold piping illustrated here indicates general rank, and the insignia on the cap is the infantry para-glider badge.

The M1944 'Ike' field jacket shown here came in a number of different patterns (note the khaki lace around the cuffs), and was usually worn with light khaki shirt and tie. This major-general's olive-drab trousers are tucked into lace-up para boots. On his jacket he wears a number of badges and insignia. On his right breast he wears a unit citation badge, while on his left is the army paratrooper badge above an infantry combat badge. The latter was always worn over the pocket and was made of silver and blue enamel. Instituted on 15 November 1943, it was awarded for exemplary behaviour in combat. The winged parachute on the left breast was always worn above the pocket and ribbons; as it was also always worn on field uniforms.

The 82nd Airborne Division, nicknamed the 'All America', fought in Sicily, and Normandy, at Nijmogen and in the Ardennes.

| Date: | May 1944 |
|---|---|
| Unit: | 82nd Airborne Division |
| Rank: | Major-General |
| Theatre: | northwest Europe |
| Location: | England |

# *Major-General US 6th Army New Guinea*

**The figure shown here is wearing a light khaki service uniform as worn by US officers in the Pacific theatre from 1943 onwards. All officers wore the 12.7mm (0.5in) olive-drab cuff bands, and those of general rank sported the letters 'US' in gold on gold, while the gold piping on the cap also indicated general rank.**

In the US Army generals wore their rank badges on both sides of the shirt collar; they wore from one to four five-pointed stars on the left front of the overseas cap. This cap, a light khaki version of the garrison cap, was known as the 'chino'. The rank of US generals has been denoted by different numbers of silver stars since 1780, when there were only two general ranks: brigadier and major-general.

In the Pacific theatre the development of army clothing was necessarily dictated by climate and by the unique combat conditions experienced there. As mentioned earlier (see page 63), this meant that the original standard tropical combat uniform gave way to more practical dress. Practical matters also ruled when it came to insignia. In general, no insignia or rank badges were worn on the battlefield, though there were various unit markings that were painted on the back of the helmet which were only visible from the rear.

The campaign in the Pacific, from the army's point of view, was spearheaded by the US 6th Army, which was activated in January 1943 and fought a grim island-hopping campaign to regain those possessions lost to the Japanese. By the end of the war the 6th consisted of three corps of 10 divisions.

| | |
|---|---|
| *Date:* | *June 1944* |
| *Unit:* | *US 6th Army* |
| *Rank:* | *Major-General* |
| *Theatre:* | *Pacific* |
| *Location:* | *New Guinea* |

# Officer
# US Women's
# Army Corps

This female officer is wearing a dark olive-drab cap and tunic with a light khaki shirt and tie. The badge on the cap is the badge of the US Army, which was worn by all ranks on their peaked caps. The badge depicts the American eagle with the stars and stripes set on a shield on the eagle's chest. In its right claw was held a sprig of laurel and in the other a bundle of arrows. The motto *E Pluribus Unum* was on a scroll spread above the wings, while above that was a round cloud with 13 stars at its centre. This badge is still worn by members of the US Army.

Officers' cap badges were made of brass or gilded brass, and averaged 75 x 65mm (2.95 x 2.55in) in size. The officers of the Women's Army Corps wore a different eagle (though not the one illustrated here) which consisted of an eagle on its own, with no embellishments.

On this figure's tunic can be seen the officers' collar patches of the US Women's Army Corps: the US national insignia at the top and underneath the badges depicting the head of Pallas Athene, the Greek goddess of war (worn by all ranks of the WAC). The olive braid on her tunic cuffs denotes her officer status.

Though women did not undertake frontline duties on the ground or in the air, unlike their Russian contemporaries, the introduction of large numbers of female recruits into the US Army was of crucial importance to the American war effort, freeing men for frontline duties.

| | |
|---|---|
| **Date:** | *June 1944* |
| **Unit:** | *US Women's Army Corps* |
| **Rank:** | *Officer* |
| **Theatre:** | *Pacific* |
| **Location:** | *Pearl Harbor* |

# *Private Infantry Division 1st Army*

**For the campaign in Normandy in June 1944 the US Army issued this two-piece camouflage suit, not realising that the soldiers of the Waffen-SS also sported camouflage uniforms. The result was that American soldiers who were wearing the suit were immediately mistaken for the enemy. The suit was immediately withdrawn.**

Despite this mistake, by the time of the D-Day landings the US Army had produced a practical and hard-wearing uniform for its frontline divisions: it consisted of M1 steel helmet, M1941 field jacket, olive-drab trousers, canvas gaiters and russet leather ankle boots.

This soldier is armed with the reliable Garand semi-automatic rifle and a captured German Walther automatic pistol in its holster. The US contribution to the Normandy landings consisted of the US 1st Army under General Bradley, which landed at Omaha and Utah Beaches. Despite the bloodshed at Omaha, the two beaches were secured and a beachhead established. From an initial strength of just seven infantry and two airborne divisions, American forces poured into Normandy to give Bradley 21 divisions by 1 August.

The US infantry division of 1944, of which this soldier is a member, comprised a headquarters company, infantry gun company, anti-tank company, service company and three infantry battalions, each made up of 860 men. The division had a strength of 14,253 men and was often reinforced by armour, artillery and anti-aircraft units.

| | |
|---|---|
| *Date:* | *6 June 1944* |
| *Unit:* | *infantry division* |
| *Rank:* | *Private* |
| *Theatre:* | *northwest Europe* |
| *Location:* | *Normandy* |

# Private 101st Airborne Division

**By the final winter of the war American troops had received the M1943 combat uniform, which included the single-breasted tunic with four patch pockets illustrated here. The tunic itself was made from an olive-drab water-repellent and windproof cotton and was issued with a detachable pile fabric liner.**

The 101st was one of two American airborne divisions which served in northwest Europe, the other being the 82nd. The airborne division had an original strength of 8505 men, but by September 1944 this number had increased to 12,979. It comprised two infantry parachute regiments, each of 2364 men in three battalions, a regimental headquarters and a service company; one infantry glider regiment of 2978 men in three battalions, a regimental headquarters, a service and an anti-tank company; one anti-tank and anti-aircraft battalion; divisional artillery, consisting of three batteries of 75mm (2.95in) pack howitzers; and various support units. It was a small, highly mobile airborne unit which could be inserted behind enemy lines.

Like most US soldiers fighting in harsh winter conditions, this private has additional equipment to keep him warm, such as rubber overboots with metal snap fasteners worn over the leather boots. By this late stage of the war in 1944, most US troops had already received the M1943 field dress, but some still had to endure the M1941 jackets and woollen service dress trousers.

| | |
|---|---|
| *Date:* | *November 1944* |
| *Unit:* | *101st Airborne Division* |
| *Rank:* | *Private* |
| *Theatre:* | *northwest Europe* |
| *Location:* | *Belgium* |

# Private 1st Ranger Battalion

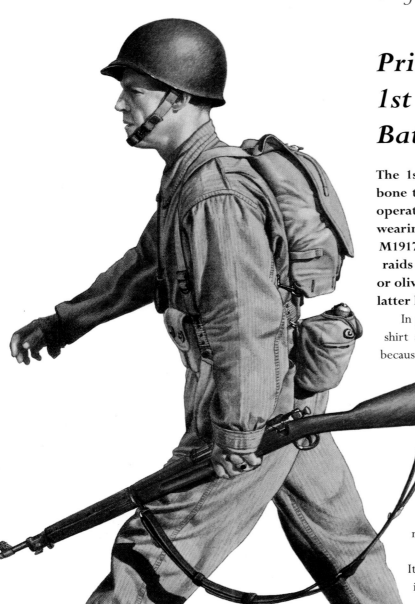

**The 1st Rangers wore a one-piece herringbone twill work suit during training and on operations, as shown here. This Ranger is wearing the Mk 1 helmet, which replaced the M1917A1 helmet in autumn 1942 (in many raids Rangers wore the wool knit skull cap or olive-drab M1941 wool knit 'jeep' caps; the latter had a small, stiff bill and knit ear flaps).**

In general, the Rangers preferred to wear a wool shirt and trousers in the deserts of North Africa because they kept the fast-moving soldiers warm and negated the need to carry blankets. The figure shown here carries the M1928 haversack on his back and a water bottle fitted to his belt. His webbing equipment is standard issue. Non-standard equipment included the Fairburn Sykes Commando knife, the scabbard of which was generally sewn directly to the trouser leg. Also, many Rangers carried M1938 wire cutters.

The 1st Rangers were heavily involved in the Italian campaign, having been involved in the fighting in Sicily and in mainland Italy. In August 1944 the battalion was deactivated, having been decimated in the fighting. It received Presidential Unit Citations for its actions at El Guettar and Salerno, and was credited with participation in several campaigns, four of which involved amphibious landings.

| | |
|---|---|
| *Date:* | *August 1944* |
| *Unit:* | *1st Ranger Battalion* |
| *Rank:* | *Private* |
| *Theatre:* | *United States* |
| *Location:* | *Camp Butner, North Carolina* |

# Private 1st Infantry Division

This is the final version of the combat uniform worn in northwest Europe by the US Army. The troops had received the M1943 combat uniform, a single-breasted tunic with four patch pockets and matching trousers, all made from an olive-drab windproof and water-repellent cotton. It was issued with a detachable pile fabric liner. The high lace-up brown leather combat boots replaced canvas gaiters and ankle boots.

This soldier has camouflage netting over his helmet and a cartridge belt with ammunition pouches for his .3in Browning Automatic Rifle Model 1918. The bipod has been removed to save weight.

In 1944 the US Army started wearing a wool field jacket very similar to the British battledress blouse. Other ranks wore a standard pattern jacket, though officers had many different models.

| | |
|---|---|
| *Date:* | *April 1945* |
| *Unit:* | *1st Infantry Division* |
| *Rank:* | *Private* |
| *Theatre:* | *northwest Europe* |
| *Location:* | *Geske* |

# Officer 10th Mountain Division

**In June 1943 the US Army authorised the formation of the 10th Light Division (Pack Alpine) using the 87th Mountain Infantry Regiment as its nucleus. The flood of skiers, sportsmen and climbers into the division gave it an eventual strength of more than 14,000 men.**

Following intensive courses in skiing and rock climbing, the recruits were instructed in tactical skills during arduous winter exercises. When it joined the US 5th Army in Italy in January 1945 the 10th Mountain was the best trained division in the US Army. It spearheaded the attack on Mount Belvedere and then took part in the Allied drive through the Po Valley and on to Verona. By the time Germany surrendered on 5 May 1945, the division had been in action for 114 days and had lost more than 4000 killed and wounded.

The division's greatest exploit occurred in north Italy in February 1945. Prior to the seizure of Bologna and the clearing of the Po Valley, the division cleared a series of keenly defended ridges that dominated the main road between Rome and Bologna. It cost the division a total of 850 casualties, including 195 dead.

This officer wears the typical attire for the campaign in the mountains of northern Italy: wool trousers, khaki temperate shirt and a cotton bandolier for storing ammunition for his personal weapon, which is an M1 semi-automatic rifle. Around his waist is an officer's pistol web belt. The division's sleeve insignia comprised two crossed swords in red on a blue background.

| | |
|---|---|
| **Date:** | *May 1945* |
| **Unit:** | *10th Mountain Division* |
| **Rank:** | *Officer* |
| **Theatre:** | *Mediterranean* |
| **Location:** | *Italy* |

# Paratrooper 82nd Airborne Division

**The Americans were slow starters when it came to parachute forces, the first being formed in June 1940, stimulated by the German successes with airborne units. The first proper jump uniform consisted of a Riddle helmet, one-piece olive-drab sateen overall and high lace-up jump boots with rubber soles.**

The Americans differed from their British and German counterparts in that they did not wear a smock over their equipment; instead, every piece of kit that could become entangled with the rigging lines of a parachute was strapped to the body with lengths of webbing. The Americans also addressed the problem of safety, issuing each paratrooper with two parachutes: the main one was worn on the soldier's back and a reserve was strapped horizontally to the front of the body.

This soldier wears the standard American parachute uniform, which was similar to the M1943 combat dress but had different pocket arrangements. Note the water bottles attached to his woven waistbelt. His weapon is the .45-calibre M1 Thompson submachine gun, the famous 'Tommy Gun'. Fed from either a 20- or 30-round box magazine, as well as a drum magazine, the Thompson was a touch heavy, but it was well made, robust and reliable – all important qualities which endeared it to paratroopers who were fighting behind enemy lines. The 'All American' shoulder sleeve insignia of the division was worn on the left upper arm.

| | |
|---|---|
| *Date:* | *May 1945* |
| *Unit:* | *82nd Airborne Division* |
| *Rank:* | *Private* |
| *Theatre:* | *northwest Europe* |
| *Location:* | *Germany* |

# US Marine 1st Marine Defense Battalion

**This uniform is typical of US Marine attire in the early stages of the Pacific war. The Marine wears a light khaki uniform, canvas leggings and brown leather boots. His helmet is the World War I-vintage M1917 model, while his weapon is the .3in M1903 rifle with bayonet attached. The bag-like appendage over his shoulder is a gas respirator case.**

This Marine is part of the 1st Marine Defense Battalion, which numbered 450 men and was tasked with defending Wake Island. The first Japanese amphibious assault on the island – on 8 December 1941 – was beaten off by the Marine defenders. On 23 December the Japanese returned with 1000 troops. This time they were more successful and they soon had the small Marine detachment surrounded. With no hope of relief the defenders had no choice but to surrender. Nevertheless, the Marines were able to inflict many casualties on the enemy as well as sinking two destroyers and inflicting damage on other light vessels.

Marine Defense Battalions had a strength of around 1000 men each and comprised anti-aircraft, artillery and special weapons elements. In 1944, in an effort to increase the strength of the six Marine divisions, 17 of the 20 defense battalions were redesignated anti-aircraft battalions which meant that some of their personnel transferred to anti-aircraft units, while those remaining were transferred to line infantry regiments.

| | |
|---|---|
| *Date:* | *December 1941* |
| *Unit:* | *1st Marine Defense Battalion* |
| *Rank:* | *Marine* |
| *Theatre:* | *Pacific* |
| *Location:* | *Wake Island* |

# Gunnery Sergeant US Marine Corps

This gunnery sergeant is in full dress uniform. Such attire continued to be worn during the war as full dress or optional walking-out dress, by members of the Marine detachments in Washington and in London, England.

Rank is indicated by the chevrons on the upper sleeve. The US Marines employed three types of chevron for NCO ranks: gold on a red background for the blue dress uniform; green on red for the green winter uniform; and black on light khaki for the summer shirt. The gunnery sergeant rank insignia comprised three chevrons and two arcs, as shown here. Until September 1942 chevrons were worn on both upper sleeves, thereafter on the left upper sleeve alone.

Service stripes, each representing four years of service, were worn on the outer part of the forearm of the left sleeve in colours matching those of the chevrons worn higher up on the arm.

On his white and blue dress peaked cap this gunnery sergeant wears the emblem of the Marines Corps in brass. The emblem itself comprised the American Eagle above the globe, which is superimposed upon a foul anchor. The service medals worn on the left side of his chest are, from left to right, for service in Nicaragua, the Marine Corps expeditionary badge and a Purple Heart. Below these medals he sports two proficiency badges: the expert rifleman's badge, which has four requalification bars, and the pistol competency badge.

| | |
|---|---|
| *Date:* | *December 1941* |
| *Unit:* | *Marine Corps* |
| *Rank:* | *Gunnery Sergeant* |
| *Theatre:* | *USA* |
| *Location:* | *Washington* |

# Captain US Marine Corps

**The US Marine Corps was a special fighting unit which had its own traditions, uniforms and organisation. In 1912 a new so-called 'green' uniform was issued for the Marines in place of the existing khaki model. However, production problems meant that the new uniform did not enter service until 1914. After further modifications, which occurred in 1929, the uniform was finalised – as is illustrated here.**

The Sam Browne belt for officers was replaced by a matching cloth belt with a two-pronged metal buckle in 1942, and a peaked cap which was also part of the uniform was made of matching green material with black leather peak and chin strap, with bronzed corps badge on the front. On the crown officers wore a green lace quatrefoil, while the campaign hat had a narrower brim than the army pattern, and the cords were green with red flecks.

The badges worn on the collar are the standard emblem of the Marines minus the rope. Collar badges were similar to those on the cap, with variations in silver and gilt, brass and bronze, according to the type of uniform. However, whatever the metal, all collar badges were worn in pairs with the anchors facing inwards.

This captain is wearing the M1917 service helmet and the French *Croix de Guerre* on his breast (which was awarded to the 5th and 6th Marines for service in France during World War I). Note his high lace-up boots.

| | |
|---|---|
| *Date:* | *January 1942* |
| *Unit:* | *US Marine Corps* |
| *Rank:* | *Captain* |
| *Theatre:* | *northwest Europe* |
| *Location:* | *Iceland* |

# Private US Marine Corps

**This battle-weary Marine in the New Guinea theatre wears the M1 helmet with webbing cover. The two-piece herringbone-twill fatigue suit shown here was introduced in 1942 and the woven belt was usually only worn by officers. However, this particular Marine is wearing it with magazine and field dressing pouches attached.**

The New Guinea theatre proved a difficult environment for such marines. The humid heat meant that it was essential for each soldier to carry plenty of dressings, as even minor scratches and wounds could quickly become infected. On jungle operations the uniform soon became drenched in sweat and water, making it very heavy. For this reason it was eventually withdrawn from service.

At the beginning of the war the Marine Corps was made up of the 1st and 2nd Marine Divisions, though both were below strength and did not reach adequate manning levels until the middle of 1942. The corps numbered 20,000 men in 1939 and 65,881 by the time the US entered the war in December 1941. By the war's end there were 450,000 Marines – an army in itself – and it even had its own air force!

The Marines performed two basic, though essential, functions: to conduct their own amphibious operations, and to act as land troops on behalf of the US Navy. During World War II the Marine Corps expanded massively as they carried out a series of grim island-hopping operations in the Pacific against the Japanese.

| | |
|---|---|
| **Date:** | October 1943 |
| **Unit:** | US Marine Corps |
| **Rank:** | Private |
| **Theatre:** | Pacific |
| **Location:** | New Guinea |

# US Marine 2nd Marine Division

**This Marine is wearing the two-piece 'dunga-ree' uniform, which differed from the army pattern in that it had a flapless pocket on the left breast. His gaiters are worn under his trousers and on his feet he wears russet-brown boots. His helmet has a 'beach' design camouflage cover, which was indicative of the gradual encroachment of camouflage onto the Marine uniform. First came the camouflaged helmet cover, then the camouflaged poncho and finally a complete one-piece camouflage jungle uniform.**

This survivor of the bloody battle on Tarawa has captured two Japanese trophies: a sword and a water bottle. The action to take Tarawa was one of the costliest battles in US military history. Some 5000 men of the 2nd Marine Division landed on the island in November 1943, and by the end of the first day 1500 of them were dead or wounded. Next day the divisional reserve landed and 344 officers and men were killed or wounded by withering Japanese gunfire. By the time the defenders had been flushed out of all their positions, after five days of vicious fighting, all but 17 of the Japanese garrison were dead and the Marines had lost 985 killed and 2193 wounded. Despite overwhelming US superiority in terms of firepower, Tarawa was eventually won by the raw courage of the individual Marine. Tactics, because of the terrain, could only consist of frontal assaults, in which the US Marines did not falter.

| | |
|---|---|
| **Date:** | *November 1943* |
| **Unit:** | *2nd Marine Division* |
| **Rank:** | *Marine* |
| **Theatre:** | *Pacific* |
| **Location:** | *Tarawa* |

# US Marine 2nd Marine Division

This rather weary figure is wearing the two-piece herringbone-twill fatigue suit, brown boots and M1 steel helmet with the 'beach' camouflage cover described on page 78. The weapon slung over his shoulder is the M1 Garand semi-automatic rifle. Also visible are his water bottle and pouches carrying rifle ammunition, and on his left breast the letters 'USMC'.

This soldier is a member of the 2nd Marine Division, which first saw action in World War II when the 2nd Marines Regiment, a part of the division, took part in the Guadalcanal operation. Soon afterwards the remainder of the regiment was landed to take part in mopping up Japanese forces on Tulagi and its neighbouring islands. The regiment then moved to Guadalcanal itself to join the 1st Marine Division's offensive along the north coast, which was the first large-scale Allied victory against the Japanese. As usual, the Japanese fought with tenacity, despite the fact that many of them were starving. In 1943 the division provided the bulk of the forces used to take Tarawa and the rest of the Gilbert Islands in the Pacific, and also saw action in the Mariana Islands in 1944.

The shoulder sleeve insignia of the 2nd Marine Division followed the style of the 1st Marine Division, with a figure '2', in the form of a snake, inscribed with the same battle honour. The badge was superseded by another pattern, showing a hand holding a torch and the Southern Cross, the whole on an arrowhead-shaped red background.

| | |
|---|---|
| *Date:* | *November 1943* |
| *Unit:* | *2nd Marine Division* |
| *Rank:* | *Marine* |
| *Theatre:* | *Pacific* |
| *Location:* | *Tarawa* |

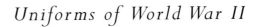

# Pilot
# US Marine
# Corps

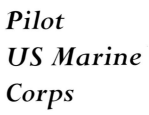

**This pilot serving in the equatorial Pacific wears lightweight clothing, which contrasts sharply with the heavy and bulky clothing of flying personnel in the European theatre. He carries an inflatable life vest worn over his light khaki flying overalls; his basic equipment hanging on his belt includes a field-dressing pouch on his right side, a pouch containing two automatic pistol magazines, and a water bottle carrier.**

His flying helmet is made of leather, though fabric helmets were also widely used, and his goggles are tinted for protection against glare from the sun.

Marine aviators first served in World War I, flying with British and French units. By the end of the war they numbered 2462 men and 340 aircraft. At the beginning of World War II, marine aviation had only 251 aircraft and 708 pilots. When the two brigades of marines were reorganised into divisions in February 1941, their air support groups were redesignated 1st and 2nd Marine Aircraft Wings (MAWs). By January 1945, the number of pilots had risen to 10,412, an additional three MAWs had been formed, and the total number of squadrons had reached 132. Ironically, marine aviators tended to engage in air-to-air combat rather than be involved in the support of marine amphibious landings. This is because the raids were often beyond the range of the marines' land-based aircraft.

| | |
|---|---|
| *Date:* | *June 1943* |
| *Unit:* | *United States Marine Corps* |
| *Rank:* | *Pilot* |
| *Theatre:* | *Pacific* |
| *Location:* | *Bougainville* |

# Technician 5th Grade USAAF

**The air units of the US Army were officially placed under a centralised command and became the United States Army Air Forces (USAAF) on 20 June 1941. As USAAF was part of the army, air force personnel also wore army uniforms. The technician shown here is wearing the Class A uniform with steel helmet, which was worn for ceremonial occasions, and his weapon is the US M1903 Springfield rifle.**

The insignia which identifies this soldier as a member of the air force are on the collar and sleeve. Like their army counterparts, USAAF members wore chevrons (both actual chevrons and arcs) on their upper sleeves. Technicians' grades were introduced in January 1942 and were denoted by the initial 'T' below the chevrons (unofficial versions sported a small winged propeller in place of the Technicians' 'T'). All chevrons were 80mm (3.2in) wide and were machine embroidered in either olive-drab silk or sandy-grey silk, all on a dark blue background. Each oblique single olive-drab stripe worn on the left forearm, as here, denoted three years of honourable Federal service.

Despite its size and resources, the air force arose from humble beginnings. In June 1941, for example, it consisted of 9078 officers, 143,563 enlisted men and approximately 6000 aircraft. However, by the time it reached its peak in March 1944, USAAF numbered nearly two and a half million men and 250,000 aircraft.

| | |
|---|---|
| *Date:* | *December 1942* |
| *Unit:* | *USAAF* |
| *Rank:* | *Technician 5th Grade* |
| *Theatre:* | *Mediterranean* |
| *Location:* | *Morocco* |

# Captain
# 7th Air Force
# USAAF

**This officer is wearing a so-called Shearling flying suit with B-3 jacket and A-3 trousers. On his head is the B-2 flying cap, which was fleece lined and had ear flaps. The flying jacket and trousers were also fur lined for protection against the freezing temperatures at high altitudes. It was also standard practice to wear A-6 fur-lined flying boots when in the air. The khaki drill dress – peaked cap, beige shirt and tie, beige trousers or 'pinks' and brown shoes – was usually worn under the flying suit, though the shoes were reserved for the ground.**

In the Pacific theatre there were no less than seven American air forces: the 5th, based in Australia; the 7th, based in Hawaii; the 10th, which supported combat operations in Burma and Thailand; the 11th, based in Alaska; the 13th, which carried out strategic bombing and provided tactical support in the Solomons; the 14th, which originated from the 'Flying Tigers' and operated in China; and the 20th, which was activated in April 1944 to fly B-29s to fulfil the role of a main strategic bomber force.

This flying suit was worn circa 1944, by which time the American air effort in the Pacific had switched from supporting naval and land forces operations to being a strategic one, with long-range bombers pounding the Japanese homeland.

| | |
|---|---|
| *Date:* | *January 1944* |
| *Unit:* | *7th Air Force* |
| *Rank:* | *Captain* |
| *Theatre:* | *Pacific* |
| *Location:* | *Hawaii* |

# Major-General 9th Air Force USAAF

**This senior officer is wearing the typical service dress for members of the air force in the European Theatre of Operations (ETO). Rank insignia is worn on the shoulder straps and on the left side of the overseas cap (two stars for major-general).**

The shoulder sleeve insignia shows him to be a member of the 9th Air Force. This organisation had begun operations in the Middle East in mid-1942, attacking enemy supply lines in the eastern Mediterranean and cooperating closely with the British 8th Army in pushing the Afrika Corps westwards. Later, on 16 October 1943, when it became the tactical arm of the US Army Air Force in Europe, the 9th provided escort and medium bombing support. Later, it also supported the D-Day landings. Its war record amounted to 9,497 enemy aircraft destroyed and 582,701 tons of bombs dropped.

The 9th's shoulder sleeve badge received its official approval on 16 September 1943. The design for this and other insignia was taken from the fuselage markings of US aircraft between the wars, which depicted a white five-pointed star with a round red centre set on a round blue background. The star insignia was to remain the main emblem in all USAAF insignia.

The silver wings worn on the breast shows him to be a senior airman (the different branches of the USAAF were identified by silver aviation qualification badges or 'wings' worn on the left breast above medal ribbons).

| | |
|---|---|
| *Date:* | *June 1944* |
| *Unit:* | *9th Air Force* |
| *Rank:* | *Major-General* |
| *Theatre:* | *northwest Europe* |
| *Location:* | *East Anglia* |

# *Captain 8th Army Air Force*

**This pilot of a P-51B Mustang is wearing a leather flying jacket, over the top of which is a life-preserving jacket. In Europe and North Africa flying personnel wore either a one-piece beige flying suit or a fleece-lined leather two-piece flying suit with helmet and a cap with peak and earflaps. This captain of the 8th Air Force wears his rank insignia on the left side of his overseas cap, while his olive-drab trousers are tucked into his A-6 flying boots.**

The Mustang aircraft fulfilled a vital role in USAAF's strategic bombing campaign in Europe during World War II. Though the Boeing B-17 Flying Fortress that carried out the majority of the bombing raids was armed with 15 machine guns for defensive purposes, and even though the bombers flew in 'box' formations, they were still vulnerable to German fighters. It was not until early 1944 that the Mustangs began to arrive, thus giving the bomber fleets fighter escort throughout their journeys.

At the peak of its strength the 8th Air Force numbered just over 40 heavy bombardment, 15 fighter and two reconnaissance groups. And in a total of 1,034,052 flights it claimed 20,419 enemy aircraft for its own loss of 11,687 aircraft. Its targets were at first limited to military locations in France, but this was later expanded to include the strategic bombing of Germany's industrial bases. Until effective fighter escorts could be arranged for the bomber fleet, American losses to German aircraft were high.

| | |
|---|---|
| *Date:* | *July 1944* |
| *Unit:* | *8th Army Air Force* |
| *Rank:* | *Captain* |
| *Theatre:* | *northwest Europe* |
| *Location:* | *East Anglia* |

# Aircrewman 8th Army Air Force

From 1943 onwards, crews of heavy bombers began to wear protective body armour as a defence against shrapnel. The so-called flak suit was designed in October 1942 by Brigadier-General Grow in conjunction with the Wilkinson Sword Company. It consisted of manganese steel plates, which could stop a .45 calibre round at close range. As such, it soon became extremely popular with bomber crews and resulted in a reduction in aircrew casualties. It weighed around 9kg (20lb), but this did not deter wearers, and by 1944 some 13,500 were in service with the 8th Army Air Force.

This aircrewman is wearing olive-green flying overalls, brown leather boots and the standard peaked cap. In their effort to personalise their uniforms, airmen often removed the stiffener from their peaked cap to give it a 'crushed' look.

The 8th Army Force was formed on 28 January 1942 at Savannah, Georgia, as the air component of the proposed invasion of the northwest coast of Africa. But due to the escalation of the war in the Pacific the 8th was diverted to Britain to take part in the bombing campaign against Germany. For this it was proposed the 8th should muster 33 bomber groups, 12 fighter groups and 15 transport and observation aircraft groups – in all, 3500 aircraft. The bombers consisted of B-17 Flying Fortresses and B-24 Liberators, which flew in 'combat boxes', the bombers grouped together for maximum protection.

| Date: | July 1944 |
|---|---|
| Unit: | 8th Army Air Force |
| Rank: | Aircrewman |
| Theatre: | northwest Europe |
| Location: | East Anglia |

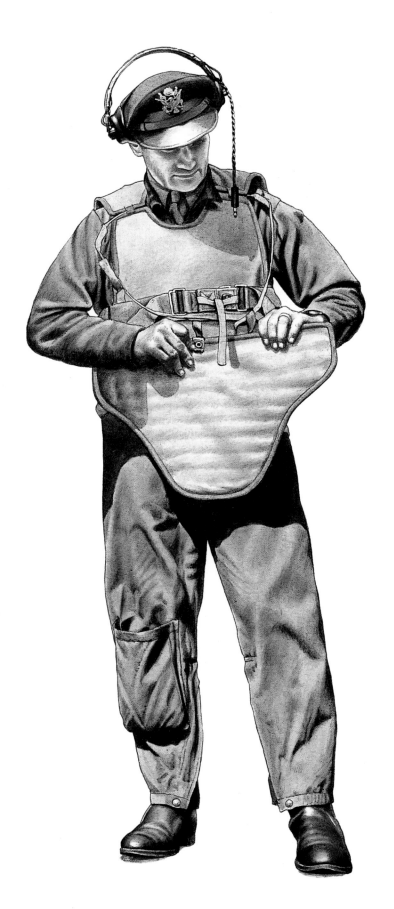

# Bombardier 322nd Bombardment Group

**This figure is 1st Lieutenant Benjamin McCartney, who is wearing the light uniform of the US Army Air Force (USAAF). Under his life jacket he wears a light khaki shirt, the rest of his clothing being khaki dress trousers, russet shoes and the standard officers' peaked cap.**

On his shirt collar Lieutenant McCartney wears a single silver bar to denote his rank. Aviation personnel used the rank insignia of their parent service. Thus USAAF had those of the US Army. McCartney's unit is the 322nd Bombardment Group, which was activated in Florida on 19 June 1942 and comprised the 449th, 450th, 451st and 452nd Squadrons. Initial training started with the B-26 Marauder bomber, but when ordered to Britain the group experienced a shortage of aircraft and the first air squadron did not arrive until March 1943.

The 322nd Bombardment Group was attached to the 3rd Bomb Wing, which had adopted a strategy of 'zero' altitude bombing in order to avoid German flak and also to maximise the number of missions possible under low cloud cover. However, this strategy was not without its risks, and on 17 May 1943 the group lost an entire strike force on a low-level attack (just one of the hard lessons the Americans learned in the skies over Europe). Nevertheless, by October the 322nd had completed 34 missions, and on the 16th of the month the Group was assigned to the Ninth Air Force to support forthcoming ground operations following the Allied invasion of Europe.

| | |
|---|---|
| *Date:* | *June 1944* |
| *Unit:* | *322nd Bombardment Group* |
| *Rank:* | *Bombardier* |
| *Theatre:* | *northwest Europe* |
| *Location:* | *England* |

# Technical Sergeant Grade 2 9th Army Air Force

**This ground crew member is wearing an olive-drab pullover of the 9th Army Air Force in Britain. On his head he wears the standard fatigue 'baseball' cap. His rank insignia is worn on the sleeves. Ground crews fulfilled vital functions in keeping the aircraft in flying order so that they could perform their missions.**

Each army air force was organised in essentially the same way, though there were differences due to climatic and geographic conditions and also because of tactical considerations. The smallest unit for administrative purposes was the group of two to four squadrons. The group always trained together, and combined its administrative services if the squadrons happened to be stationed at a permanent base. Essentially, the air group was the air force equivalent of an army regiment.

In Europe the various army air forces were involved in the fighting in the Mediterranean – both in North Africa and in Sicily and mainland Italy – and in the skies over northwest Europe. And the Americans also worked in close conjunction with the British and other Allied air forces. The efforts of the ground crews ensured that the Americans were able to put hundreds of aircraft into the air at this crucial time. Up to 1 March 1944, for example, the 8th and 9th Army Air Forces flew a total of 107,001 sorties, losing 1509 aircraft in the process.

| | |
|---|---|
| *Date:* | *January 1945* |
| *Unit:* | *9th Army Air Force* |
| *Rank:* | *Technical Sergeant Grade 2* |
| *Theatre:* | *northwest Europe* |
| *Location:* | *East Anglia* |

# Bomber Crewman 8th Army Air Force

**This Boeing B-17 Fortress crewman is wearing the intermediate wool and alpaca-lined flying suit, complete with life jacket, A-11 helmet, B-8 flying goggles and A-10 oxygen mask. To combat the freezing temperatures encountered when flying at high altitudes, this bomber crewman wears fur-lined flying boots.**

The crew of the B-17 consisted of 10 men: pilot, co-pilot, navigator, bomb aimer, flight engineer, wireless operator and four gunners (two waist gunners, a ventral turret gunner and a tail gunner). For defence purposes the navigator manned two window machine guns, while the bomb aimer was responsible for the forward-firing armament and the flight engineer was responsible for manning the two dorsal weapons. Therefore, in total the B-17 had a defensive armament of 15 machine guns of various calibres.

However, and despite the fact that American bombers flew in defensive formations, daylight raids by the Americans still suffered heavy casualties at the hands of the Luftwaffe. During the raid on Schweinfurt on 14 October 1943, for example, out of the total of 291 bombers which took part, 60 B-17s were shot down by the German Air Force and a further 133 were damaged. This raid, known as the 8th Army Air Force's 'Black Thursday', resulted in a reappraisal of the 8th's daylight bombing policy, despite the fact that three out of the five German ball-bearing factories which the 8th had targeted had in fact been badly damaged.

| | |
|---|---|
| *Date:* | *February 1945* |
| *Unit:* | *8th Army Air Force* |
| *Rank:* | *Aircrewman* |
| *Theatre:* | *northwest Europe* |
| *Location:* | *East Anglia* |

# Lieutenant
# US Navy Aviator
# USS Enterprise

**This naval aviator is wearing the standard green service dress of pilots of the US Navy. He sports a khaki drill shirt, which is worn buttoned-up with black tie, the shirt bars on the collars indicating his rank. In addition, the black lace stripes and star on the cuffs are also rank indicators. On his left breast he wears the Naval Aviator wings. These were adopted in 1919 and were used throughout World War II by pilots of the US Navy, Marine Corps and Coast Guard.**

As was standard practice in the navy, the peaked cap matches the colour of the rest of the uniform (the exception was the white cover, which was worn with either the white or the blue uniform). The cap band is black, which matches the background of the cap badge. The visor is made of black leather, with a chin strap of gold braid. Until May 1941 the eagle on the cap badge faced to the left; afterwards it faced to the right, towards the wearer's sword arm. There were two types of gold embroideries used for the peaked cap's visor: a double row of gold oak leaves and acorns for flag officers and a single row for the ranks of captain and commander. After 1 January 1944 the visor embroideries were worn only on formal occasions; at other times a plain visor was worn by all.

In the early stages of the war in the Pacific, an American carrier group with more than one carrier was usually divided in order to launch or recover its aircraft. By 1943, though, task forces stayed together to increase the effectiveness of Combat Air Patrols.

| | |
|---|---|
| *Date:* | *December 1941* |
| *Unit:* | *USS Enterprise* |
| *Rank:* | *Lieutenant* |
| *Theatre:* | *Pacific* |
| *Location:* | *central Pacific Ocean* |

# Chief Petty Officer Task Force 34

The basic American naval uniform that was worn in World War II was a development of the uniform which entered service in the American Civil War, albeit subsequently modified. Officers and chief petty officers wore the uniform which is illustrated here: the peaked cap with either blue or white top, overseas cap, reefer jacket with white shirt and black tie, and matching trousers with black shoes and socks. Both the greatcoat and the raincoat were double-breasted with two rows of four buttons down the front.

As a chief petty officer, this figure wears chevrons and a branch badge on the left sleeve. The rating badge consisted of an eagle, chevrons, arc and speciality badge. The eagle and branch badges were white. Chief petty officers and petty officers with at least 12 years' service, and holding three consecutive good conduct awards or an equivalent outstanding record, were entitled to wear gold chevrons and silver embroidered eagle and speciality mark on the blue uniform.

This figure wears four stripes on his cuff, each one denoting four years' service. The branch badge is that of a machinist, indicating that he is a member of the engineering corps (speciality badges were introduced in 1841). The badges were either dark blue for white uniforms or white or silver embroidery for blue uniforms. The badge on the peaked cap is a special badge for petty officers.

This figure is serving aboard one of the more than 100 ships used in the invasion of North Africa.

| | |
|---|---|
| **Date:** | *November 1942* |
| **Unit:** | *Task Force 34* |
| **Rank:** | *Chief Petty Officer* |
| **Theatre:** | *Mediterranean* |
| **Location:** | *Atlantic Ocean* |

# *Petty Officer 1st Class Task Force 34*

This petty officer wears the so-called square rig for ratings. During cold weather ratings also wore a shortened overcoat or pea-coat, which had two rows of large plastic buttons sporting the American Eagle in front. On his head this petty officer wears the white fatigue cap, which replaced the unpopular 'Donald Duck' cap (it had associations with the Walt Disney character).

His three seaman grades are identified by the white tape stripes on the cuff, and his rank and radio speciality badges are worn on the left sleeve. Newly recruited sailors became Apprentice Seamen and wore a single white stripe on both cuffs of the jumper. They later graduated to Seaman 2nd Class with two stripes, or Fireman 3rd Class (retaining the single stripe). The stripes themselves were 5mm (0.2in) wide, the double and treble cuff markings being joined together by vertical stripes. The whole insignia was approximately 120mm (4.7in) long.

According to normal practice, this petty officer's eagle and speciality badge are white and the chevrons red. As a member of Task Force 34, he assisted in the US landings in North Africa. The force included 30 transports and was supported by the Royal Navy. The American Chiefs of Staff were opposed to the landings, arguing that they were a diversion from the actions in the vital northwest European theatre. However, the landings (codenamed 'Torch'), took place on 8 November 1942. It was the largest amphibious operation attempted at the time, with more than 100,000 troops.

| | |
|---|---|
| *Date:* | *November 1942* |
| *Unit:* | *Task Force 34* |
| *Rank:* | *Petty Officer 1st Class* |
| *Theatre:* | *Mediterranean* |
| *Location:* | *Atlantic Ocean* |

# *Petty Officer 3rd Class* *USS* Saratoga

**The US Navy employed thousands of non-Americans to provide service on board ships and to keep its supply lines running smoothly. This figure illustrates one such individual, a Samoan, who wears a lava-lava with the speciality mark of a baker cook on it. On his standard Navy undershirt he wears the ribbon of the Purple Heart. His dress is completed by the red turban, waist sash and four bands below the badge.**

In the Pacific the Americans established two commands: the Pacific Ocean Area under the command of Admiral Chester W Nimitz and the South West Pacific Area under the leadership of General MacArthur (the naval force which supported MacArthur was under the command of Admiral Halsey).

Such were the military resources of the United States that she was able to maintain both commands with ease, and by the middle of 1943 Admiral Nimitz's 5th Fleet had become the largest naval force the world had ever seen. The fleet comprised 3 task forces: TF50, a fast carrier force with 11 aircraft carriers, 6 battleships and 6 heavy cruisers; TF54, which comprised the amphibious assault force; and TF57, which controlled all shore-based ships plus repair ships, destroyer tenders and tugs.

Although US Navy auxiliaries, such as the petty officer illustrated here, performed seemingly mundane and manual tasks in the navy, they were, in fact, indispensable to the eventual US victory in the Pacific theatre.

| | |
|---|---|
| *Date:* | *November 1943* |
| *Unit:* | *USS* Saratoga |
| *Rank:* | *Petty Officer 3rd Class* |
| *Theatre:* | *Pacific* |
| *Location:* | *The Solomons* |

# Ensign
# US Atlantic
# Fleet

**This naval ensign wears the standard officers'
service dress with white cap cover. On his
cuffs he wears the lace rank distinction
stripes and the five-pointed star of a line officer. Cuff stripes on the blue service dress were
in gold. At the beginning of the war the
stripes were worn all around the cuff, but
later they were placed on the outside only,
from seam to seam.**

From 1 January 1944 only the shorter cuff stripes
were allowed on the service dress. The single stripe
illustrated here indicates this figure's ensign rank,
which on the shoulder straps was also indicated by one
medium gold lace ring and one gilt metal bar on the
shirt collar and side cap. The aiguillette was worn by
presidential aides.

Although to the Americans the Atlantic Ocean was
a secondary theatre in comparison with the Pacific,
nevertheless, the US Navy devoted substantial
resources towards winning the Battle of the Atlantic.
By 1944, for example, there were seven escort carrier groups with a total of seven carriers and 97
destroyers, which were committed to the destruction
of German U-boats and to the protection of Allied and
neutral vessels. This substantial force was aided by the
division of the Atlantic into sea frontiers, each being
an area of ocean that extended from a section of coast
out to sea for more than 320km (200 miles). The
commander in each sea frontier controlled all the vessels inside his area for the duration of their voyage
there.

| | |
|---|---|
| **Date:** | *June 1944* |
| **Unit:** | *US Atlantic Fleet* |
| **Rank:** | *Ensign* |
| **Theatre:** | *Atlantic* |
| **Location:** | *Washington* |

# Landing Signals Officer USS **Princeton**

**In the US Navy flight deck personnel on aircraft carriers adopted coloured helmets, baseball caps, T-shirts and jackets with their name, rank and role often painted in black on the front and back. Coloured helmets were used in order to indicate specific functions on the carriers. For example, aircraft captains wore red; aircraft handlers, grey; fire details and firemen, red; arresting gear details, green; hangermen, yellow; and ordnance men, pink.**

This landing signals officer is signalling to the pilot of an aircraft coming in to land on the deck of the USS *Princeton* during the Battle of Leyte Gulf. He is wearing the light khaki cotton or poplin officers' service dress shirt and light khaki trousers, with yellow slipover and helmet.

Though the USS *Princeton* was sunk at the Battle of Leyte Gulf, nevertheless the action crippled Japan's naval fleet and air force, and also led to a serious reduction in its ground-force strength in the Philippines (some 135,000 Japanese soldiers were also marooned behind the US advance). At Leyte Gulf the Japanese lost 4 carriers, 3 battleships, 6 heavy and 4 light cruisers, 11 destroyers and a submarine. The Americans lost only a light carrier, 2 escort carriers, 2 destroyers and a destroyer escort. On land, the Japanese suffered 70,000 casualties during the campaign, while the Americans suffered 15,584.

| | |
|---|---|
| *Date:* | *October 1944* |
| *Unit:* | *USS Princeton* |
| *Rank:* | *Landing Signals Officer* |
| *Theatre:* | *Pacific* |
| *Location:* | *Leyte Gulf* |

# *Great Britain*

*The British serviceman went to war in 1939 with weapons and equipment developed before or during World War I, expecting to fight a similar conflict. Despite the defeats of 1940-41, the fighting spirit of the average British 'Tommy' remained unchanged: one of dogged determination in the attack and steadfastness in the defence.*

# Lance-Corporal 4th Infantry Division

**The British Army had first introduced a khaki service dress in 1902, though it was not until 1913 that it became mandatory for all ranks on every occasion except when full dress was required.**

The service dress for other ranks comprised a single-breasted khaki serge tunic with stand-and-fall collar, five metal general service-pattern buttons in front, patch breast and side pockets with flap and button, and matching shoulder straps. Non-cavalry personnel wore khaki and serge pantaloons, while mounted troops sported Bedford cord pantaloons. Both categories wore black ankle boots and khaki puttees. The greatcoat was single-breasted with five buttons, fall collar and matching shoulder straps. The head-dress worn by British Army personnel consisted of the M 1916 helmet (later to be called the Mk 1), stiff peaked cap and the side cap, though many regiments retained their own distinctive head-dress, as has the figure shown here.

This lance-corporal of the Black Watch, a Highland regiment, is wearing a cutaway version of the service dress tunic, which was called a doublet. His head-dress is called a 'Tam o'Shanter' and has a khaki pom-pom or touri. Note the red hackle, which was worn by members of the Black Watch in place of a cap badge. His left sleeve carries a number of insignia, including, from the shoulder down, the formation sign of the 4th Infantry Division, a lance-corporal's chevron and proficiency badges of a driver and rifle marksman.

| | |
|---|---|
| *Date:* | *May 1940* |
| *Unit:* | *4th Infantry Division* |
| *Rank:* | *Lance-Corporal* |
| *Theatre:* | *northwest Europe* |
| *Location:* | *France* |

# Captain Grenadier Guards

**This captain is a member of the British Expeditionary Force (BEF), which was sent to France in September 1939. The force eventually comprised 152,031 troops, 21,424 vehicles and all necessary logistical backup. By April 1940 the BEF numbered 394,165 men, however it did little except take up its position in the line and establish supply depots. When the German attack came in the West in May 1940, the BEF was unable to halt the *Wehrmacht*.**

This figure appears to date from World War I rather than 20 years later – indeed, many BEF officers thought the campaigns would be very similar. With the khaki service dress officers wore an open tunic with light khaki shirt and tie, matching khaki pantaloons, puttees and brown ankle boots, although long khaki trousers with brown shoes were also worn. Officers in cavalry units, mounted officers in unmounted units, as well as staff and general officers, could also wear cord breeches and brown leather field boots.

This officer is in one of the five regiments of Foot Guards, which retained a number of regimental distinctions on their service dress. Instead of using 'pips' to denote rank, the Guards employed a system of either miniature stars of the Orders of the Garter (Grenadiers, Coldstream and Welsh Guards), Thistle (Scots Guards) or Shamrock (Irish Guards). The combined belt, cross strap and sword frog seen here was called a 'Sam Browne' after its inventor; the medal ribbon worn on his left breast is the British War Medal 1914–20.

| | |
|---|---|
| *Date:* | *May 1940* |
| *Unit:* | *Grenadier Guards* |
| *Rank:* | *Captain* |
| *Theatre:* | *northwest Europe* |
| *Location:* | *France* |

# Lance-Corporal 1st Anti-Aircraft Division

**As a result of the contribution made by women during World War I, through such organisations as the Women's Army Auxiliary Corps (WAACs), women were already serving in the British Army when World War II broke out.**

The Auxiliary Territorial Service (ATS), one of whose members is shown here, received royal assent on 9 September 1939. At the beginning of the war members of the ATS were employed as cooks, clerks and drivers, having the rather dubious status of camp followers. In the spring of 1940 some ATS telephonists and drivers were sent to France, but it was not until after Dunkirk that the ATS was expanded and its members were given full military status. ATS personnel fulfilled vital functions in the army, such as searchlight, radar and artillery operatives.

This ATS lance-corporal is wearing a privately bought field service cap with a khaki pattern uniform. The unit emblem on the upper sleeve is that of the 1st Anti-Aircraft Division, which was committed to the aerial defence of London against the Luftwaffe in 1940–41. As she is attached to the Royal Artillery, she wears its badge on the left breast.

The ATS had its own organisation and administrative system based on platoons, companies and groups. Platoons contained 23–75 women; two to five platoons made up a company; and groups were formed from a number of companies, each having a minimum strength of 250 women. It made a significant contribution to the war effort.

| | |
|---|---|
| *Date:* | *September 1940* |
| *Unit:* | *1st Anti-Aircraft Division* |
| *Rank:* | *Lance-Corporal* |
| *Theatre:* | *northwest Europe* |
| *Location:* | *London* |

# Sergeant Welsh Guards Household Division

This sergeant is wearing khaki service dress with knickerbockers and long puttees, an arrangement which was out of date by 1940 – the date of this figure – having been replaced largely by the battledress. The latter had first been worn in 1937, and consisted of a baggy waist-length blouse and long baggy trousers, which were gathered at the ankle. Despite this attempt at modernisation, the uniform was rather impractical and difficult to wear smartly, though easy and relatively cheap to manufacture. The summer battledress was made out of denim and was rather more light-weight.

Nevertheless, the old khaki service dress continued to be worn, as illustrated here. This NCO is wearing a leather jerkin lined with thick khaki cloth over his jacket, which had first been worn in World War I and was both comfortable and practical. The other equipment worn on the body includes the 1937-pattern webbing and gas mask carried in the 'ready' position, on the chest. His weapon is the .303in rifle No 1 SMLE (Short Magazine Lee-Enfield) Mk 3, a very effective, reliable and robust rifle.

This figure is a sergeant of the Welsh Guards, one of the five regiments of foot guards in the British Army, which at the outbreak of war in 1939 numbered 227,000 soldiers, including British forces in India and Burma. This number included two regiments of the Household Cavalry, 20 regiments of line cavalry and 64 line infantry regiments.

| | |
|---|---|
| *Date:* | *September 1940* |
| *Unit:* | *Welsh Guards* |
| *Rank:* | *Sergeant* |
| *Theatre:* | *northwest Europe* |
| *Location:* | *Pirbright* |

# Captain 3rd King's Own Hussars

**In the deserts of North Africa cavalry officers often wore brightly coloured service caps with embroidered badges, as shown here. On his shoulders this captain of the 3rd King's Own Hussars wears metal rank 'pips' which are fastened to detachable khaki drill shoulder straps.**

At the beginning of the desert war the British Army tropical uniform was rather impractical: it contained a ridiculous amount of starch and needed much ironing. When hostilities commenced in 1940 a uniform of a more practical nature emerged, which soon became universal to all ranks.

Officers wore a tropical version of the khaki service dress, which was manufactured from khaki-drill, gabardine or from barathea. The arrangement comprised tunic, shirt and tie, shorts or long trousers, which were worn either with puttees and ankle boots or with khaki socks and shoes. Cavalry troops wore breeches with either field boots or puttees. At the front all ranks donned a khaki-drill shirt, pullover, and long trousers or shorts (in general, the uniform for officers was made of better cloth and was better tailored than that for other ranks).

For their part, officers wore corduroy trousers and rubber-soled suede 'chukka' boots, as shown here. The suede boots were not part of the official uniform but were good for desert wear. This officer's 1937-pattern webbing has a pouch on the right for a compass, while on the left is a pouch for ammunition. His weapon in the holster is the reliable Webley revolver.

| | |
|---|---|
| *Date:* | *October 1941* |
| *Unit:* | *3rd King's Own Hussars* |
| *Rank:* | *Captain* |
| *Theatre:* | *Mediterranean* |
| *Location:* | *North Africa* |

# Corporal Hampshire Regiment

**This NCO is wearing the new battledress and a Mk 1 helmet with elasticated chin strap. The single-breasted blouse is made of a rough serge with a stand-and-fall collar, fly front, pleated breast patch pockets with flap and concealed button. The buttons are green and, curiously, were made of a vegetable compound.**

At the waist the blouse is gathered into a waistband and secured with a flat metal buckle to the right of centre. On the trousers, and in addition to the normal hip and side pockets, is a large patch pocket with a flap on the left thigh, as can be seen here. At the bottom of the trousers is a tab and a button, which enables them to be fastened around the ankle when worn with black ankle boots.

The 1937-pattern webbing carries a binocular case on his left and a service respirator on his chest, in the so-called 'ready' or 'alert' position.

The rubber 'Wellington' boots are indicative of the kind of campaign the British expected to fight in France in 1940. They were not standard issue, but were made available in very wet weather to soldiers serving in the trenches. But the boots were not needed; there was no trench warfare in the West in 1940, only an ignoble retreat to Dunkirk and then evacuation to Britain – for the lucky ones.

Fortunately, due to the French Army's efforts in holding back German forces, plus Hitler's decision to halt his Panzers outside Dunkirk, 224,320 British and 141,842 Allied soldiers were evacuated – an achievement which boosted British morale.

| | |
|---|---|
| **Date:** | *June 1940* |
| **Unit:** | *Hampshire Regiment* |
| **Rank:** | *Corporal* |
| **Theatre:** | *northwest Europe* |
| **Location:** | *France* |

# Private The East Yorkshire Regiment

**During the so-called 'Phoney War' on the Western Front in the winter of 1939–40 (the only Allied move during this period was a tentative French probe towards Saarbrüken) the main policy was one of blockade and defensive fortification to exhaust German strength. This private on duty on the Maginot Line – the sophisticated series of strongholds and fortifications along France's eastern border – is wearing a specially manufactured snow suit over his battledress. He carries ammunition for his Lee-Enfield No 1, Mk 3 rifle in a cloth bandolier.**

The East Yorkshire was one of the line regiments; it was the backbone of the British Army. In wartime this regiment was grouped in infantry divisions, which comprised three infantry brigades of three battalions each and three regiments of field artillery – giving a total strength of 13,600 men. Each infantry battalion, numbering 33 officers and 780 men, was divided into four rifle companies, each having a headquarters and three platoons. In addition, the battalion had a headquarters company which comprised six platoons, namely: signals, anti-aircraft, mortar, carrier, pioneer and administration.

The infantry regiment was more of an administrative unit, but one which was ideal for recruitment and morale purposes. This was because members were invariably being recruited from the area in which the regiment was based, thus creating a high level of *esprit de corps*.

| | |
|---|---|
| *Date:* | *January 1940* |
| *Unit:* | *The East Yorkshire Regiment* |
| *Rank:* | *Private* |
| *Theatre:* | *northwest Europe* |
| *Location:* | *Maginot Line* |

# Private 49th Infantry Division

**This private of the British Army is one of the thousands who took part in the Norwegian campaign in April 1940. He is wearing the heavy and uncomfortable 'Tropal' coat, which was lined with kapok. For added warmth he is also wearing a 'balaclava helmet'. His gas mask is in the ready position and the two pouches slung over his shoulder hold ammunition for his Bren machine gun.**

At the beginning of World War II, the British Army was a large organisation, which comprised 227,000 men, including those who were serving in India and Burma. The army was organised into two regiments of Household Cavalry, 20 regiments of cavalry of the line, five regiments of foot guards, 64 regiments of infantry of the line, the Royal Artillery, the Royal Tank Regiment and auxiliary units and services. Supporting the regular organisation was the Territorial Army of 204,000 officers and men organised into a field force consisting of nine infantry divisions, one mobile division, two cavalry brigades and an anti-aircraft corps of five divisions.

The calibre of the British 'Tommy' was high, though he was often let down in other respects. Hitler's comments regarding the state of the British Army were entirely apt: 'The British soldier has retained the characteristics which he had in World War I. Very brave and tenacious in defence, unskilful in attack, wretchedly commanded. Weapons and equipment are of the highest order, but overall organisation is bad.'

| | |
|---|---|
| **Date:** | April 1940 |
| **Unit:** | 49th Infantry Division |
| **Rank:** | Private |
| **Theatre:** | Arctic |
| **Location:** | Narvik |

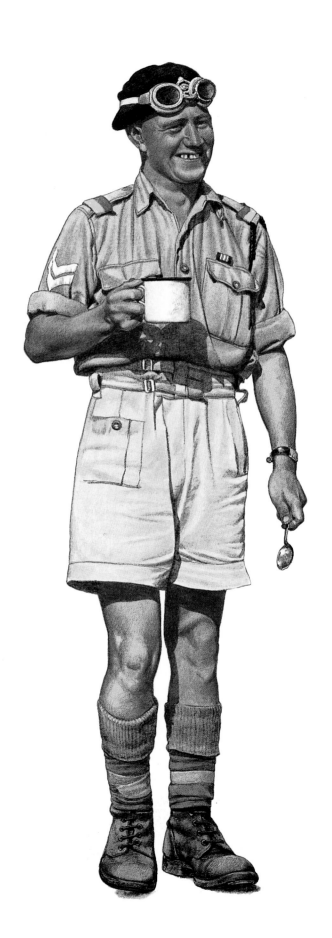

# Corporal 6th Royal Tank Regiment

**This NCO is wearing the distinctive head-dress of the Royal Tank Regiment: black beret with silver cap badge. The rest of his dress is standard desert wear: khaki shirt and shorts, socks, short puttees and leather ankle boots. Note the coloured flashes or slides on the shoulders straps and the black lanyard, which were worn by troops of the 6th Royal Tank Regiment. A .38 Enfield No 2 Mk 1 revolver is carried in the special holster issued to tank crews, which was usually worn lower and strapped to the thigh.**

In cooler climes British armoured crews wore a one-piece black denim overall over the battledress, complete with a khaki or black fibre helmet, gloves and goggles. However, the overall and helmet were soon relegated to training crews, with armoured crews reverting to standard clothing and denims.

In the Middle East the British had begun preparing for armoured desert warfare in 1938 with the formation of the Matruh Mobile Force, which became the Mobile Division in October 1939. The division was made up of the Light Armoured Brigade (7th, 8th and 11th Hussars), Heavy Armoured Brigade (1st and 6th Royal Tank Regiments), and units of the Royal Horse Artillery and infantry. In April 1940, the armoured units were reorganised: the Light Armoured Brigade became the 7th Armoured Brigade and the Heavy Brigade became the 4th Armoured Brigade. The resulting formation was called the 7th Armoured Division.

| | |
|---|---|
| *Date:* | *January 1941* |
| *Unit:* | *6th Royal Tank Regiment* |
| *Rank:* | *Sergeant* |
| *Theatre:* | *Mediterranean* |
| *Location:* | *North Africa* |

# Sergeant
# No 1 Commando
# *HMS* Campbeltown

**This British Army Commando took part in the raid against the dry-dock in the French port of St Nazaire in late March 1942. By this time the Allies had been suffering heavy losses in the Atlantic from U-boat attacks. In addition, enemy warships stood ready to strike out into the Atlantic and attack Britain's weak lifeline. The dry-dock at St Nazaire was the largest in the world and could accommodate German capital ships, therefore it had to be destroyed.**

The Commando assault force from No 2 Commando, plus special demolition teams from Nos 1, 2, 3, 4, 5, 6, 9 and 12 Commandos, plus sailors, numbered 611 men. The raid was a success, though the British lost 197 men killed and 200 captured. But their sacrifice resulted in the destruction of the dry-dock and the end of German capital ships venturing into the Atlantic.

This Commando is one of the demolition parties. He wears a khaki battle dress, scrubbed anklets and ammunition boots with thick rubber soles. He wears a naval roll-neck sweater and a lifebelt under his blouse (the inflation tube for the lifebelt can just be seen). On his back he wears a rucksack filled with explosives, while the large pouches contain grenades and ammunition for his Browning semi-automatic pistol, which is carried in his holster. Like most Commandos, he also carries a Fairburn-Sykes Commando dagger. The raid was marked by courage of the highest order, with no less than five Victoria Crosses being awarded to those involved.

| | |
|---|---|
| *Date:* | *28 March 1942* |
| *Unit:* | *No 1 Commando* |
| *Rank:* | *Sergeant* |
| *Theatre:* | *northwest Europe* |
| *Location:* | *St Nazaire* |

# Lance-Corporal Royal Military Police

**This Military Policeman (MP) is serving with the 46th (North Midland and West Riding) Division in the Italian campaign. He wears a steel helmet with painted band and the letters 'MP' on it. On his right sleeve he wears a blue armlet which sports the same letters. The greatcoat is of a special pattern which was issued to motorcyclists. MPs always maintained a high standard of appearance; indeed, they were expected to set an example to their fellow troops.**

For the invasion of Sicily and Italy the British 8th Army was organised as follows: XIII Corps, comprising the 5th and 50th Divisions and the 231st Brigade, and XXX Corps, made up of the 51st Division and 1st Canadian Division. The invasion of Sicily began on 25 July 1943 and was over by 17 August. Southern Italy was invaded on 3 September 1943 when troops of the 8th Army crossed the Straits of Messina. Six days later the US 5th Army landed at Salerno. The 5th was made up of both American and British troops. The British element, X Corps, comprised the 7th Armoured Division, 46th and 56th Infantry Divisions and the 23rd Armoured Brigade. In taking Salerno the cost to British units was 725 officers and men killed, 2739 wounded and 1800 missing. Naples fell on 1 October and the advance on Rome began 11 days later.

| | |
|---|---|
| **Date:** | *October 1943* |
| **Unit:** | *46th (N. Midland & W. Riding) Division* |
| **Rank:** | *Lance-Corporal* |
| **Theatre:** | *Mediterranean* |
| **Location:** | *Naples* |

# Lance-Corporal Home Guard Herts Regiment

On 14 May 1940, Anthony Eden, the British Secretary of State for War, broadcast an appeal for fit men between the ages of 16 and 65 to enrol in an organisation to be called the Local Defence Volunteers (LDV), or Home Guard, as it was popularly known. By 20 May nearly 250,000 volunteers had come forward, to be increased by a further 50,000 by the end of the month. By the end of July 1940 the Home Guard numbered 500,000 all ranks – a tribute to the patriotism of the British people.

One of those who volunteered is this lance-corporal illustrated here. At first LDV recruits wore their own clothes with a khaki armlet on their upper right arms, which carried the letters LDV in black. But there were limited weapons for the eager new recruits. Eventually, however, both uniforms and arms were made available.

This LDV recruit is wearing the light working version of the battle dress – known as denims – and on his field-service cap he wears the cap badge of the Hertfordshire Regiment. On his left sleeve is the Home Guard shoulder title, and below that the HTS badge (denoting Hertfordshire) and his battalion number. The medal ribbons on his chest are from World War I, and include the British War Medal 1914–20 (far left). The web ammunition pouches were specially produced for the Home Guard, while his US Enfield .30in M1917 rifle carries a red band to indicate it fires non-standard ammunition (.30in instead of .303in calibre).

| | |
|---|---|
| *Date:* | *September 1940* |
| *Unit:* | *Home Guard, Hertfordshire Regiment* |
| *Rank:* | *Lance-Corporal* |
| *Theatre:* | *northwest Europe* |
| *Location:* | *southeast England* |

# Sergeant 6th Battalion Grenadier Guards

**This NCO in Tunisia is wearing serge battle dress with regimental shoulder title and sergeant's chevrons. His steel helmet has a hessian cover, while around his ankles he wears 1937-pattern web anklets and ammunition boots.**

In his hands this sergeant is holding a captured German 7.92mm MG 34 machine gun, the first of a category of weapons known as 'general purpose' machine guns. The attached bipod allowed the gun to fulfil the role of squad light automatic weapon; when fitted to a tripod the MG 34 became a medium machine gun.

The 6th Battalion, Grenadier Guards, was raised at Caterham, Surrey on 18 October 1941, and left England on 16 June 1942 for Syria. In November 1943 the battalion toured northern Syria, and made its combat debut at the Battle of the Horseshoe on 16/17 March 1943.

The battalion entered into a period of refitting following the end of the North African campaign. On 9 September 1943, it landed at Salerno in Italy — the first Grenadier battalion to set foot on mainland Europe since the evacuation at Dunkirk. The battalion was withdrawn from the line and reorganised following its sterling efforts at the action for Bare Back Ridge at Camino in early 1944. Most of its men were subsequently assigned to the 5th Battalion while the others were assigned to the Reinforcement Training Depot. The 6th Battalion was disbanded on 4 December 1944.

| | |
|---|---|
| *Date:* | *17 March 1943* |
| *Unit:* | *6th Battalion, Grenadier Guards* |
| *Rank:* | *Sergeant* |
| *Theatre:* | *Mediterranean* |
| *Location:* | *Tunisia* |

# Warrant Officer 77th Indian Brigade

At the beginning of the war in the Pacific theatre, British Army troops wore the same khaki drill uniform as their comrades in the Middle East. However, this uniform was found to be unsuitable for jungle operations as it was the wrong colour, sandy yellow, and was uncomfortable. In 1942 a new jungle-green uniform was introduced. It was made of a jungle-green cellular material and comprised a bush jacket, shirt and both long and short trousers. The head-dress varied, though in battle either the steel helmet or slouch hat were favoured. Webbing was often painted dark green or black to make it more resistant to moisture.

This 'Chindit', a member of a long-range penetration group that operated behind Japanese lines in Burma (named after the *Chinthe*, the mythical creatures that guard the temples of Burma) is kitted out to resist the dreadful monsoon climate and dense jungle of Burma. Clothing was worn for ease of movement as opposed to military etiquette. Therefore, this soldiers is wearing a long-sleeved light khaki shirt and drill trousers. His rather battered headgear consists of slouch hat with light khaki puggaree. This head-dress is normally associated with Australian or New Zealand forces, but it was also extremely popular with the Chindits. His footwear consists of standard ammunition boots and web anklets, which were often discarded in battle. In his holster he carries an American Smith and Wesson pistol. Chindit clothing was standard, although months spent in the jungle reduced it to rags.

| | |
|---|---|
| *Date:* | *April 1943* |
| *Unit:* | *77th Indian Brigade* |
| *Rank:* | *Warrant Officer* |
| *Theatre:* | *Pacific* |
| *Location:* | *Burma* |

# Lieutenant Long Range Desert Group

This figure is Lieutenant 'Tiny' Simpson, who is wearing the heavy knit 'commando' sweater favoured by many members of Britain's special forces during the war. He wears it with battle dress trousers and black ammunition boots. He has a 1937-pattern web belt with pistol holder and ammunition pouch around his waist. On his head he wears the black beret of the Royal Tank Regiment.

Lieutenant Simpson was a member of the Long Range Desert Group (LRDG), which was a British reconnaissance and intelligence-gathering unit raised in July 1940. In the field LRDG patrols were armed with American M1 carbines and Thompson submachine guns. The men used Colt automatic pistols as their personal weapons. Bren machine guns and PIAT anti-tank weapons were only taken on offensive action missions.

Every man was issued with IS9 escape aids, a Bergen backpack, and the Thompson Black sleeping bag or the heavier Baxter, Woodhouse and Taylor version with waterproof cover.

Clothing generally was a mixture of British and Commonwealth issue, supplemented by American items. Steel helmets were never used and parachute jumps were carried out in the original British-style sorbo rubber helmets, which were discarded on the ground in favour of cap comforters or the distinctive LRDG sand-coloured beret (some men, though, such as Lieutenant Simpson here, retained the black beret originally worn in the desert campaign).

| | |
|---|---|
| *Date:* | *June 1944* |
| *Unit:* | *Long Range Desert Group* |
| *Rank:* | *Lieutenant* |
| *Theatre:* | *Mediterranean* |
| *Location:* | *Yugoslavia* |

# Private
# 4th Infantry Division
# Eighth Army

The uniform of the typical 'Tommy' during the Italian campaign. On his back this private wears the 1937-pattern web equipment, under the top flap of which he has stowed his battle dress. The Mk 1 helmet is worn with a camouflage net, to which strips of green and brown hessian were often added. Standard equipment carried with the 1937-pattern web kit included a pick, which doubled up as an entrenching tool, while inside the pack were a mess tin and cover, emergency rations, fork and spoon, cardigan, socks, cap comforter and washing kit.

Other items carried, which are not part of this figure's attire, included a groundsheet fastened beneath the pack flap, a gas mask carried on the left hip and a water bottle on the right hip.

By November 1943 the Eighth Army in Italy numbered 351,000 officers and men. The average size of a division, including support units, was around 40,000 men. However, attrition rates were high: between September 1943 and March 1944 the army suffered 46,000 battle casualties, of which 58 per cent were from the infantry arm. By February 1944, the infantry battalions of the 1st and 56th Divisions were operating with only 72 per cent and 68 per cent respectively of their establishments. When the Allies entered Rome on 4 June 1944, total British and Commonwealth casualties since the crossing from Sicily numbered 73,122, comprising 14,331 killed, 47,966 wounded and 10,825 missing.

| | |
|---|---|
| *Date:* | *June 1944* |
| *Unit:* | *4th Infantry Division* |
| *Rank:* | *Private* |
| *Theatre:* | *Mediterranean* |
| *Location:* | *Rome* |

# Lieutenant 1st Glider Pilot Regiment

**This figure is Lieutenant J. F. Hubble of the 1st Glider Pilot Regiment, who is wearing a paratrooper's Denison smock with ordinary battle-dress trousers. The Denison smock started to enter service in late 1941, and was usually worn either over or instead of the battle dress blouse. On his head Lieutenant Hubble wears a fibre protective helmet, under which is a Type C flying helmet with Type F oxygen mask. The wings on his left breast indicate that he is a qualified glider pilot.**

Glider pilot wings were always worn on the left breast, above the pocket, and all parachutists and glider pilots, other than those in the regular army, wore a white parachute or a glider embroidered in pale blue on the forearm of the left sleeve. At Arnhem so many glider pilots were lost that trainee pilots had their courses cut short and were made into second pilots, their badge comprising smaller wings, with a gold 'G' set in a gold ring. The red beret that Lieutenant Hubble carries in his right hand is the famous British Para headgear.

The British 6th Airborne Division had a strength of 12,000 men in anticipation of D-Day, comprising two parachute brigades and one airlanding brigade. The division's job was to drop its men in advance of the beach landings in order to secure vital canal and river bridges and to knock out enemy coastal batteries. The division deployed a large number of gliders. On 6 June, for example, 250 landed south-east of Ranville to bring in the 6th Air-Landing Brigade.

| | |
|---|---|
| *Date:* | *6 June 1944* |
| *Unit:* | *1st Glider Pilot Regiment* |
| *Rank:* | *Lieutenant* |
| *Theatre:* | *northwest Europe* |
| *Location:* | *Normandy* |

# *Corporal 6th Rajputana Rifles Eighth Army*

The Indian head-dress was normally the khaki puggaree, which varied in shape according to the religion and tribe of the wearer. In general, however, Muslims wore the pointed kullah or skull cap inside the puggaree and one end of the puggaree was formed into a large comb which stood up behind the kullah, while the other end of the puggaree hung down behind to the small of the back, and was used to protect the face from dust and sandstorms.

Sikhs wore the Sikh puggaree with their uncut hair in buns, which was normally tied with a red cloth. The Jats and other Hindus wore their puggaree as appropriate to their particular tribe or clan. This Naik of the 6th Rajputana Rifles in North Africa is wearing the standard Indian Army dress with distinctive puggaree bearing his regimental badge. Under his pullover he is wearing a typical collarless shirt, which was manufactured in grey material. His belt and pouches are Indian pattern, as is his bayonet.

Units of the Indian Army had begun to move to strategic points of the Empire before the war broke out, in anticipation of the struggle ahead. At the beginning of August 1939, for example, the 11th Infantry Brigade, which included the 6th Rajputana Rifles, left for Egypt. It was followed on 23 September by the 5th Indian Brigade and a Divisional Headquarters, both becoming part of the 4th Indian Infantry Division.

| | |
|---|---|
| *Date:* | *June 1944* |
| *Unit:* | *6th Rajputana Rifles* |
| *Rank:* | *Corporal* |
| *Theatre:* | *Mediterranean* |
| *Location:* | *Italy* |

# Royal Marine No 40 Commando 2 Commando Brigade

**The first of the Royal Marine Commandos was formed in February 1942, when Combined Operations Headquarters decided to establish a Royal Marine Commando of volunteers from the Royal Marine Division. It came into existence on 14 February at Deal in Kent, commanded by Lieutenant-Colonel J. Picton (who was killed in the abortive Dieppe raid in August 1942).**

The Royal Marines previously had worn army-pattern khaki service dress, but this was replaced at the beginning of the war with standard army khaki battle dress. The only insignia worn was the straight red and blue 'Royal Marine' shoulder flash. Royal Marine commandos wore battledress with straight woven blue shoulder flashes with 'Royal Marines', the number of the Commando above and the word 'Commando' below in red.

This Royal Marine of No 40 Commando wears the khaki serge battle dress with 1937-pattern webbing equipment and anklets. Under his helmet netting is tucked a field dressing, while his weapon is the Thompson M1928A1 submachine gun.

By the end of 1942 there were six Commandos in existence – Nos 40, 41, 42, 43, 44 and 45 – and by March 1944 these six had been joined by another, No 48. In November 1943, 2 Special Service (renamed Commando) Brigade was formed in Italy, comprising Nos 2, 9, 40 and 43 Commandos, together with the Belgian and Polish troops of No 10 (Inter-Allied) Commando.

| | |
|---|---|
| *Date:* | *April 1945* |
| *Unit:* | *No 40 Commando* |
| *Rank:* | *Marine* |
| *Theatre:* | *Mediterranean* |
| *Location:* | *Italy* |

# *Airman*
# *Bomber Command*
# *Royal Air Force*

**This airman is wearing a thermally insulated jacket and trousers made from glazed sheepskin, which was produced by the Irvin Parachute Company. These suits could be wired to give electrically heated gloves and socks – to warm the hands and feet of those flying aircraft at bitterly cold high altitudes.**

By the outbreak of World War II the RAF had 1000 Fairey Battles and 1000 Bristol Blenheims. High hopes were attached to both these light bombers, but when it came to the test in early 1940, they were shot down in droves by anti-aircraft fire and enemy fighters.

Tragic though it was, such huge losses forced the RAF to think of other options. One of these was strategic bombing at night, initially with Wellingtons, Whitleys and Hampdens. Originally it was believed that the Short Stirling was the aircraft that would prove the decisive factor in the campaign, but on operations it was discovered that its altitude ceiling put it in among the worst of the enemy flak. Alternative aircraft were needed.

First came the Halifax, then the Avro Manchester. The latter at first proved troublesome due to problems with its Vulture engines. However, the manufacturer switched to four Merlin engines on a longer wingspan. The resulting aircraft was the Lancaster, one of the greatest aircraft of the war and the undoubted star of Bomber Command. In many ways the Lancaster was a vindication of pre-war thinking about the potential decisiveness of strategic bombing.

| | |
|---|---|
| *Date:* | *September 1939* |
| *Unit:* | *Bomber Command* |
| *Rank:* | *Airman* |
| *Theatre:* | *northwest Europe* |
| *Location:* | *England* |

# *Bomber Crew 102 Squadron Royal Air Force*

**Accompanying the British Expeditionary Force (BEF) in France at the beginning of the war was an Air Component of two bomber-reconnaissance squadrons, four fighter squadrons, six army cooperation squadrons and two flights of a headquarters communication squadron. An additional Royal Air Force (RAF) component was an Advanced Air Striking Force of medium bombers from Bomber Command, though they were not under the operational command of the BEF.**

One of bomber command's aircrew is shown here. A member of a Whitley bomber crew, he wears an 'Irvin Harnsuit' over his service dress. The 'Harnsuit' had an inflatable lifebelt and three attachment points for the parachute. In addition, he is equipped with a type B helmet and an oxygen mask with a fitted microphone and oxygen tube. His boots are of the 1936 pattern: polished black leather with sheepskin lining.

The Whitley, though virtually obsolete at the outbreak of war, had the honour of being the first RAF aircraft to drop bombs on Germany since 1918, on 19 March 1940. Thereafter, these solid bombers undertook missions as far afield as Milan and Pilsen.

After 1942 the Whitley served mainly as a carrier of experimental radars and countermeasures. Its defensive armament included one machine gun in the nose turret and four in the tail turret (which was power-driven). A typical bomb load was made up of 3175kg (7000lb) of bombs carried in cells in the fuselage and the inner wings.

| | |
|---|---|
| *Date:* | *May 1940* |
| *Unit:* | *102 Squadron* |
| *Rank:* | *Aircrew* |
| *Theatre:* | *northwest Europe* |
| *Location:* | *England* |

# Leading Aircraftwoman Women's Auxiliary Air Force

Women had served in the British air force since the beginning of World War I. The original Women's Royal Air Force was disbanded in 1920, but in 1938, with war in Europe looming, women were again recruited into the Auxiliary Territorial Service. Units of the latter were attached to the RAF and eventually became the Women's Auxiliary Air Force (WAAF).

Members of the WAAF wore blue-grey uniforms like those of their male counterparts, though their rank titles were different. WAAF officers and NCOs wore special peaked caps, while other ranks sported dark blue berets (later changed to a head-dress similar to that worn by their senior officers). The pay was two-thirds that of the men depending on the duties performed and the rank held.

This leading aircraftwoman is wearing the women's version of the standard RAF service dress as worn by members of the WAAF. On her left sleeve she wears an RAF eagle above the letter 'A' (denoting auxiliary), together with the flash of a wireless operator and a horizontal propeller, indicating the rank of leading aircraftwoman. The RAF eagle was usually worn on both the upper sleeves by all those below the rank of warrant officer 1st class. The badge was adopted in 1918 and was originally red on a khaki uniform, though it was later changed to light blue when the blue-grey uniform was introduced. Like the RAF eagle, the rank and trade badges are embroidered in light blue on a dark blue background.

| | |
|---|---|
| **Date:** | *May 1940* |
| **Unit:** | *Women's Auxiliary Air Force* |
| **Rank:** | *Leading Aircraftwoman* |
| **Theatre:** | *northwest Europe* |
| **Location:** | *Kent* |

# Sergeant 11 Group Royal Air Force

**This NCO is wearing the standard issue service dress for other ranks in the RAF. It was identical in cut to the one worn by officers, though it was made of serge. Before the outbreak of war the RAF uniform differed little from that of the British Army, though of course it was in blue-grey. As shown here, all ranks had an open tunic which was worn with collar and tie, with black shoes and socks. Poor-weather attire included a double-breasted greatcoat with matching cloth belt, mackintosh and raincoat.**

This sergeant is wearing a Mk 1 steel helmet, though the most common form of head-dress was the field service cap, or the stiff peaked cap with metal cap badge. Rank is indicated by the three chevrons on each upper arm, which are embroidered in worsted on a black background (dark blue was also used). When wearing overalls, both officers and other ranks wore rank badges on dark blue armlets, and NCOs also wore their rank badges in this manner with shirt-sleeve order. The top NCO rank was flight sergeant, which differed from the ranks shown here by having a crown above the three chevrons.

By the date of this figure – July 1940 – the RAF had a total of 530 fighter aircraft deployed to meet the Luftwaffe's bombers and fighters, plus another 289 in reserve. Though the Luftwaffe outnumbered its British enemy, RAF Fighter Command was able to prevent the Germans gaining air superiority over England and thus effectively prevented an invasion, though the margin of victory was slim.

| | |
|---|---|
| *Date:* | *July 1940* |
| *Unit:* | *11 Group* |
| *Rank:* | *Sergeant* |
| *Theatre:* | *northwest Europe* |
| *Location:* | *Home Counties* |

# Pilot
# No 112 Squadron
# Royal Air Force

**This pilot is wearing flying overalls and the 'seat-type' parachute pack which was issued to pilots of single-seat fighters. Its quick-release device (the metal disc) is situated at the front, while the parachute release handle lies under his left forearm. His leather flying helmet is the RAF 'B' type, with provision for external wiring. On his feet he wears non-issue civilian shoes.**

No 112 Squadron was reformed on 16 May 1939, and was equipped with Gloster Gladiator biplanes and shipped to Egypt as part of the Suez Canal force. With the outbreak of war the squadron was involved in patrols over the Western Desert, which included taking part in the defence of Athens and covering the retreat of British troops from Greece. The squadron was then redeployed to Egypt and re-equipped with Curtiss Tomahawk fighters. The latter were poor for fighter duties, but were ideal for supporting ground units against the Africa Corps.

The squadron distinguished itself in the North African desert, carrying out many bomber-escort and ground-attack missions. After the end of the North African campaign, the squadron took part in the Sicilian and Italian campaigns, supporting Allied landings. No 112 Squadron ended the war equipped with North American Mustangs, having supported the Allied landings in France in 1944. It was disbanded at the end of the war, but was then reformed and went on to serve the RAF until 1957 as part of the Tactical Air Force.

| | |
|---|---|
| *Date:* | *November 1941* |
| *Unit:* | *No 112 Squadron* |
| *Rank:* | *Pilot* |
| *Theatre:* | *Mediterranean* |
| *Location:* | *North Africa* |

# Sergeant No 120 Squadron Coastal Command

**It was the job of RAF Coastal Command to oppose the German U-boat threat in the Atlantic Ocean. At first this was a forlorn task; Coastal Command had just 196 aircraft in Britain, and of these only the 12 Lockheed Hudsons and 18 Short Sunderlands could operate more than 480km (300 miles) from their bases.**

However, by September 1941 long-range Consolidated Liberators had entered service with No 120 Squadron, and then with Nos 59 and 86 Squadrons. As a result, German U-boats could be driven into the Bay of Biscay — where they came within range of other RAF aircraft. The first U-boat sunk by Coastal Command was U-55 on 30 January 1940.

The figure illustrated here is Sergeant Harold Oliver. He is wearing the flying suit which was typical of those crews who flew with Coastal Command on long missions over the Atlantic and the Arctic. Sergeant Oliver was a Liberator pilot, and so his attire reflects the two attributes which were essential to flights of 12 hours or more: comfort and practicality. His polo-neck sweater — which is called a Frock White sweater — and Irvin sheepskin jacket over a pre-war flying suit, provided both. On his feet he wears a pair of 1941-pattern flying boots with brown rubber soles and brown suede uppers. Between the outer suede and sheepskin lining is a splinter-proof interlining of 30 layers of parachute silk. On his head he wears a side cap which sports the yellow badge of RAF other ranks.

| | |
|---|---|
| *Date:* | *June 1943* |
| *Unit:* | *No 120 Squadron* |
| *Rank:* | *Sergeant* |
| *Theatre:* | *Atlantic* |
| *Location:* | *Bay of Biscay* |

# *Wing Commander No 85 Squadron Royal Air Force*

**Wing Commander John Cunningham is wearing pre-war black flying overalls, a silk scarf and black shoes. In his hands he carries a leather flying helmet and oxygen mask. Wing Commander Cunningham was a night-fighter ace who first joined the RAF when he became a member of No 604 Squadron. On the outbreak of war Cunningham's squadron was equipped with Bristol Blenheim twin-engined fighters. The unit was assigned to convoy patrol duties, which were carried out until June 1940.**

The squadron then began training for night fighting, receiving its first Bristol Beaufighters in September 1940. On 20 November Cunningham scored his squadron's first night victory with his aircraft, and won the Distinguished Flying Cross in January 1941 following his third victory. By April 1941 he had scored 10 victories, three during one night alone. A DSO followed, and in August Cunningham was promoted to the rank of wing commander and took command of No 604 Squadron.

By this time Cunningham was the RAF's most successful and experienced night-fighter pilot, and was involved in developing new tactics and equipment. By June 1942 he had scored 16 victories, and was given a rest in a staff post. However, following this he took command of No 85 Squadron and gained a further four victories. This final addition to his score made him the second highest-scoring RAF night-fighter pilot of World War II.

| | |
|---|---|
| *Date:* | *June 1943* |
| *Unit:* | *No 85 Squadron* |
| *Rank:* | *Wing Commander* |
| *Theatre:* | *northwest Europe* |
| *Location:* | *southern England* |

# *Head Officer Royal Observer Corps Royal Air Force*

**The Observer Corps was established in 1918, and by 1929 had become part of the RAF under the Air Ministry. It was just one of many such organisations created during the war, and it gave civilians the chance to contribute to national defence. In April 1941, on account of its sterling service in World War I, the 30,000-strong corps was granted a royal warrant and became the Royal Observer Corps.**

At first, corps recruits wore civilian dress, with just a blue and white vertically striped armlet with 'Observer Corps' in red letters to denote membership. However, in June 1941 the RAF-type grey serge battle dress was adopted, as shown here. In addition to the black beret, a black steel helmet, on which 'Observer Corps' was sometimes painted in white, was worn on duty.

The Royal Observer Corps badge, worn on the beret and left breast, depicted an Elizabethan Coast Watcher holding a torch above the motto 'Forewarned is Forearmed', surrounded by a wreath and ensigned by the Royal Crown. Officers wore the initials ROC on their collar lapels, while other ranks sported an embroidered breast badge, showing the RAF eagle surrounded by the title 'Royal Observer Corps', which was set in a ring surmounted by the Crown. This officer wears a Spitfire badge on his left sleeve. This was the mark of a master spotter, a rank introduced in January 1944. ROC personnel provided invaluable service throughout the war, especially during the Battle of Britain.

| | |
|---|---|
| *Date:* | *June 1944* |
| *Unit:* | *Royal Observer Corps* |
| *Rank:* | *Head Officer* |
| *Theatre:* | *northwest Europe* |
| *Location:* | *Kent* |

# Wing Commander No 617 Squadron Royal Air Force

**Wing Commander Guy Gibson wears standard RAF battle dress with fleece-lined flying boots. The latter, besides keeping their wearer warm, could be adapted for use in enemy territory. A small knife was provided so the upper part could be detached from the shoe. In this way the boots could be turned into walking boots. The inflatable life-jacket is the standard type, known as Type LS yellow, while on his head Gibson wears an officer's service cap. In his hand he carries a Type C flying helmet. Note the shoulder straps showing his rank.**

Guy Gibson led the famous 'Dam Buster' squadron – No 617 – in the spring of 1943. His flying experience (with No 106 Squadron) was second to none, but what was exceptional about Gibson was that he was an inspired leader, and a tough commanding officer where flying was concerned (he always kept a loaded revolver on his desk). The breaching of the Ruhr dams in May 1943 totally vindicated the RAF's faith in him, for it was Gibson's skill, as much as the detailed planning and innovative bouncing bombs, which resulted in his success. Of the 19 Lancasters and 133 men which had set out to attack the dams, nine aircraft and 56 men failed to return. Gibson received the Victoria Cross, and 33 other men were also decorated.

Gibson always led from the front and spared no effort in helping his fellow pilots. His Victoria Cross was well earned, and was a just reward for a very brave pilot who later gave his life for his country.

| | |
|---|---|
| *Date:* | *May 1943* |
| *Unit:* | *No 617 Squadron* |
| *Rank:* | *Wing Commander* |
| *Theatre:* | *northwest Europe* |
| *Location:* | *England* |

# *Flying Officer No 617 Squadron Royal Air Force*

**This flying officer is a member of the Royal Australian Air Force serving in 617 Squadron, and flying in a Lancaster bomber. He is wearing standard British Royal Air Force battle dress, over which he wears an inflatable life vest.**

On his upper left arm can be seen this officer's nationality badge. During World War II large numbers of foreign nationals served with the RAF. As a mark of identification they wore nationality titles. In general, officers wore curved titles embroidered in light blue on a grey-blue background, while others had titles in light blue on a dark blue or black background which was usually rectangular. All ranks wore red and khaki shoulder titles on tropical uniforms.

There were variations in nationality badges. Some had the RAF eagle and nationality title combined in the same badge, and different styles of lettering were also applied. Thus, for example, there were titles depicting the eagle above the initials 'USA'. Conversely, British airmen serving in Canada started wearing the 'GT. BRITAIN' title. All Commonwealth nations, colonies and British territories were represented in this form.

This flying officer is a member of a night-bombing force, which relied on the skill and judgement of the aircraft in the Pathfinder Force. The Pathfinder navigators identified the target and dropped incendiary marker bombs on the intended target so that the follow-on bombers would know where to drop their bombs.

| | |
|---|---|
| *Date:* | *June 1944* |
| *Unit:* | *No 617 Squadron* |
| *Rank:* | *Flying Officer* |
| *Theatre:* | *northwest Europe* |
| *Location:* | *England* |

# Squadron Leader Royal Air Force Volunteer Reserve

**Before the war in the tropics RAF personnel wore the Wolseley helmet with puggaree and flash in RAF colours on the left side (or the pith hat in India), khaki drill tunic, shirt, tie, long or short trousers, khaki woollen stockings and black shoes or boots. Towards the end of the war in the Far East, officers wore jungle-green clothing and the slouch hat.**

This officer of the Royal Air Force Volunteer Reserve is wearing the RAF's tropical dress, but has kept the cap from the blue-grey service uniform. His rank insignia is worn on the shoulder straps. On tropical uniforms rank badges were embroidered or woven in red on a light khaki background. Senior officers had two medium rings with one narrow ring between, or three or four medium rings of black and light blue lace on the cuffs and shoulder straps. Junior officers sported one narrow ring, or one or two medium rings of black and light blue lace on the cuffs and shoulder straps. This officer's reserve status is indicated by the letters 'VR' on the collar, while on his left breast he wears the observers' half-wing qualification badge. His appearance contrasts sharply with the more relaxed look of the British Armed Forces in the Pacific theatre at the end of World War II.

By the date of this figure, July 1945, the strength of the RAF in the Far East numbered 207,632 officers and men, of which 13,225 were RAF officers and 118,582 British other ranks. In addition, the Royal Indian Air Force had a strength of 29,201 officers and men by August 1945.

| | |
|---|---|
| ***Date:*** | *July 1945* |
| ***Unit:*** | *Royal Air Force Volunteer Reserve* |
| ***Rank:*** | *Squadron Leader* |
| ***Theatre:*** | *Pacific* |
| ***Location:*** | *India* |

# Groundcrew Fire-fighting Unit Royal Air Force

**This rather futuristic-looking individual is dressed in an asbestos suit, which was designed to provide maximum protection from the heat and flames generated by burning kerosene. These suits were issued to groundcrew of RAF airfield firefighting units, as well as of Royal Navy ships which carried aircraft. The wearer could see through the tinted reinforced glass plate.**

The threat of fire, either from accidents or from attack by enemy aircraft, has always been a danger for military aircraft, particularly carrier aircraft. However, in the Far East this threat was even greater due to Japanese kamikaze attacks on British and American aircraft carriers.

In general, the RAF in the Pacific theatre was under strength in comparison with its Japanese counterpart. Also, the aircraft available to the RAF — the Brewster Buffalo fighter and Vildebeest torpedo-bomber — were totally outclassed by the Japanese Zero (although at the time the Far East was way down on the RAF's list of priorities).

It was not until 1943–44, with the arrival of the Spitfire and Thunderbolt, that the situation reversed itself. One of the main problems with regard to operating in the Far East was the difficulty of building and operating airfields in terrain which did not lend itself to flat and open spaces. Once the RAF had gained aerial superiority this meant that it could provide air support to ground formations, as well as carry out strategic bombing against Japanese targets.

| | |
|---|---|
| *Date:* | *June 1945* |
| *Unit:* | *Southeast Asia Command* |
| *Rank:* | *Private* |
| *Theatre:* | *Pacific* |
| *Location:* | *Malaya* |

# Captain
# Home Fleet
# Royal Navy

**The British naval uniform which was worn during World War II actually dated from the uniform which was worn in the middle of the nineteenth century. The basic uniform for officers is shown here. It consists of a peaked cap, double-breasted 'reefer' jacket, white shirt and black tie, long trousers which matched the jacket, and black shoes and socks. There was also a double-breasted greatcoat, which was worn with brown leather gloves.**

Royal Navy officers' caps were made of blue navy cloth and were fitted with peak, chin strap and a black mohair band 44.5mm (1.75in) wide. The cap badge itself consisted of a wreath of gold laurel leaves surrounding a silver anchor with the Royal Crown above embroidered in gold and silver. The anchor could either be embroidered in silver or partly made of silver metal. The chin strap was made of black patent calf leather, and the peak of the cap of senior officers who were entitled to wear embroidery was covered with blue cloth and bound with leather.

This figure's rank of captain is denoted by the four gold rings around each cuff and the single row of oak leaves on the cap's peak. In the Royal Navy rank insignia for officers consisted of rows of gold lace on the cuffs, with the uppermost stripe curled into a circle. The width of stripes for captains was 14mm (0.55in). In between the gold rings, this figure sports his arm of service colour – purple – indicating he is an engineer.

| | |
|---|---|
| *Date:* | *January 1940* |
| *Unit:* | *Home Fleet* |
| *Rank:* | *Captain* |
| *Theatre:* | *northwest Europe* |
| *Location:* | *Great Britain* |

# Chief Petty Officer
# *Home Fleet*
# *Royal Navy*

In the Royal Navy the uniforms for chief petty officers were basically the same as those for officers except that the former had a special cap badge and wore rating badges on the sleeves. The everyday chief petty officer uniform is illustrated here: a single-breasted jacket with three buttons on the cuffs (a double-breasted jacket was worn on all other occasions). The same basic uniform was also worn by petty officers and by various junior ratings who were not members of the seamen branch.

In the tropics, chief petty officers wore a white cap cover, a single-breasted white tunic with a stand-collar, open patch breast pockets and four brass buttons, long white trousers and white canvas shoes.

Rate and non-substantive badges were red for blue uniforms, blue for white uniforms and embroidered in gold for the No 1 uniform. Chief petty officers wore gold badges on the right forearm of the white tunic, above the three buttons. The chief petty officer pictured here wears the non-substantive badge of a gunner's mate on his jacket collar. This non-substantive badge consisted of two crossed guns with a crown above and star below (the gun was the first device to be adopted in 1860, when it resembled an old cannon, with the more modern version entering into use in 1903).

At the outbreak of war in 1939 the Royal Navy was the most powerful navy in the world, having bases around the globe and a massive number of ships.

| | |
|---|---|
| **Date:** | *January 1940* |
| **Unit:** | *Home Fleet* |
| **Rank:** | *Chief Petty Officer* |
| **Theatre:** | *northwest Europe* |
| **Location:** | *Scapa Flow* |

# Petty Officer Home Fleet Royal Navy

**Royal Naval ratings wore the so-called 'square rig' shown here, which was to be the model for the uniforms of many navies worldwide. At the beginning of the war the cap tally that displayed the name of the ship was officially replaced by a tally bearing just the letters 'HMS', or 'His Majesty's Ship', without the ship's name. This was a simple security measure in time of war.**

Although not shown here, Royal Navy ratings were also issued with a single-breasted greatcoat, instead of the short winter coat worn in some navies. This had five black plastic buttons in front, an adjustable belt at the back and could be worn open or closed.

For everyday work, ratings wore a blue boiler suit, or one of the many other types of protective clothing worn in the navy. In cold weather, ratings were issued with a thick woollen pullover and sea socks to be worn inside rubber boots, a knitted woollen cap comforter and the ubiquitous duffle coat. Attire for rough seas consisted of waterproof clothing, especially the oilskin 'sou'wester' and coat.

This petty officer wears his non-substantive badge on his right sleeve, which identifies him as a gunlayer first class (two stars and crossed guns), while on his left sleeve is the substantive or rank badge for petty officer: crown and crossed anchors (petty officers' rates were unified in 1913, when that of 2nd petty officer was abolished). Note the two good conduct chevrons on his left upper sleeve.

| | |
|---|---|
| *Date:* | *May 1940* |
| *Unit:* | *Home Fleet* |
| *Rank:* | *Petty Officer* |
| *Theatre:* | *Atlantic* |
| *Location:* | *Atlantic Ocean* |

# Rating
# *HMS* Warspite
# *Royal Navy*

**The rating pictured here is a member of one of HMS *Warspite*'s anti-aircraft gun crews. His clothing is typical of that worn by British naval gun crews during World War II and consists of a duffle coat, over which he wears a life vest, and bell-bottom trousers tucked into Wellington boots.**

He wears a steel helmet, which was standard issue for those seamen exposed to aerial attack. As a gunner, he wears an asbestos anti-flash hood, which was a form of protection against the sudden flash-fires resulting from the ignition of gun magazines (the Royal Navy used flashless cordite, which meant that at night her ships could fire unseen at an enemy whose flashes lit up the night sky).

HMS *Warspite* was launched in 1913 and saw service in World War I. At the beginning of World War II she was armed with eight 15in guns in four turrets and eight 6in guns, as well as eight 4in, 32 two-pounder and 16 0.5in anti-aircraft guns. She served at Narvik in April 1940 and in the Mediterranean in 1941. She was badly damaged during the evacuation of Crete in May 1941, and underwent repairs in the United States before returning to the Mediterranean in 1942. HMS *Warspite* went on to support the Allied landings in Europe, and though she was nearly sunk on one occasion, stayed in service until late 1945.

During the Crete battle the Royal Navy lost 2011 men, though it still managed to stave off the German efforts to send reinforcements to the island by sea, and evacuate Allied defenders from Sfaika.

| | |
|---|---|
| ***Date:*** | *March 1941* |
| ***Unit:*** | *HMS* Warspite |
| ***Rank:*** | *Rating* |
| ***Theatre:*** | *Mediterranean* |
| ***Location:*** | *off Crete* |

# Lieutenant-Commander Royal Navy

**Lieutenant-Commander Kimmins of the Royal Navy is wearing the same uniform as he wore during a combined operation in Norway: a naval service dress under an army helmet and leather jerkin. His web equipment is the 1937-pattern, while the binoculars are marked with the broad white arrow which indicates they are the property of the War Department. The white lanyard is attached to a folding jack knife.**

On his cuffs Kimmins wears the rank distinctions for lieutenant-commander: two medium 14mm (0.5in) wide gold lace rings with one narrow 'half stripe' 6.5mm (0.25in) wide between, with a curl on the upper ring. Above the lace rings are the pilot's wings of the Fleet Air Arm.

In addition to its commitments in the Atlantic Ocean with regard to protecting convoys and searching for enemy vessels, the Royal Navy was heavily engaged in convoy duties in the Arctic Ocean, in escorting Allied supplies to the Soviet Union. Surprisingly, given German superiority in 1941, these convoys met little resistance. The six convoys which sailed during autumn 1941, for example, delivered 120,000 tons (121,900 tonnes) of supplies with only minimal losses. However, the following year German aerial and submarine attacks inflicted heavy losses. The worst of these attacks was on the PQ 17 convoy, which landed 150,000 tons (152,500 tonnes) but had another 100,000 tons (101,500 tonnes) sunk by the Germans.

| | |
|---|---|
| *Date:* | *August 1941* |
| *Unit:* | *Royal Navy* |
| *Rank:* | *Lieutenant-Commander* |
| *Theatre:* | *Arctic* |
| *Location:* | *North Cape* |

# *Petty Officer Convoy Duties Royal Navy*

**This petty officer serving aboard an escort vessel in the Atlantic Ocean is holding a shell for a 4.7in gun. He wears a peaked cap which displays the special badge for petty officers. The rest of his uniform consists of a balaclava helmet, duffle coat and sea socks and boots. The duffle coat was also issued in dark blue and white, though the colour shown here was the most common.**

Following the German conquest of western Europe in 1940, Britain's ability to wage war was threatened by the presence of enemy U-boats in her waters. Before the war very little attention had been paid to the convoy system as a whole, despite the fact that it had proved to be highly effective during World War I. And it would not be until after the heavy losses experienced during the early months of World War II that the Admiralty would finally decide to reinstate the convoy system. However, there was a dire shortage of escort vessels at this time, and it was not until the end of 1941 that coast-to-coast convoys were made possible.

Britain operated a convoy system which was centred around the three bases of the Western Approaches: Liverpool, Greenwich and Londonderry, in Northern Ireland. A total of 70 destroyers and 95 smaller ships in 25 escort groups were involved. An escort group usually consisted of about eight ships, though sometimes only six were available. At sea every attempt was made to keep the group together for maximum effectiveness.

| | |
|---|---|
| *Date:* | *June 1941* |
| *Unit:* | *Royal Navy* |
| *Rank:* | *Petty Officer* |
| *Theatre:* | *Atlantic* |
| *Location:* | *Atlantic Ocean* |

# Gunlayer 2nd Class Royal Navy

**This figure wears the typical action rig, which was worn by naval gun crews during World War II. Over this he wears a one-piece blue overall with a canvas money belt. Under the steel helmet he wears an anti-flash hood, while his hands are protected by special gauntlets. This was a dangerous job and clean underwear was essential as dirty underclothing could easily cause any wounds to become infected.**

The blue overall illustrated here was just one of many types of working clothing worn throughout the navy during the war. The 'stoke hole' boots shown here were often worn without laces so that in the event of a ship evacuation the sailor could kick them off easily before jumping into the sea. On his upper right sleeve this sailor wears the non-substantive badge of a gunlayer.

Despite the adoption of the convoy system by the navy (see page 132), British losses at the hands of German U-boats were massive. This was particularly the case in the period 1941–43, when U-boat packs roamed the ocean from their bases on the French Atlantic coast. In June 1941 alone, for example, 300,000 tons (301,000 tonnes) of Allied shipping was sunk in the Atlantic. It was only the massive allocation of resources, plus the new anti-submarine techniques and the increasing numbers and quality of escort vessels, which gave the Allies eventual victory over the U-boats. By October 1943, the Battle of the Atlantic had been won.

| | |
|---|---|
| **Date:** | *June 1941* |
| **Unit:** | *Royal Navy* |
| **Rank:** | *Gunlayer 2nd Class* |
| **Theatre:** | *Atlantic* |
| **Location:** | *Atlantic Ocean* |

# 2nd Officer Women's Royal Naval Service

**The Women's Royal Naval Service (WRNS) was formed in November 1917, its members becoming known as 'Wrens' on account of the service's initial letters. The service was disbanded after World War I but reformed in 1939. The commanding officer was Director Vera Laughton Mathews, who at first wore four blue stripes on her cuffs, which was the equivalent of Rear-Admiral.**

The figure illustrated here holds the rank of 2nd Officer, which was equivalent to the rank of lieutenant in the Royal Navy. All Wren officers wore special cap badges on their tricorne hats. These cap badges were smaller than those worn by their male colleagues and, in addition, the six-leaved wreath was embroidered in blue silk. Officers also wore special blue stripes on the cuffs, as shown here, and shoulder straps, with a diamond instead of a curl. Shoulder straps with rank insignia were worn on the greatcoat and on the tropical rig.

The uniform shown here is the standard women's version of the naval service dress with tricorne hat, reefer (nicknamed the 'monkey jacket') and matching skirt. Note the rank distinction on her cuffs showing two blue stripes 12.7mm (0.5in) in width, sandwiched between which is a white stripe indicating paymaster branch.

At the beginning of the war, all Wren ratings were issued with pull-on hats, but these were recalled in late 1942 and replaced by tricorne hats or round hats, according to the rating.

| | |
|---|---|
| *Date:* | *January 1942* |
| *Unit:* | *Women's Royal Naval Service* |
| *Rank:* | *2nd Officer* |
| *Theatre:* | *northwest Europe* |
| *Location:* | *Whitehall* |

# *Warrant Officer Pacific Ocean Force Royal Navy*

**This British naval engineer stationed in the Pacific theatre in World War II is wearing working garb. His Royal Navy officers' peaked cap has a white cover which matches the colour of his overalls. He has strong gloves on his hands, and his laceless shoes can be kicked off quickly in an emergency.**

At the beginning of the war in the Far East the Royal Navy had a sizeable contingent — five battleships, three light aircraft carriers, seven cruisers and sixteen destroyers — though their overall quality left a lot to be desired. The carriers, for example, were no match for their Japanese adversaries. This force was under the command of Admiral Sir James Somerville, who managed to keep it from being destroyed in the Indian Ocean despite the string of Japanese victories in 1941–42. Ironically, Somerville's force was broken up not by the enemy but by the re-starting of Arctic convoys to Murmansk. Nevertheless, by the summer of 1944 Somerville had received the carriers *Victorious* and *Illustrious*.

In the event, Somerville was replaced by Admiral Sir Bruce Fraser in August 1944, and by January 1945 the British Pacific Fleet comprised one battleship, four aircraft carriers, three cruisers and ten destroyers, and was based at Sydney, Australia. Though this was an excellent force, it paled in comparison with the American fleets in the region. In March 1945, for example, the British Pacific Fleet was but one component of Admiral Spruance's US Fifth Fleet of more than 1200 vessels.

| | |
|---|---|
| *Date:* | *June 1943* |
| *Unit:* | *Pacific Ocean Fleet* |
| *Rank:* | *Warrant Officer* |
| *Theatre:* | *Pacific* |
| *Location:* | *Indian Ocean* |

# Admiral Mediterranean Fleet Royal Navy

**Before and during World War II, Royal Navy officers wore the white uniform which is shown here. However, in February 1938 a new tropical uniform was introduced, consisting of white shirt, white shorts, white stockings and canvas shoes, or black stockings and black leather shoes.**

Here, Admiral Sir John Cunningham, Naval Commander-in-Chief Levant, wears regulation navy whites. The cap was either made with a white top, or a washable white cover was put over the blue cloth cap. On his shoulders Cunningham carries his rank badges.

Shoulder straps were worn with greatcoat, watch-coat, white tunic and white mess jacket. All straps were made of blue cloth, except those of engineer, medical officers and accountant officers of flag rank, which were made of appropriate distinction cloth, with gold lace on top and a leather backing. Flag officers like Cunningham had 51mm (2in) wide lace sewn along the shoulder straps, which left a narrow piping of blue or other coloured distinction cloth exposed all around. The shoulder straps themselves were 133mm (5.25in) long and 57mm (2.25in) wide and had a button at the top and a leather tongue at the back. On his straps Cunningham wears a crown, crossed sword and three eight-pointed stars.

On his left side Cunningham wears the Order of the Bath, and below that the Norwegian Royal Order of St Olaf and the Royal Greek Order of George I. His sword is the regulation M1891 naval officers' sword.

| | |
|---|---|
| **Date:** | *September 1943* |
| **Unit:** | *Mediterranean Fleet* |
| **Rank:** | *Admiral* |
| **Theatre:** | *Mediterranean* |
| **Location:** | *Cairo* |

# Lieutenant Royal Naval Volunteer Reserve

**This lieutenant is wearing the uniform for land operations in the tropics. During the war the most popular uniform for wear in these conditions was the white-topped hat or khaki drill sun helmet, khaki drill shirt or Royal Marine-pattern tunic, and khaki drill long or short trousers.**

This officer also wears the 1937-pattern web equipment over his khaki drill jacket and leather leggings, which were standard issue for officers wearing landing rig (the navy adopted khaki battledress in 1941, which was worn with naval head-dress). Throughout the war Royal Navy officers played an invaluable part in the supervision of amphibious landings.

The lieutenant here is a member of the Royal Naval Volunteer Reserve, which was instituted in 1903. Its officers wore waved stripes of gold braid, which can be seen on the shoulder straps of this officer. The stripes were 9.5mm (0.4in) wide and they were worn parallel to each other and surmounted by a squarish, waved curl. Distinction cloth was placed between the stripes.

In general, in the Mediterranean theatre during the war, Royal Navy badges of rank were worn on the shoulder straps and sometimes painted on the steel helmet as well. Officers in the civil branches of the navy wore coloured backing or 'lights' to the rank lace on the shoulder straps, while cadets and midshipmen had a stripe of the same coloured cloth on their shoulder straps.

| | |
|---|---|
| **Date:** | *September 1943* |
| **Unit:** | *Royal Naval Volunteer Reserve* |
| **Rank:** | *Lieutenant* |
| **Theatre:** | *Mediterranean* |
| **Location:** | *Sicily* |

# Sub-Lieutenant *HMS* Shakespeare *British Pacific Fleet*

**The figure shown here is Sub-Lieutenant A. Lloyd Morgan, who served aboard the submarine *Shakespeare* in the Pacific theatre during the war. As a member of the Royal Naval Volunteer Reserve, he wears khaki drill shirt and shorts, with rank insignia on the shoulder straps (some officers, like the sub-lieutenant pictured here, wore their rank distinction lace on khaki drill slides on the shoulder straps which were provided with the shirt or bush jacket, while others wore blue shoulder straps).**

Although the names sounded similar, the Royal Naval Volunteer Reserve and Royal Naval Reserve were totally different organisations. The latter was formed in 1859 and its cadre of offices was organised five years later. Members of the Volunteer Reserve wore a square curl on their rank insignia, whereas members of the Royal Naval Reserve had a star-shaped curl and 'wavy' rank lace (the letters 'RNVR' were sometimes worn on cuffs above buttons by chief petty officers, while cadets and midshipmen wore maroon loops or collar patches).

Sub-Lieutenant Lloyd Morgan's uniform appears to be quite informal, a style which was typical of uniforms aboard both allied and axis submarines, given the nature of these vessels. He wears the standard Royal Navy officers' peaked cap with white cover. The uniform illustrated here became the standard attire for British Royal Navy officers in the Far East, and replaced the white service dress introduced in 1938.

| | |
|---|---|
| *Date:* | *May 1945* |
| *Unit:* | *HMS* Shakespeare |
| *Rank:* | *Sub-Lieutenant* |
| *Theatre:* | *Pacific* |
| *Location:* | *Indian Ocean* |

# *Italy*

*Due to the defeats suffered by Italy in World War II, the average Italian serviceman has been viewed, unfairly, as a coward. Participating in an unwanted conflict, equipped with sub-standard hardware and often poorly led, it is not surprising that he performed badly. However, Italy did not lack for courage, and over 200,000 men were killed in the war.*

# Lieutenant Infantry Division Italian Army

In the Italian Army tropical clothing closely followed the cut of the army's temperate uniform, but was made of a light khaki drill material. Italian soldiers also wore a semi-official bash jacket, or *sahariana*, which must have been very comfortable as it was taken up and worn by both British and German soldiers in North Africa.

This infantry lieutenant is wearing typical dress for tropical regions. On the front of his side cap, called a *bustina*, he sports his infantry cap badge with the regimental number in the centre of the grenade. The badge is embroidered in gold and was used during the period 1933–43.

The shoulder straps bear two stars for a lieutenant, although this officer's collar stars were common to all arms and ranks. Italian officers wore their rank badges on the head-dress and on both forearms and on the jacket. In the cases of the black uniform, white summer uniform and colonial uniform, the badges were worn on shoulder boards instead of on the forearms.

1st lieutenants wore a small bar at the outside end of the shoulder board instead of the two stars illustrated here. The rank of 1st lieutenant was given to officers after 12 years' service as a lieutenant. In general, as the war progressed Italian rank badges gradually became smaller, and those which had been originally made of gold were later produced in yellow silk instead. The stars on his collar were common to all arms and ranks in the Italian Army.

| | |
|---|---|
| **Date:** | *August 1940* |
| **Unit:** | *infantry division* |
| **Rank:** | *Lieutenant* |
| **Theatre:** | *Mediterranean* |
| **Location:** | *Sidi Azeis* |

# Colonel 36th Infantry Regiment

**In the Italian Army the standard uniform for other ranks was made of a coarse, dark, grey-green cloth, while officers wore a uniform made of a much lighter shade of twill, which was called a *cordellino* (shown here). Officers had two basic uniforms. The service dress consisted of a khaki version of the grey-green uniform, which, with a few additions, could also be worn as full dress.**

This colonel of the 1940 French campaign is wearing a gold-embroidered pattern cap badge on his cap; this is unusual because on the field service uniform the cap badge was normally embroidered in black thread. The madder red (called *robbio*) backing on the cap and rank badges was only worn by colonels commanding a regiment. The rank badges worn on the forearm were gold braid stripes 10mm (0.4in) in depth, while the 17mm (0.7in) gold stripe was the basic insignia of senior rank.

Italian collar patches were rectangular in shape. According to regulations they were 60mm (2.4in) long, though as the war progressed they gradually became shorter. The crown and swords on this figure's breast is the badge indicating promotion due to meritorious service in the field, while above the medal ribbon can be seen a metal eagle, indicating that he is a graduate of the war academy.

The Italian campaign in France, which began on 10 June 1940 and ended 15 days later, was a disaster for the Italian Army. The Italians suffered over 4000 casualties, the French only 200.

| | |
|---|---|
| *Date:* | *June 1940* |
| *Unit:* | *36th Infantry Regiment* |
| *Rank:* | *Colonel* |
| *Theatre:* | *Mediterranean* |
| *Location:* | *southern France* |

# Corporal
# VI Eritrea Battalion
# Italian Colonial Army

**Italy was an imperial power at the beginning of the war, and as such she employed colonial troops to fulfil a number of roles. For example, the** *Sahariani*, **for example, were excellent desert fighters, and had their own transport and artillery. However, this force was the exception, and most of Italy's colonial forces were poorly armed and trained.**

The figure shown here is from Italian East Africa. As a corporal in the Italian Colonial Army he is wearing the uniform laid down in the 1929 regulations. The head-dress was called a *tarbusc*, and its tassel identifies the wearer as a member of the VI *Eritrea* Battalion, as does the coloured sash. The rank chevrons are worn on the right sleeve, above the three stars which denote 10 years' service. His rifle is the Mannlicher-Carcano M91/38, a bolt-action weapon.

The Italian Army of East Africa boasted 88,000 Italian troops and 200,000 colonial troops at the beginning of the war. Italian military doctrine stressed the primacy of the offensive; indeed, defensive action was seen as being only a temporary measure, and an impressive force committed to the attack. However, it was a force with a number of inherent weaknesses, such as an obsolete artillery arm and almost non-existent supplies of ammunition and equipment. Its commander was the Duke of Aosta, who knew that his force could only hold out for six months if war came. He was right; in January 1941 the British invaded Ethiopia, and within four months the Duke had surrendered all his troops to the enemy.

| | |
|---|---|
| **Date:** | *June 1940* |
| **Unit:** | *VI* Eritrea *Battalion* |
| **Rank:** | *Corporal* |
| **Theatre:** | *Africa* |
| **Location:** | *Ethiopia* |

# *Corporal*
# Milizia Volontaria
# Per La Sicurezza

The Italian Fascist Militia (*Milizia Volontaria Per La Sicurezza*) – or the Black Shirts as it was more commonly known – was formed in 1922 by Mussolini, its commander, from bands of ex-servicemen. The militia was organised along ancient Roman lines, complete with legions and cohorts. At the beginning of the war the Black Shirts had three divisions, while other battalions raised were used to reinforce infantry divisions. The quasi-Roman force was organised into 133 legions, each with two battalions (one of men aged between 21 and 36 and a second territorial battalion with men up to the age of 55).

From June 1940 MVSN members serving with the Italian Army wore a standard grey-green uniform. However, some black was retained in the form of black tie, black collar patches with silver fascio (bundle) and the black fez with tassel. The fascio was the emblem of the Fascist Party. It was meant to symbolise the unity of the people and to demonstrate that unity is strength – a notion that singularly failed in Italy during the war. Badges of rank were similar to those worn in the army, except that a lozenge-shaped loop replaced the army oval loop on the uppermost bar.

The fascist militiaman shown here wears the Italian Army uniform with black trimmings. He wears the medal ribbons of the Crown of War Merit, Ethiopian Campaign, Volunteer in Spain and 10 years' service in the MVSN. His special dagger denotes his Black Shirt allegiance.

| | |
|---|---|
| *Date:* | *January 1940* |
| *Unit:* | *MVSN* |
| *Rank:* | *Corporal* |
| *Theatre:* | *Mediterranean* |
| *Location:* | *Sicily* |

# *Private Army Group Albania Italian Army*

Italy was one of the first countries to adopt a 'shirt and tie' uniform: a grey-green single-breasted tunic, which was designed to be worn open with matching shirt and tie. It had five buttons in front, a pleated patch breast and side pockets with flap and button. The shoulder straps were made of the same cloth as the tunic and had pointed ends, while the cuffs were round and plain for officers and pointed for other ranks.

In 1939 a new tunic with matching cloth belt was issued to other ranks in the infantry and unmounted arms, while cavalry and artillery retained their traditional tunic with the half-belt at the back. Other ranks now sported pantaloons with puttees or woollen socks and ankle boots, while mounted personnel wore breeches with black leather leggings and ankle boots.

This soldier is ill-equipped to fight a winter campaign – his greatcoat is made of a cheap, coarse cloth and is not even double-breasted. No special winter clothing was issued by the Italians, and the only troops to have even adequate cold-weather attire were the mountain troops. Note the two ammunition pouches carried at the front of the belt – a distinctive feature of the Italian Army.

This infantryman was a participant in the campaign against Greece, when an Italian army of 160,000 men attacked from Albania. Expecting an easy victory, the Italians – and the rest of the world – were surprised when the Greeks repulsed the invasion.

| | |
|---|---|
| *Date:* | *December 1940* |
| *Unit:* | *Army Group Albania* |
| *Rank:* | *Private* |
| *Theatre:* | *Mediterranean* |
| *Location:* | *Albania* |

144

# *Tankman*
# Ariete *Division*
# *Italian Army*

The Italian Army before the war was poorly equipped with armour: its armoured divisions had only light tanks and were incapable of providing a spearhead into enemy territory which matched that of their German counterparts. Things improved slightly during the course of the war with the introduction of a better medium tank, the M13/40, together with self-propelled guns and heavier divisional weapons. However, even with these, Italian capabilities fell well short when compared with their British armoured counterparts in North Africa.

A typical Italian armoured division contained one tank regiment, which normally had three battalions, though some had five. Each battalion had a complement of 457 men and 55 tanks, divided into a headquarters company, a reserve company of six to eight tanks and three tank companies. There were four armoured divisions in the Italian Army in World War II: *Ariete*, *Littorio*, *Centauro* and *Giovani Fascisti*. The clothing worn by tank crews was based on that worn in France and consisted of overalls, crash helmet and three-quarter length leather coat.

In the 1930s troops belonging to armoured and motorised divisions wore rectangular collar patches or 'flames' on their blue collars. As a result, in 1940 they adopted their own collar patches by sewing the flames on rectangular blue backgrounds (units equipped with tankettes sported a white double flame).

| | |
|---|---|
| *Date:* | *January 1941* |
| *Unit:* | Ariete *Division* |
| *Rank:* | *Tankman* |
| *Theatre:* | *Mediterranean* |
| *Location:* | *North Africa* |

# *Corporal* Gruppi Sahariana

**Italian colonial troops wore the Italian Army uniform combined with many colourful traditional native features, such as turbans of different colours, sandals instead of boots and a red tarbush. This corporal is wearing the white full-dress jacket with *sirical* trousers. His coloured sash indicates that he is a member of the 3rd Service Group, while the rank badge on his right sleeve is the pattern introduced in 1939 when Libyans were granted Italian nationality.**

In the Italian Army only sergeants and sergeant-majors were designated as non-commissioned officers (NCOs). Both of these ranks wore gold chevrons, while corporals wore black woven chevrons on both forearms, over the cuffs. Before the war these chevrons were adopted in shorter, inverted form on the upper sleeves, and during the war itself corporals and corporal-majors were issued with red chevrons. The chevrons were woven as a ribbon, then cut and sewn in 'V' form on grey-green material, ready to be stitched on to the wearer's sleeves.

By 1942, the date of this figure, Italy had suffered a military disaster in North Africa, following the British offensive led by General Wavell in late 1940 and early 1941. During this engagement the British Western Desert Force of 31,000 men destroyed 9 Italian divisions and captured 130,000 men, 400 tanks and 1290 artillery pieces. The British suffered a mere 500 killed and 1373 wounded, and had achieved this spectacular victory with obsolete equipment.

| | |
|---|---|
| *Date:* | *January 1942* |
| *Unit:* | Gruppi Sahariana |
| *Rank:* | *Corporal* |
| *Theatre:* | *Mediterranean* |
| *Location:* | *North Africa* |

# Private Royal Carabinieri

**The popular image of the Italian Army in World War II is one of incompetence and apathy. In general this image was correct: the population as a whole was not enthusiastic about the war and a severe shortage of strategic raw materials meant the army was totally ill-equipped to fight a modern war of manoeuvres. Against an almost medieval army of Ethiopians in 1935 the Italian army performed well enough, but when it was confronted with European armies, such as the French and British, its shortcomings were starkly revealed.**

That is not to say that the Italians did not have excellent individual units – they did – but the quality of such units was never enough to compensate for the deficiencies.

The Royal *Carabinieri* was the senior arm of the regular army and had fine traditions. It comprised hand-picked men who, in addition to their military duties, carried out police tasks. The distinctive insignia on its uniform consisted of an exploding grenade cap badge over a tricolour in national colours, and special collar patches. On the tropical uniform all Italian troops wore a circular cockade sporting the national colours, over which was worn a brass arm-of-service badge. The *Carabinieri* retained its black tie for special occasions.

Note the bandolier, which was only issued to mounted or motorised personnel. By 1942 the puttees were beginning to look distinctly outdated.

| | |
|---|---|
| *Date:* | *January 1942* |
| *Unit:* | *Royal* Carabinieri |
| *Rank:* | *Private* |
| *Theatre:* | *Mediterranean* |
| *Location:* | *Tunisia* |

# *Sergeant*
# Polizia Africa Italiana

**As in all armies, the military police fulfilled many important functions. This sergeant of the *Polizia Africa Italiana* is wearing standard Italian Army tropical uniform which comprises side cap (*bustina*), jacket (*sahariana*), breeches and leather leggings for motorised personnel.**

The standard-issue tunic had four patch pockets and a cloth belt which was fastened with two grey-green buttons (though this NCO has a brown leather belt). The *bustina* replaced the peaked cap on active service (in 1942 a new *bustina*, which had a peak similar to the one worn by Africa Corps personnel, was introduced; it was found to be very good for wear in hot climates).

Note the blue *aiguillette* and the 9mm Beretta M38A submachine gun slung over his shoulder. Submachine guns were something of a luxury in the Italian Army, as the standard-issue personal weapon was the bolt-action rifle and many units had a shortfall of hardware.

By 1942 the Italians were forced to play a subsidiary role alongside the Africa Corps; indeed, it was only the arrival of the Germans in North Africa in February 1941 that prevented a total Italian collapse. Though Rommel used many Italian divisions during his offensives in 1941–42, the old problems of lack of manpower and equipment, combined with low morale, were never resolved – with inevitable results. That said, the Italian soldier often fought with courage, but was let down by poor leadership and equipment.

| | |
|---|---|
| *Date:* | *February 1942* |
| *Unit:* | Polizia Africa Italiana |
| *Rank:* | *Sergeant* |
| *Theatre:* | *Mediterranean* |
| *Location:* | *North Africa* |

# Captain 184th Parachute Division

In 1942 a new and distinctive field uniform was introduced for paratroopers: this was a combination of the existing field tunic and the *sahariana*. It was open at the neck, had neither collar nor lapels, and the sleeves fastened tightly at the wrist. The trousers were worn with a matching cloth belt and were baggy and fastened at the ankle.

As can be seen from this figure, the Italian parachute uniform pattern closely resembled that of the Germans (in many cases Italian paras were issued with German clothing and equipment). This figure wears the special steel helmet specially developed for the paras, which had a forked chin strap and leather nose pad in front. The smock and helmet cover was made from both German and Italian camouflage material, and the sleeveless canvas waistcoat contained integral pouches on the front and back for submachine-gun magazines. This figure's weapon is the Beretta M38A submachine gun, which was only issued to special units.

The two airborne divisions – the *Nembo* and *Folgore* – were each organised into two parachute regiments, each of four battalions. An artillery regiment of two batteries was divided among the parachute regiments. The parachute battalion comprised a headquarters unit and three parachute companies and had a strength of 326 men. Its armament was good: 54 light machine guns and 62 semi-automatic rifles, and at the divisional level there was a motorcycle company, an 81mm mortar company and an engineer company.

| | |
|---|---|
| *Date:* | *December 1942* |
| *Unit:* · | *184th Parachute Division* |
| *Rank:* | *Captain* |
| *Theatre:* | *Mediterranean* |
| *Location:* | *Tunisia* |

# *Major-General Co-Belligerent Forces*

**The first Italian unit to fight on the Allied side following Italy's desertion from the Axis cause was the First Motorised Combat Group. It saw action in the Cassino sector of Monte Lungo, in the autumn of 1943. It had a strength of 295 officers and 5387 men, and did much to convince the Allies of Italy's determination to fight against Nazi Germany.**

At the beginning of Italy's new war her pro-Allied troops wore the grey-green or khaki Italian uniforms with the insignia of the House of Savoy on the breast. However, a severe lack of clothing meant that the Italian troops were soon wearing Allied dress, typically British uniforms with Italian insignia. A rectangular badge in the national Italian colours was introduced to be worn high on the left sleeve to differentiate the Italians from the rest of the Allied troops.

This senior officer commanding the Combat Group 'Lightning', wears the Italian military dress which was typically worn during the later stages of the war. He wears British battledress with khaki beret, though all his insignia is Italian. Rank badges were worn on the cuffs and on the left side of the beret (rank badges on the sleeves were embroidered in cherry red for medical generals, on violet for commissariat generals and on grey-green for all other generals). On his collar this major-general wears the light-blue collar patches of the paratroopers, while high on his left sleeve he sports the combat group's formation sign: Italian Tricolour with a black bolt of lightning.

| | |
|---|---|
| *Date:* | *May 1944* |
| *Unit:* | *Co-Belligerent Forces* |
| *Rank:* | *Major-General* |
| *Theatre:* | *Mediterranean* |
| *Location:* | *Italy* |

# *Militiaman*
# Legion
# Tagliamento

On 25 July 1943, Mussolini was deposed in Italy and replaced by a new head of government, Badoglio. The new Italian government agreed terms of surrender with the Allies, and in September 1943 monarchist Italy changed its loyalties and declared war on its former ally, Germany. Meanwhile, Mussolini established the Northern Italian Social Republic in Salo.

This move effectively split Italian army units into two distinct lines. The nucleus of Mussolini's army, which consisted of four German-trained divisions, wore the Italian uniform and had German equipment and Roman-inspired badges and emblems (the Italian Army was ruthlessly disarmed by Germany following Italy's surrender).

The paramilitary illustrated here is wearing the uniform that was typical of the fascist side in Italy at the end of the war. He is a Legionary 'M' (for Mussolini) of the Republican National Guard (GNR). His black head-dress is similar to the pattern worn in dark red by the elite riflemen, known as *bersaglieri*. The Legion badge, a silver fascio on a red letter 'M', was worn on the collar of the black shirt or on black collar patches.

The other equipment on his uniform is of German origin, including the Luftwaffe belt and 'potato masher' grenades. His weapons, however, are of Italian origin: the standard MVSN-pattern dagger and Beretta M38A submachine gun, a popular weapon due to its reliability and robustness.

| | |
|---|---|
| *Date:* | *June 1944* |
| *Unit:* | *Legion Tagliamento* |
| *Rank:* | *Militiaman* |
| *Theatre:* | *Mediterranean* |
| *Location:* | *northern Italy* |

# *Air Marshal Italo Balbo Italian Air Force*

**Air Marshal Italo Balbo, pictured here, is wearing a combination of tropical and temperate uniform. Essentially the uniform of the Italian Air Force was the same as that worn by the army, the main difference being that it was manufactured in grey-blue cloth. Minor differences included pointed pocket flaps as opposed to the straight flaps, which were a feature of army uniforms.**

Air Marshal Balbo wears a peaked cap with distinctive embroidered *greca*, the mark of general officers and marshals. The cap badge comprises a spread eagle surrounded by a laurel wreath and surmounted by the Royal Crown. Large gold embroidered badges were worn on the peaked cap by officers, warrant officers and sergeants. Generals of air squadrons and above, wore cap badges with purple-red backing under the crown.

At the beginning of the war some of the 'frills' which were a feature of the air force uniform disappeared, such as the shoulder straps and full-dress belt, plus the coloured backing to the rank distinction badge which indicated the branch to which the wearer belonged.

Air Marshal Balbo carries rank insignia on the shoulder boards of his *sahariana*. On his left breast he sports a pilot's qualification badge. Balbo was a popular figure in the fascist movement, but he was accidentally shot down by Italian anti-aircraft fire near Tobruk shortly after the Italian declaration of war in the summer of 1940 — an ominous portent.

| | |
|---|---|
| *Date:* | *May 1940* |
| *Unit:* | *Italian Air Force* |
| *Rank:* | *Air Marshal* |
| *Theatre:* | *Mediterranean* |
| *Location:* | *North Africa* |

# *Major*
# *One Group*
# *Italian Air Force*

There were two types of flying suit worn in the Italian Air Force during the war. The winter model was lined and made of brownish olive-green material, whereas the summer uniform was made of white linen. Both were manufactured in one- or two-piece versions; the one-piece is shown here. This item was often worn with khaki drill shorts or other types of trousers. The helmet was also made of white linen.

As Italian officers' service jackets had no cuffs, rank stripes were applied 90mm (3.5in) from the lowest edge of the sleeve and were 80mm (3in) long. The rank stripes were made of gold lace, the narrow ones being 12mm (0.5in) in width and the larger base stripes 22mm (0.9in) in width. On his left breast this air force major wears his squadron badge.

In 1940 the Italian Air Force comprised 12,000 pilots and aircrew, 6100 non-flying officers and 185,000 other ranks. The squadron was the basic tactical unit; it had a strength of nine aircraft and another three in reserve. Two or three squadrons formed an air group, while two or more groups formed a wing or *stormo*. On occasion, two to three wings would combine to form an air division.

The largest overseas deployment of Italian air assets was in North Africa, but the large losses suffered at the hands of the British in late 1940 and early 1941 required a large-scale reinforcement. However, shortages of fuel and spare parts greatly reduced the air force's overall effectiveness.

| | |
|---|---|
| *Date:* | *June 1940* |
| *Unit:* | *One Group* |
| *Rank:* | *Major* |
| *Theatre:* | *Mediterranean* |
| *Location:* | *Libya* |

# *Major*
# *Southern Zone*
# *Italian Air Force*

**The pilot shown here is wearing a leather flying jacket over his service dress and a leather flying helmet. On his cuffs he wears his rank badges: officers' rank stripes were made of gold lace, the narrow ones being 12mm (0.5in) wide and the larger base stripes being 22mm (0.9in) wide.**

On his left breast he wears the qualification badge of a torpedo bomber. Such badges were worn by pilots, observers and aircrew members. The first two were modified in the early 1930s to become a stylish, contemporary design with the fascio added to the bottom. Before these changes, some pilots had been granted special badges with coloured letters enamelled in the centre. Pilots who had flown high-velocity aircraft had a red 'V' on the badge, others had an 'S' for flying at high altitudes, and those who crossed the Atlantic were granted a badge with a blue 'A' on it. Though pilots wore the new badges with the fascio, the majority of observers wore the new-pattern badge without the fascio.

Aviators were granted metal breast badges for good performance. There were three grades of badges, in gold, silver and bronze, though in the case of the former, only the central device was gilded. During the war the badges of the first two grades were made of aluminium, and the central device of those of the first grade was painted yellow.

There were four territorial Air Zones in Italy: Northern, Central, Southern and South-Eastern. There was also a large Italian air presence in Libya and a smaller one in East Africa.

| | |
|---|---|
| *Date:* | *June 1942* |
| *Unit:* | *Southern Zone* |
| *Rank:* | *Major* |
| *Theatre:* | *Mediterranean* |
| *Location:* | *North Africa* |

# Major-General Italian Social Republic Air Force

The air force of Mussolini's Italian Social Republic (RSI) was formed on 27 October 1943. The very fact of its existence was due entirely to the efforts of one man: Lieutenant-Colonel 'Iron Leg' Botto, an officer of great organisational talents. When Italy signed an armistice with the Allies the Germans immediately seized Italian aircraft and equipment, plus pilots and technicians. Botto managed to retrieve most of these, though the RSI Air Force did not become operational until October 1944 due to German attempts to incorporate it into the Luftwaffe.

With the establishment of the RSI, the Italian Air Force uniform underwent a number of changes. The crown on the cap badge and shoulder straps was replaced by a winged bird, as can be seen here. Rank distinction rings on the cap band were abolished, and instead officers wore German-pattern chin cords, while generals sported gold embroidery on the cap peak. On the collar the *gladio* replaced the five-pointed star.

By this late stage of the war, October 1944, many fascist Italian airmen were serving alongside Luftwaffe personnel, or had been trained by the German Air Force. As a result, they wore German Air Force uniform with German or Italian rank badges. Note that this figure wears the ribbon of the Iron Cross 2nd Class in his button-hole.

The RSI Air Force was not large, but it did have a good fighter and torpedo-bomber arm. Its bomber squadron was sent to the Eastern Front.

| | |
|---|---|
| *Date:* | *October 1944* |
| *Unit:* | *Italian Social Republic Air Force* |
| *Rank:* | *Major-General* |
| *Theatre:* | *Mediterranean* |
| *Location:* | *northern Italy* |

# *Ranking Lieutenant Taranto Command Italian Navy*

**This officer of the Italian Navy wears the typical Italian service dress with peaked cap and 'reefer' jacket. In addition to the peaked cap officers also wore a blue field cap with matching cloth peak. Italian Navy officers, chiefs and senior petty officers wore the peaked cap with a gold embroidered naval badge, which consisted of an oval shield, surrounded by six laurel leaves, and the whole ensigned by the crown.**

Shoulder straps of naval officers were made of navy blue cloth and were similar in shape and size to those of the flag officers. Senior officers' shoulder straps had a gold embroidered border stripe and crown and rank stars; those of the junior officers had the crown and stars only. A small embroidered bar on the outer end of the shoulder strap was worn by 1st lieutenants. Gold lace stripes were worn on the cuffs, senior officers having a large stripe 20mm (0.7in) wide and from one to three narrower stripes 12mm (0.5in) wide. The top stripe had a curl in it, and the stripes and curl were sewn on navy blue cloth or distinction cloth, according to the corps.

At the beginning of the war the Italian Navy boasted 4 battleships, 8 heavy cruisers, 14 light cruisers, 128 destroyers, 115 submarines and 62 motor-torpedo boats. In addition, there were four battleships fitting out. Its strength was 4180 officers and 70,500 ratings. It was an impressive force, though the absence of radar and a fleet air arm was eventually to give the advantage to the British in the Mediterranean.

| | |
|---|---|
| *Date:* | *June 1942* |
| *Unit:* | *Taranto Command* |
| *Rank:* | *Ranking Lieutenant* |
| *Theatre:* | *Mediterranean* |
| *Location:* | *Mediterranean Sea* |

# Sergeant-Major Italian Marine Infantry

**Marine officers wore grey-green army service dress, while other ranks wore the uniform illustrated here: this was a grey-green version of the blue jumper with matching trousers, complete with puttees and pantaloons. Further items worn by other ranks included a green beret, a green version of the naval jumper, which could be worn with white shirt, blue jean collar, black scarf and white lanyard, or with just a green polo-necked pullover.**

In North Africa marines wore a light khaki drill beret, shirt, *sahariana*, pantaloons, long trousers or shorts, puttees, woollen stockings or webbing gaiters, and ankle boots or shoes. There was also a khaki drill version of the jumper, which had pointed cuffs and a rectangular collar edged with two white stripes. All members of the marines wore scarlet collar or cuff patches with the lion of St Mark in gilt metal or yellow embroidery.

The various arms within the regiment wore a distinguishing yellow metal badge above the rank chevrons. Officers wore naval rank badges, while this sergeant-major has one narrow red stripe between two others, all in lace and inverted on the upper sleeves.

Note the webbing equipment, which was manufactured by the Mills Company of Great Britain. His dagger is similar to the one worn by the Fascist Militia. It had dubious military value though its symbolic importance was great – a mark of an individual's devotion to the cause.

| | |
|---|---|
| **Date:** | *February 1942* |
| **Unit:** | *Italian Marine Infantry* |
| **Rank:** | *Sergeant-Major* |
| **Theatre:** | *Mediterranean* |
| **Location:** | *Sicily* |

# Seaman Italian Social Republic Navy

**Few Italians actually joined Mussolini's Fascist Navy, nevertheless there were a number of uniform changes to the attire of the Italian Social Republic Navy which were implemented after September 1943. These changes included replacing the crown on the cap badge with a winged bird, and replacing the five-pointed star on the ends of the collar with the** *gladio.*

The lace rings on the cap band were also abolished and instead lieutenants wore a blue and gold chin cord, while senior officers wore an all-gold one. In addition, the traditional sailor's hat was replaced by a blue beret which had a small yellow metal anchor on the front.

The seaman pictured here is wearing the traditional 'square rig', which was worn in navies throughout the world, complete with webbing, which was manufactured in Great Britain. He wears a steel helmet which carries the second pattern anchor painted on the front.

As with the army and the air force, the Italian Navy suffered a series of spectacular defeats by the Allies in the war, notably at Taranto and Matapan. By September 1943, the Italian Navy had lost a battleship, 13 cruisers and 24,660 men. Following the Italian Armistice, Mussolini's navy was only one-twentieth the size of the Co-Belligerent Fleet. The latter comprised 5 battleships, 8 cruisers, 33 destroyers, 39 submarines, 12 motor-torpedo boats, 22 escorts and 3 mine-layers.

| | |
|---|---|
| *Date:* | *October 1944* |
| *Unit:* | *Italian Social Republic Navy* |
| *Rank:* | *Seaman* |
| *Theatre:* | *Mediterranean* |
| *Location:* | *northern Italy* |

# *Japan*

*Japan mobilised 9,100,000 men for her army, navy and air force and her armed forces carried all before them in the Pacific and Far East in 1941-42. Fanatical courage and resilience characterised Japan's fighting man. But in the war of hardware that was to follow, fanaticism was not enough to defeat the economic might of the United States.*

# Private Imperial Japanese Army

**The Japanese Army adopted khaki after World War I, and thereafter adjusted its uniforms to suit conditions in the Far East. In 1938, for example, the single-breasted tunic with stiff stand collar was replaced by one with a softer stand-and-fall collar. Both tunics had breast and side pockets with flap and button, matching pantaloons, which were worn with puttees criss-crossed with khaki tapes, and black canvas boots.**

The Japanese M90 greatcoat was single-breasted with a fall collar and two rows of six buttons in front and slanting side pockets with flap, while the M98 greatcoat was double-breasted.

The Japanese head-dress consisted of a soft field cap with matching peak, brown leather chin strap and detachable neck guard. On the front of the cap was a five-pointed star. Throughout the war caps were made of different types of materials, including straw, while others were painted for camouflage purposes and covered in twigs and leaves to break up their outline. The cap itself was often worn under the circular steel helmet, which was painted a mustard colour and had a yellow five-pointed star on the front. At the beginning of the war in China in 1937, there were two types of steel helmet in use, but the first was phased out by World War II.

In the Far East theatre Japanese soldiers wore cotton drill uniforms, the standard lightweight tunic being single-breasted with a stand-and-fall collar. Matching long or short trousers were worn with leather ankle boots or *tabi*, and puttees.

| | |
|---|---|
| *Date:* | *December 1941* |
| *Unit:* | *Imperial Japanese Army* |
| *Rank:* | *Private* |
| *Theatre:* | *Pacific* |
| *Location:* | *Luzon* |

# Senior NCO Indian National Army

The Indian National Army (INA) was raised in January 1942 by the Japanese at Kuala Lumpur, with the intention of achieving Indian independence from British rule. The Japanese Army recruited from Indian prisoners of war, who were enlisted by General Mohan Singh, formally of the 14th Punjab Regiment. When Singapore fell to the Japanese in February 1942, 55,000 Indian soldiers were captured, and of these some 20,000 joined the INA. Though another 20,000 enlisted in the summer of 1942, few did so because they were pro-Japanese. Many joined to escape brutal prison camps, while others simply wanted to get back to the front – and then escape to British lines.

The INA wore either Indian Army khaki drill uniforms with puggaree or field service side cap in khaki cloth. Japanese uniforms were also issued to INA members. A brass cap badge was worn on the left side of the side cap, which consisted of a map of India with the letters 'INA' on it.

This senior NCO is wearing the old Indian Army khaki drill uniform with a khaki turban. His rank is indicated by the coloured stripes on the shoulder straps (NCOs had one to three stripes across the shoulder straps, company officers one to three stripes above the letters 'INA', field officers one to three stripes surmounted by an eight-pointed star above the letters 'INA', and general officers one to three bars surmounted by crossed sabres with an eight-pointed star above).

| | |
|---|---|
| **Date:** | *September 1942* |
| **Unit:** | *Indian National Army* |
| **Rank:** | *Senior NCO* |
| **Theatre:** | *Pacific* |
| **Location:** | *Malaysia* |

# Paratrooper Naval Parachute Troops

**Japanese naval paratroopers wore a special olive-drab uniform and an army pattern parachute helmet with yellow anchor badge on the front, and special arm badge on the upper right sleeve. Fully qualified paratroopers wore a yellow silk embroidered winged badge on the right breast.**

Japanese Army paratroopers wore German-style smocks and special leather helmets, and high lace-up leather ankle boots with rubber soles. The helmets were later replaced by canvas-covered steel items (there is photographic evidence that German paratrooper helmets were issued to Japanese parachute troops). This naval paratrooper wears the steel-pattern helmet with canvas cover, a much better item than its fibre predecessor as it gave ballistic protection for the head. The overall shown here was sometimes worn over the olive-drab naval khaki uniform, while a special weapons container which holds either a light mortar or personal weapons, is clipped to the parachute harness.

The Japanese developed a whole series of weapons for use by airborne troops during the war, such as the Model 89 50mm grenade discharger together with four grenades, a small M94 smoke candle, an anti-tank grenade and a small pick, all of which could be carried in a special canvas bag which was strapped to the soldier's leg. Attached to the other leg was a bag which contained an M2 7.7mm paratroop rifle, a bayonet, four hand grenades and thirty rounds of rifle ammunition.

| | |
|---|---|
| **Date:** | *October 1942* |
| **Unit:** | *Japanese Navy* |
| **Rank:** | *Private* |
| **Theatre:** | *Pacific* |
| **Location:** | *Pacific Ocean* |

# Rating Combined Fleet Japanese Navy

**This Japanese naval rating is wearing the white rig which was the uniform for clean work, such as office duties and general clerical work. In the winter months sailors wore regulation 'whites', and in cold weather they would wear a double-breasted peacoat with two rows of five grey metal buttons and vertical slash side pockets. In hot climes sailors wore a short-sleeved shirt with blue edging around the neck opening, white cotton jumper with or without the blue jean collar, black scarf, and blue edging around the cuffs and skirt.**

Under operational conditions sailors wore either the shirt on its own with white duck trousers, or the white duck working shirt, or even a white working overall. In action a steel helmet and life-jacket were also worn.

This rating has a single blue band around his cap, while all commissioned ranks had two blue bands. On his cap he carries a blue anchor. Officers wore a gold anchor in a ring surrounded by a gold wreath on their peaked caps, the whole ensigned by a silver cherry blossom. Petty officers wore the cherry blossom superimposed upon the anchor with an oval gold edge around it, and midshipmen had a gold foul anchor on its own. Seamen, as illustrated here, wore a plain anchor on their field caps. The colour of the emblem changed according to the colour of the cap.

The badge on this rating's left sleeve is that of Musician 3rd Class.

| | |
|---|---|
| *Date:* | *May 1942* |
| *Unit:* | *Combined Fleet* |
| *Rank:* | *Rating* |
| *Theatre:* | *Pacific* |
| *Location:* | *Philippine Sea* |

# *Lieutenant 5th Fleet Japanese Navy*

**Japanese naval officers, such as this lieutenant, wore a single-breasted blue tunic with stand collar and slash side pockets, and hook-and-eye fastening in front. The top and front edge of the collar, the front and skirt of the tunic, and the pockets, were trimmed with black silver lace, which was also used to distinguish rank on the cuffs. The figure shown here is wearing the white summer uniform for officers.**

This lieutenant wears the peaked cap with white cover and regulation whites. He carries his rank distinction badges on his shoulders. Shoulder straps were generally used on the white tunic, though they were also worn on blue and khaki tunics as well. They carried gold lace stripes, which distinguished class of rank, and silver cherry blossoms to identify individual ranks. Rank was also displayed on the cuffs thus: gold lace stripes with a curl on the blue dress uniform and overcoat, and black lace stripes on the service dress tunic (which also carried additional collar patches). Officers who were commissioned from the ranks (they could graduate to the rank of lieutenant) had silver cherry blossoms on the shoulder straps, though above a narrower gold lace stripe, of warrant officer's width. Interestingly, naval officers had the same rank titles as the officers of the army.

This lieutenant carries an undress-dirk on his left hip, suspended from a fabric belt under the tunic. Chief petty officers wore a peaked cap with special badge, and a single-breasted tunic in navy or white.

| | |
|---|---|
| **Date:** | *February 1943* |
| **Unit:** | *5th Fleet* |
| **Rank:** | *Lieutenant* |
| **Theatre:** | *Pacific* |
| **Location:** | *Tokyo* |

# Soviet Union

*Mass characterised the Russian armed forces, be it the massed infantry attacks, or the massive fleets of tanks and aircraft that beat the Germans. The average 'Ivan' was like his equipment: uncomplicated and robust. Some 13,200,000 men and women were mobilised, and their sacrifices were largely responsible for the defeat of Nazi Germany.*

# Private Infantry Division Red Army

**At the beginning of World War II the Soviet Union had the largest army in Europe (estimated at around 1.8 million men). To maintain a continuous supply of uniforms and equipment for this many men was a major undertaking, and so the state factories could only stick to tried and tested methods to ensure a steady flow of wear. This meant that the average Russian soldier was kitted out in designs which dated back to the beginning of the century. That said, these designs were actually very rugged and practical, having proved themselves in World War I.**

This private took part in the disastrous Winter War against Finland. He is wearing the distinctive pointed grey cloth helmet, known officially as the *shelm*, but nicknamed the *dubionovka* after the legendary Russian cavalry commander Budjenny. The peaked cap, or *furashka*, had a khaki top and band and its piping was in arm colour. The peak and chin strap were black, and a five-pointed red star was worn on the front. During the winter battles against the Fins the *shelm* was found to be useless against the cold, and in 1940 it was replaced by a grey cloth cap – the *ushanka* – which had fur flaps that covered the ears and the back of the neck. Typical of the so-called 'equality' in the Red Army was that officers had real fur flaps whereas other ranks had artificial fur.

This soldier is from the infantry, as indicated by the colour of the cloth star and the raspberry-red collar patches. He carries a gas mask in his canvas bag.

| | |
|---|---|
| *Date:* | *December 1939* |
| *Unit:* | *infantry division* |
| *Rank:* | *Private* |
| *Theatre:* | *Eastern Front* |
| *Location:* | *Gulf of Finland* |

# Colonel Armoured Division Red Army

In 1935 Soviet tank troops were ordered to wear a steel-grey uniform instead of the khaki service dress. This change in the dress mode was an attempt by the Red Army to enhance the importance of the tank arm in general; this was a wise move, since armour was to play a crucial part in the war on the Eastern Front in 1941–45. Ironically, during World War II Russian tank troops continued to wear their standard khaki uniforms though officers did occasionally continue to wear the grey peaked caps.

On his peaked cap this officer sports the famous 'hammer and sickle' cap badge. Actually, the first red star cap badges had a hammer and plough in the centre. It was not until later that the sickle replaced the plough as the symbol of agriculture. There were no regimental badges in the Red Army: each corps or service was represented by its colour, which was shown on the collar patches, piping and frog fasteners of the greatcoat and tunic.

This officer carries his rank insignia on his collar patches and sleeves. New rank insignia, comprising red squares, triangles and diamonds, were devised during the Revolution, and in 1924 the metal and enamel badges were moved on to collar patches. In addition, in 1935 regulations stated that officers should wear rank badges on the forearms of their tunics, jackets and greatcoats in the form of chevrons. As can be seen here, colonels wore red chevrons with gold edgings.

| | |
|---|---|
| *Date:* | *January 1940* |
| *Unit:* | *armoured division* |
| *Rank:* | *Colonel* |
| *Theatre:* | *Eastern Front* |
| *Location:* | *Kiev* |

# *Marshal of the Soviet Union Red Army*

**In 1935 the rank of Marshal of the Soviet Union was instituted. Five generals were elevated to this rank: Commissar for Defence Voroshilov, Commander of the Far Eastern Army Blyukher, Chief of Staff General Tukhachevsky, General Yegorov and Director of Cavalry Budjenny. In July 1940 a new grey parade uniform was introduced for generals and marshals in an attempt to enhance the status of senior Red Army officers.**

This figure is Marshal Timoshenko, the commander of the Kiev Military District and Commander-in-Chief of the Soviet forces during the war against Finland. He is wearing the new smart grey parade uniform, complete with red piping (marshals and generals were also issued with grey greatcoats, which also had red piping). Twin gold cords were granted to marshals and generals, which were worn on the grey peaked cap of the parade uniform. A new cap badge was also issued: a red star in brass and enamel, set in a gilded roundel, 30mm (1.2in) in diameter.

On ranks badges, gold stars replaced enamel diamonds in the collar patches of generals, while marshals wore a gold star above a laurel wreath. On the sleeves, marshals wore a large gold embroidered star above two chevrons, one above and one below a laurel wreath on a red background.

Timoshenko's decorations are, from top to bottom, the Gold Star of a Hero of the Soviet Union, two Orders of Lenin, three Orders of the Red Banner, and the Red Army 20th anniversary medal.

| | |
|---|---|
| *Date:* | *June 1940* |
| *Unit:* | *Kiev Military District* |
| *Rank:* | *Marshal of the Soviet Union* |
| *Theatre:* | *Eastern Front* |
| *Location:* | *Moscow* |

# Sergeant
# Cavalry Division
# Red Army

**This sergeant is wearing the Red Army uniform that was standard at the beginning of the war on the Eastern Front, with amendments to reflect his arm of service (cavalry). The standard khaki cotton shirt at this time had a stand-and-fall collar (though curiously this particular figure has a stand collar) and breast patch pockets with flap and button. The sleeves are gathered at the wrist and cuff, where they are fastened with two small buttons (officers wore arm of service coloured piping).**

The shirt was worn with matching khaki breeches by all ranks in unmounted units, while those soldiers in mounted units wore royal blue breeches. This sergeant wears a peaked cap with khaki top and band in arm colour.

Though seemingly outdated by 1941, cavalry units were to prove invaluable on the Eastern Front. The Red Army had 40 cavalry divisions in 1940, and during the war against Germany they carried out many useful missions: as reconnaissance, as a mobile reserve and by fighting patrols deep behind enemy lines. A Red Army cavalry division was divided into three cavalry regiments and an artillery regiment plus support units. Its paper strength was just over 5000 men, 5128 horses and 130 vehicles. The division carried a lot of firepower, including 447 submachine guns, 48 heavy machine guns, 118 light machine guns, 48 light mortars, 18 medium mortars, 8 heavy mortars, 76 anti-tank rifles, and 43 assorted anti-tank and anti-aircraft guns, in addition to 10 T-70 light tanks.

| | |
|---|---|
| *Date:* | *June 1941* |
| *Unit:* | *cavalry division* |
| *Rank:* | *Sergeant* |
| *Theatre:* | *Eastern Front* |
| *Location:* | *Kiev* |

# *Major-General Odessa Military District: Red Army*

New German-influenced uniforms were introduced for Soviet Red Army officers in December 1935. This change was carried out so that those in command could be distinguished more easily. It included a single-breasted tunic with stand-and-fall collar called a 'French', after the British general of that name who wore a khaki uniform which was copied by Russian Tsarist officers in World War I. In addition, the collar and cuffs were piped in arm colour.

The tunic could be worn with either khaki or blue trousers, piped in arm colour, and black shoes, or royal blue piped breeches and black boots (the blue trousers with generals' *lampassen* were introduced in July 1940). Following the July 1940 regulations, this major-general wears gold stars instead of enamel diamonds in his collar patches, and on each sleeve he wears a single gold embroidered star above a gold chevron with red edging at the bottom.

At the beginning of the war with Germany the Red Army was in a weakened state, Stalin having carried out his infamous purges which effectively liquidated some of the most useful senior Russian officers. The result was disaster in the Winter War against Finland, when some 200,000 Russian soldiers were killed. But this paled into insignificance when compared to the losses suffered during the first few weeks of Operation 'Barbarossa'. No amount of new dress regulations could quickly repair the damage caused by the Soviet dictator.

| | |
|---|---|
| *Date:* | *June 1941* |
| *Unit:* | *Odessa Military District* |
| *Rank:* | *Major-General* |
| *Theatre:* | *Eastern Front* |
| *Location:* | *Odessa* |

# Junior Sergeant Armoured Regiment Red Army

The tankman illustrated here is wearing the sun hat that was first introduced in March 1938 for military personnel serving in the Central Asian, North Caucasian and Trans Caucasian commands, and in the Crimea. His shirt with stand-and-fall collar has reinforcing patches on the elbows, and the same patches can be found on the knees of his trousers.

On his collar this junior sergeant wears patches which indicate his arm of service colours, together with a small metal tank badge (armour and artillery had the same coloured collar patches: black with red piping). All ranks in the Red Army wore metal collar badges. These metal badges were designed to identify the branch of service of the wearer, the reason for this being that the colours of the patch and piping were often not enough to do so. This was especially the case with officers, who all wore gold piping on the collar patches.

The first collar badges were laid down in the regulations of 31 January 1922, when around 40 badges were given official approval. Except for veterinaries, who had badges made of white metal, all ranks wore brass collar badges. The armoured troops went through a major reorganisation in the 1930s, and the actual tank badge was not instituted for the tank units of the armoured troops until 1936. Armoured artillery and other service branches wore their own badges on the black collar patches of the armoured troops.

| | |
|---|---|
| **Date:** | *July 1941* |
| **Unit:** | *armoured regiment* |
| **Rank:** | *Junior Sergeant* |
| **Theatre:** | *Eastern Front* |
| **Location:** | *Crimea* |

# Corporal Infantry Division Red Army

**The typical Red Army soldier lived a life of boredom and hardship, with few creature comforts, poor rations and, certainly before the war, sub-standard equipment. The fact that he was probably better off than the average industrial worker or collective farmer must have been small comfort. Even the quality of his clothing was poor – such was the lot of the men and women Stalin relied on to defeat the might of Nazi Germany.**

This corporal is the archetypal Russian conscript. His greatcoat was made of dark grey cloth turning, in some cases, to brown and was double-breasted with fall collar and fly front. It had turn-back cuffs which were cut at an angle with the highest point at the back, and slashed side pockets. From December 1935 officers wore a new double-breasted greatcoat with fall collar and two rows of four buttons and turn-back cuffs. The collar and cuffs were piped in arm-of-service colour.

This NCO wears the 1940-pattern steel helmet, on the front of which was sometimes painted a red star. The collar patches on the greatcoat identify his arm of service and his rank of *efreitor* (which comes from the German *Gefreiter*, meaning soldier freed from menial tasks). His equipment consists of a gas mask worn on the left and entrenching tool on the right, waist belt with ammunition pouches, and a pack which is really nothing more than a khaki cloth sack. His weapon is the 7.62mm Tokarev M1940 bolt-action rifle.

| | |
|---|---|
| *Date:* | *July 1941* |
| *Unit:* | *infantry division* |
| *Rank:* | *Corporal* |
| *Theatre:* | *Eastern Front* |
| *Location:* | *Ukraine* |

# Trooper
# Cavalry Regiment
# Red Army

**This cavalryman is wearing the special wading gear that was designed to enable Red Army soldiers to cross the plethora of rivers which criss-crossed the Soviet Union. This kit included two paddles for propulsion and a rod for measuring the depth of the water. He wears the old 1936-pattern helmet, which was eventually to be superseded by the 1940 model.**

By the date of this figure, July 1941, the Red Army was in a state of near collapse, the Germans having made massive gains and pushed the Russians back all along the front. The Soviets lost huge amounts of weapons and equipment, to say nothing of the tens of thousands of soldiers killed or taken prisoner (a major problem experienced during this period was that units completely lost their coherence, which was compounded by the inexperience of staff officers at headquarters). By the autumn of 1941 the Russian front ran from Leningrad in the north to Odessa in the south, and the Red Army had lost a third of its pre-war strength. However, it had not been totally destroyed and, surprisingly, had inflicted major losses on the Germans.

This corporal is carrying the 7.62mm Mosin-Nagant M1891/30 rifle, which was the standard personal weapon in the Red Army. It was long and rather clumsy but, like much Soviet equipment, was simple to operate, clean and very robust. As a result of this, it stayed in service until the 1950s.

| | |
|---|---|
| *Date:* | *October 1941* |
| *Unit:* | *cavalry regiment* |
| *Rank:* | *Corporal* |
| *Theatre:* | *Eastern Front* |
| *Location:* | *Leningrad* |

# Officer Infantry Division Red Army

**At the end of 1941 the Red Army, and therefore the Soviet Union, was saved from defeat largely due to the brilliant generalship of Marshal Zhukov and 'General Winter'. On 5 December 1941, in sub-zero temperatures, Zhukov hurled 720,000 men, 670 tanks, 5900 guns and mortars and 415 rocket launchers against the Germans around Moscow. It was the first success of the Red Army against the Germans, and it gave a much-needed boost to Russian morale.**

The bitter Russian winter also helped to blunt the German advance, as, unlike the Russian Army, the *Wehrmacht* was totally unprepared to fight a winter war in the Soviet Union.

The Russian winter uniform consisted of shirt, matching breeches and high black leather boots, with the addition of a grey cloth cap with grey fleece front and neck and ear flap, and issue double-breasted greatcoat.

Other types of Russian winter wear included coats made of either sheepskin (usually worn by tank crews and cavalryman) or khaki cotton duck. The officer illustrated here is wearing the most typical and distinctive type of Russian winter clothing: it comprised jacket and trousers which were both made from khaki and padded with cotton wool sewn in strips. This warm quilted outfit was called *telogreika*. Introduced in August 1941, the outfit was complemented by the felt boots or *valenki*, which were ideal for wear in the snow.

| | |
|---|---|
| *Date:* | *December 1941* |
| *Unit:* | *infantry division* |
| *Rank:* | *Officer* |
| *Theatre:* | *Eastern Front* |
| *Location:* | *west of Moscow* |

# Officer Guards Motorised Division: Red Army

**The halting of the Germans by the Russians outside Moscow at the end of 1941 did not mean defeat for the *Wehrmacht* on the Eastern Front – far from it. In early 1942 Stalin ordered a counteroffensive all along the front, but the Red Army was thrown on to the defensive once more as its armies were encircled and destroyed by the German Army Group South's own offensive.**

As a result of the German offensive, the Russians were pushed back deep into the Caucasus. The hardest fighting took place in and around Stalingrad, and it was here that the Red Army dug in and refused to budge. During the winter of 1942–43 the Russians surrounded the German 6th Army in Stalingrad, and on 2 February 1943 the city fell – a turning point of World War II.

The Red Army officer pictured here took part in the Stalingrad battles. He wears the 1940-pattern *ushanka* and the sheepskin coat, the *polaschubuk*, with 1935-pattern leather equipment for officers. The sheepskin coat was normally issued to both mounted and armoured personnel. However, it is worth noting that the image of Russian troops being fully equipped with warm winter clothing is wrong. Like the Germans, Soviet troops also suffered from exposure, not least because of problems with the logistical system. Shoe leather, for example, was in very short supply, which meant many Red Army troops had to wear ankle boots (imported from Great Britain or America) instead of boots.

| | |
|---|---|
| *Date:* | *December 1941* |
| *Unit:* | *guards motorised division* |
| *Rank:* | *Officer* |
| *Theatre:* | *Eastern Front* |
| *Location:* | *Stalingrad* |

# Private Rifle Division Red Army

**This elderly Red Army private is wearing standard Russian summer field uniform with a side cap which sports the red star. His shirt (*rubaha*) has a traditional cut and carries shoulder boards. The raspberry-red piping on the boards denotes his membership of the infantry arm. Coloured piping and bands took the place of badges in the Red Army. Thus, a sniper would wear an infantry tunic with normal infantry collar patches, plus a vertical raspberry-red stripe of material sewn along the tunic's front overlap.**

This soldier wears puttees and ankle boots due to a shortage of boots; his leather belt is another late war economy, made of webbing reinforced with leather. His pouches are made from a synthetic material and were often replaced by better-made German leather pouches.

By 1943 many infantry units in the Red Army had become motorised. The mechanised infantry brigade, for example, had three battalions of motorised infantry, each of around 650 men and armed with 50 machine guns, 250 submachine guns, six 82mm mortars and four 45mm anti-tank guns, in addition to a small number of anti-tank rifles. Transport was provided by 40–50 trucks and lorries. Three brigades of mechanised infantry, plus a separate tank brigade with artillery and self-propelled artillery units, made up the mechanised corps. With a strength of 18,000 men this was the largest and most powerful division-sized unit.

| | |
|---|---|
| **Date:** | *August 1943* |
| **Unit:** | *rifle division* |
| **Rank:** | *Private* |
| **Theatre:** | *Eastern Front* |
| **Location:** | *western USSR* |

# Tankman II Guards Tank Corps

When on duty with their vehicles Russian tank crews wore a one-piece black or dark blue overall, though during the war itself the colour of Russian overalls ranged from black to grey. Crew members also wore a brown leather (later to become black canvas) padded helmet with special ear flaps to hold microphones.

The wartime overall had a fall collar, zip fastener in front and matching cloth belt with metal buckle. There was a patch pocket with flap on the left breast and right thigh, as well as slash side pockets which gave access to the breeches' pockets.

Later on in the war the two-piece tank suits were introduced, and in the winter the Russian crews were issued with three-quarter length sheepskin coats. No insignia was worn on the overall until the end of the war, when crews taking part in the Moscow victory parade in 1945 were to sport black overalls with collar patches, shoulder boards and various decorations.

After the early reverses the Red Army organised its tanks efficiently in independent tank brigades. Each brigade of 1300 men was broken down into three battalions of 140 men and 21 tanks each. The brigade was reinforced by a submachine gun battalion of 400 men and companies of anti-tank and anti-aircraft troops. Tank brigades were formed into tank corps, which consisted of three tank brigades, a motorised rifle brigade and support units. By 1943 the Red Army had 26 tank corps.

| | |
|---|---|
| *Date:* | *July 1943* |
| *Unit:* | *II Guards Tank Corps* |
| *Rank:* | *Tankman* |
| *Theatre:* | *Eastern Front* |
| *Location:* | *Kursk* |

# Sergeant Red Army Medical Services

**Uniforms for women who served the Red Army were first introduced in August 1941, though they were quickly superseded by standard-issue clothing. This sergeant of the Red Army Medical Services wears a man's shirt with rank and arm-of-service badges on the shoulder straps.**

In 1943, all the ranks of junior commander in the Red Army underwent modifications. For example, the red enamel triangles and old collar patches were abolished and the stripes on the shoulder boards were adopted in their place. The shoulder boards of the ordinary uniform were made of coloured cloth edged with coloured piping. The rank stripes were of gold braid (and silver for the services) with additional badges, numbers and letters to identify the unit to which the wearer belonged. The service of this NCO, the medical service, can be seen clearly on the shoulder boards: dark green with red piping (officers of the commissariat had shoulder boards with red stripes and piping, and officers of the medical, veterinary and legal services had narrower boards with red stripes and red piping).

A brown leather belt was issued to junior ranks and soldiers of the Red Army in 1943, and wound stripes were instituted in July 1942. They were awarded in two classes represented by gold and red braid respectively. They were sewn above the left-hand side of the right breast pocket. The badge on this NCO's right breast was worn by all personnel in Guards units.

| | |
|---|---|
| *Date:* | *December 1943* |
| *Unit:* | *Red Army Medical Services* |
| *Rank:* | *Sergeant* |
| *Theatre:* | *Eastern Front* |
| *Location:* | *Ukraine* |

# Sniper Rifle Battalion Red Army

**The war on the Eastern Front involved the total mobilisation of Soviet society in the battle against the German invader. This meant that hundreds of thousands of women were recruited into the army, and many fought at the front. This female sniper is wearing one of the many camouflage-pattern overalls which were issued to snipers, paratroopers and assault engineers.**

Pre-war, these troops had one-piece overalls worn over standard khaki field uniforms. During the war the blue-grey overall was replaced by a khaki one with a black camouflage-pattern print. This was issued to snipers and assault engineers. One version had strips of frayed cloth sewn to the shoulder and outside sleeves. This had the effect of diffusing the wearer's outline and making a stationary figure almost invisible.

Sniping played an important part in the Red Army. Marksmen and women were tasked with singling out and killing enemy officers and radio operators, which had the effect of demoralising enemy units. The risks were high, of course, and the Germans immediately executed any snipers that they captured.

Snipers were usually attached to rifle divisions, though they operated autonomously. Each division had on average three rifle regiments made up of three rifle battalions. Each battalion had 70 machine guns.

Sniping required ice-cool nerves and lots of patience. It also required a good rifle. This markswoman is armed with a 7.62mm Mosin-Nagant M1891/30 rifle with telescopic sight.

| | |
|---|---|
| *Date:* | *July 1943* |
| *Unit:* | *rifle battalion* |
| *Rank:* | *Sniper* |
| *Theatre:* | *Eastern Front* |
| *Location:* | *Kursk* |

# *Partisan Pripet Marshes Soviet Union*

**The early massive gains made by the Germans in 1941 resulted in thousands of Red Army soldiers going into hiding (though hundreds of thousands more were killed or captured). The vast spaces of the Soviet Union meant that Russian soldiers and party officials were able to roam the countryside and organise resistance. However, until the Germans started to lose in the East and commit atrocities, there was a general reluctance to mount partisan operations against the occupying forces (which would bring immediate savage reprisals).**

In August 1943, there were 24,500 partisans operating in the Ukraine alone, and it has been estimated that up to two million partisans were operating throughout the Soviet Union as a whole. The Germans did not remain idle while this was going on: they organised 25 divisions of the SS, police and paramilitary to combat the partisan threat. This resulted in partisan losses of 85,000 (70,000 were shot and a further 15,000 died in concentration and forced labour camps).

Partisans had no uniforms as such. This figure is wearing a mixture of civilian and military clothing. He wears civilian cap and jacket with Red Army breeches, and boots from a captured German. Clothing was always a problem for the Russians on the Eastern Front, though the deluge of kit which fell into Soviet hands following the German defeat at Stalingrad certainly helped.

| | |
|---|---|
| **Date:** | *August 1943* |
| **Unit:** | *Partisans* |
| **Rank:** | *—* |
| **Theatre:** | *Eastern Front* |
| **Location:** | *Pripet Marshes* |

# Private Guards Motorised Division: Red Army

**This Red Army private is wearing a side cap (*pilotka*) and waterproof cape over the standard field uniform. The Russian ground sheet was designed so that it could be worn as a hooded cape, as illustrated here. By the date of this figure, 1944, the Red Army was on the offensive on the Eastern Front and was a far more effective organisation than it had been three years previously.**

The new Soviet rifle division of the Red Army came into being in 1942. The division had a strength of around 9500 men who were organised into three infantry regiments of 2500 men each and an artillery regiment of 1000 men, together with an anti-tank and an engineer battalion, and a company each of signals and reconnaissance troops. The rifle regiment itself was composed of three battalions of 620 men, each battalion being supported by companies of 76mm howitzers and 45mm anti-tank guns. Every battalion was made up of three rifle companies of 140 men each, a mortar and machine-gun company, together with a platoon each of anti-tank guns and rifles and signals.

Efforts were made to equip Russian infantrymen with submachine guns, and each division was to have 2000 men so armed by late 1942, but the majority were still armed with bolt-action rifles, such as this 7.62mm M44 Mosin-Nagant carbine with folding bayonet in fixed position. Soviet Guards rifle divisions were traditionally better equipped than the standard divisions.

| | |
|---|---|
| *Date:* | *March 1944* |
| *Unit:* | *guards motorised division* |
| *Rank:* | *Private* |
| *Theatre:* | *Eastern Front* |
| *Location:* | *Crimea* |

# General Voronezh Front Red Army

**The sea-green full-dress uniform for marshals and generals was introduced in 1945 specifically for the victory celebrations and parades following the defeat of Nazi Germany (before the Revolution this colour was known as Tsar's green). Marshals had heavier embroidery on the collar and cuffs than those of generals.**

The regulations of 15 January 1943 stated that the marshal's grey parade uniform had gold oak leaves embroidered on the cap band, collar and cuffs. Generals had laurel leaves embroidered on the cap band and on the collar of the tunic. On each cuff they had three gold-embroidered double bars. Marshals wore a red cap band and red piping, while generals wore cap bands and piping in their service branch colours.

The shoulder boards were made of gold braid 140 to 160mm (5.5 to 6.3in) in length and 65mm (2.5in) wide, with piping. Generals in the non-combatant services wore altogether different shoulder boards. On the boards themselves generals sported silver-embroidered stars 22mm (0.9in) in diameter. They were issued with two greatcoats, for parade uniform and ordinary wear. The buttons of both marshals and generals depicted the emblem of the Soviet Union.

The awards on his right breast are, from top to bottom: the Orders of Suvorov 1st Class, Kutusov and the Red Star; and on the left breast the Star of a Hero of the Soviet Union, three Orders of Lenin and two of the Red Banner and, underneath, the Medal for the 20th Anniversary of the Red Army and two campaign medals.

| | |
|---|---|
| *Date:* | *May 1945* |
| *Unit:* | *Red Army* |
| **Rank:** | *General* |
| *Theatre:* | *Eastern Front* |
| *Location:* | *Moscow* |

# *Lieutenant Ukrainian Front Red Army Rifles*

**This officer is an infantryman, as indicated by the red piping and band on the peaked cap and the red piping on the shoulder straps. He is wearing the 1943-pattern shirt (*rubaha*), with belt and pistol holder.**

Shoulder boards, which were worn on the field shirt/tunic, were all khaki red with red stripes and with piping in the colours of the wearer's branch of service. Two red stripes distinguished senior commanders, while commanders had only one stripe along the centre of the board (the two stars worn by this figure on his shoulder boards denote the rank of lieutenant). The shoulder boards of junior commanders and privates were edged with coloured piping, and the former also wore their rank stripes in the service branch colours.

In 1943 junior ranks and soldiers in the Red Army were issued with a brown leather belt, which had a rectangular brass buckle with the hammer and sickle within the star in the centre. This belt was worn with all uniforms and also on the greatcoat.

This officer is a veteran, as indicated by the awards on his right breast, which are: the Orders of the Red Star and the War for the Fatherland with the Guards Badge below. On his left breast he wears two campaign medals.

The Soviet Union had some 9 million members of the armed forces when it entered the war in 1941. Four years later, the figure had increased to 12.4 million. Of these, 6 million were members of the Red Army.

| | |
|---|---|
| *Date:* | *May 1945* |
| *Unit:* | *Red Army Rifles* |
| *Rank:* | *Lieutenant* |
| *Theatre:* | *Eastern Front* |
| *Location:* | *Berlin* |

# *Junior Lieutenant Byelorussian Front Red Army*

**The new dress regulations of 1943 were to change the entire structure of the Red Army. The traditional collar patches were abolished and all rank badges were transferred on to piped shoulder boards. Commanders were provided with a khaki parade uniform consisting of a peaked cap and a single-breasted tunic with five brass buttons and straight collar, as here. The tunic had no pocket at the front and had two false pockets at the back.**

The same peaked cap was worn with both the parade and the ordinary uniform, the coloured band identifying the branch of service of the wearer. Coloured collar patches served the same purpose, and they also displayed the rank of the wearer, senior commanders having two bars and commanders having only one. Note the cuff patch denoting this figure's rank of commander.

Russian engineers and technical staff wore silver embroidered bars with a single, gold-wire ornament, while the rest of the Red Army wore gold bars with a silver ornament, thus distinguishing technical personnel from artillery and armoured troops, who also wore black collar patches.

In addition, the Red Army had two types of shoulder board: those made in gold or silver braid, and the field ones made of khaki material. The boards themselves were 60mm (2.3in) in width and had stripes and piping which identified the branch of service of the wearer.

| | |
|---|---|
| *Date:* | *May 1945* |
| *Unit:* | *Red Army* |
| *Rank:* | *Junior Lieutenant* |
| *Theatre:* | *Eastern Front* |
| *Location:* | *Berlin* |

# *Major*
# *Red Army*
# *Air Force*

The Russian air force was a branch of the Red Army and not an independent arm. In August 1924 a blue service uniform was introduced, and this underwent modifications in December 1935, when it was restricted for wear as a service, a full and as walking-out dress. The basic uniform of the air force was the same as the uniform of the army, but with air force personnel being distinguished by their light blue collar patches and piping. This light blue colouring was later to appear on the shoulder straps.

New collar patches were introduced for the Russian air force in 1935: these patches were light sky blue with gold piping for officers and black piping for political personnel and other ranks. The winged propeller and rank insignia were placed on the patches as illustrated here. Rank badges in the form of red enamelled diamonds, rectangles, squares and triangles, each corresponding to a specific rank, were introduced in 1924.

The gold and red chevrons which can be seen on this major's forearm were adopted by the Russian air force in 1935 and subsequently modified five years later in 1940. Originally gold chevrons were sported by generals and red chevrons worn by other officers, but in 1940 a single large gold chevron with a narrow red stripe at the bottom and a gold star above was prescribed for generals. The chevrons prescribed for other officers displayed a combination of gold and red stripes.

| | |
|---|---|
| *Date:* | *June 1940* |
| *Unit:* | *Red Army Air Force* |
| *Rank:* | *Major* |
| *Theatre:* | *Eastern Front* |
| *Location:* | *Kiev* |

# Lieutenant
# Red Army Air Force
# Arctic Circle

**This fighter pilot is wearing a pre-war leather flying coat with flying helmet. Note the rank badges displayed on his collar patches. Lieutenants were identified by square red enamelled badges, in this case two, plus the winged propeller.**

At the beginning of Operation 'Barbarossa' the Red Army Air Force was in the throes of a reorganisation, with commanders endeavouring to modernise the arm following its poor showing in the 'Winter War' against Finland. When the Germans attacked in June 1941 the Red Army Air Force was totally unprepared and, as a result, the Luftwaffe was able to destroy 1489 Soviet aircraft on the ground and 322 in the air at a loss of only 35 aircraft of its own. Unfortunately, this defeat proved to be a foretaste of things to come.

As the war dragged on, the Germans continued to inflict staggering losses on the Russian air force. Even if Soviet aircraft managed to engage the enemy in the air, Red Army Air Force aircraft and pilots were no match for the Germans. By late November 1941, the Germans claimed to have destroyed 16,000 Soviet aircraft with the loss of 3453 damaged or destroyed of their own.

The winter of 1941–42 gave the air force a respite, allowing the Russians to devote time to training aircrews and developing models, such as the *Ilyushin Il-2* and *Yak* and *Lavochkin* fighters. In addition, the re-siting of the aircraft industry east of the Urals put it out of range of German bombers.

| | |
|---|---|
| *Date:* | *September 1941* |
| *Unit:* | *Red Army Air Force* |
| *Rank:* | *Lieutenant* |
| *Theatre:* | *Eastern Front* |
| *Location:* | *Murmansk* |

# Senior Political Officer
# Red Army Air Force

**The senior political officer pictured here is wearing the 1935-pattern blue service dress of the Red Army Air Force, although the black piping on his collar patches and the absence of rank chevrons on the cuffs identifies him as a commissar. Red Army regulations stated that commissars were required to wear a red cloth five-pointed star on both cuffs, though this particular officer seems to have removed them.**

In addition to the blue service dress shown here, air force personnel were also issued with greatcoats. There were two versions of the latter: officers' greatcoats were double-breasted and had two rows of four brass buttons, while other ranks were issued with single-breasted greatcoats with five brass buttons. The officers' version had slanting side pockets with flap, turn-back cuffs and half-belt at the back fastened with a button at each end. As well as the blue peaked cap and the side cap, there was a blue cloth helmet called a *shelm*, which was later to be replaced by the fur cap (*ushanka*).

By 1942 the Red Army air force industry had recovered sufficiently enough to make possible an increase in the size of air force units. For example, fighter and ground-attack regiments had three squadrons each, giving them a total strength of 32 aircraft. The Russians also organised massive air armies, which in 1942–43 numbered just under 1000 aircraft each. Two years later this had increased to between 2500 and 3000 aircraft per army.

| | |
|---|---|
| *Date:* | *August 1942* |
| *Unit:* | *Red Army Air Force* |
| *Rank:* | *Senior Political Officer* |
| *Theatre:* | *Eastern Front* |
| *Location:* | *Leningrad* |

# Lieutenant Kiev Region Red Army Air Force

**New regulations introduced on 15 January 1935 brought many changes to the uniforms of air force officers. For example, new tunics were introduced for the purpose of showing insignia, and all officers had shoulder boards of gold lace for parade and service uniform, or plain cloth ones for wearing on the field uniform.**

The cloth shoulder boards had blue piping and dark red stripes running down the centre. Lieutenants, such as the officer pictured here, had one stripe and silver stripes 13mm (0.5in) in diameter. The parade dress tunic sported collar patches and double bars on the cuffs. The patches were blue with one or two embroidered stripes according to class of rank, which was also shown by the double bars on the cuffs.

This officer wears the Guards Badge and the wound badges introduced in July 1942 on his right breast (red for a light wound, gold for a serious wound). On his left breast he wears the Order of the Red Star.

By the beginning of 1944 the Red Army Air Force boasted 11,000 military aircraft which were deployed against a German strength of less than 2000. During the four-year war on the Eastern Front the Russians managed to build a staggering 137,271 aircraft in total, and also received another 2000 Allied Lend-Lease aircraft. It was this massive numerical superiority which was to give the Red Army Air Force victory in the East.

| | |
|---|---|
| *Date:* | *December 1944* |
| *Unit:* | *Kiev Region* |
| *Rank:* | *Lieutenant* |
| *Theatre:* | *Eastern Front* |
| *Location:* | *Kiev* |

# Seaman
# Northern Fleet
# Red Navy

**The uniform of the Red Navy followed that of other navies, though with two distinct features. First, the Red Navy was the only navy in which the sailor's traditional square rig was worn with petty officer's peaked cap; second, the sailor's uniform combined the colours blue and black.**

Officers wore a black uniform which comprised a peaked cap, 'reefer' jacket with white shirt and black tie, black trousers and black leather shoes. Officers also wore a black double-breasted greatcoat which had two rows of six gilt metal buttons. Ratings, such as the one illustrated here, wore a dark blue jumper (*flanelevka*) and black bell-bottom trousers. This rating wears the single-breasted greatcoat issued for wear in cold weather. It had six yellow metal buttons, and replaced the short pea-coat.

Russian black cap tallies carried the name of a fleet, such as the Northern Fleet, or the name of a ship's crew, in gilt cyrillic letters. At the beginning of the war all ranks wore their rank badges on the cuffs. These badges were in gold on blue, or light blue on white uniforms for officers, and red or yellow on all uniforms for ratings.

Russian naval conscripts would usually serve for a period of five years in one of the four fleets – Baltic, Northern, Black Sea and Pacific – or in one of the flotillas which operated in the lakes and seas of the Soviet Union. In 1939 the Soviet Navy had a strength of 40,000 men. Of this number, around 22,000 were serving at sea in the various fleets.

| | |
|---|---|
| *Date:* | *September 1939* |
| *Unit:* | *Northern Fleet* |
| *Rank:* | *Seaman* |
| *Theatre:* | *Arctic* |
| *Location:* | *Archangel* |

# Pilot
# Arctic Fleet: Air Force
# of the Red Navy

**In 1941 the Soviet Naval Air Service possessed a total of 2581 aircraft, though 90 per cent of them were at this time obsolete. These aircraft were organised into four Naval Air Forces corresponding to the Russian fleets: namely the Baltic, Northern, Black Sea and Pacific fleets. Russian naval aviation also possessed a number of specialist mining and torpedo units, which were organised into divisions, brigades and regiments.**

In general Russian naval pilots wore navy uniforms along with various kinds of flying clothing, as illustrated here by this Russian flying officer. Naval pilots also wore one-piece blue overalls, with their rank distinction lace displayed on the cuffs. Thereafter, with the reintroduction of shoulder boards, naval air force personnel wore light blue piping. Naval aviators and flight engineers wore the same badges as their army counterparts on the upper left sleeve of their blue jackets. Flying helmets were usually made of brown leather.

This flying officer is a member of the Arctic Fleet, as indicated by his warm footwear and quilted trousers. In addition to the four Naval Air Forces, the navy had more than 1600 flying boats – Beriev Be-2s, Chetverikov MDR-6s and Consolidated Catalinas – organised in maritime reconnaissance regiments. By the later stages of the war the Russians had achieved total air superiority over the Germans, and so their outdated naval aircraft were able to operate with impunity.

| | |
|---|---|
| *Date:* | *August 1941* |
| *Unit:* | *Arctic Fleet* |
| *Rank:* | *Pilot* |
| *Theatre:* | *Arctic* |
| *Location:* | *Archangel* |

# Seaman
# Baltic Fleet
# Red Navy

**At the beginning of the war against Nazi Germany, the Red Navy lacked anti-submarine warfare vessels, minesweepers and support craft. As a consequence, during the first six months of the war in the Baltic the Soviets lost 25 submarines for the loss of only three German cargo ships. Many of the Red Army's ships were old, and many of its bases and training areas were being overrun as the Germans advanced east.**

For Red Army ratings working in warm weather the uniform consisted of working clothing made of natural undyed linen (ratings wore their number on a patch on the left breast). Working clothing was often dyed blue, and in winter fur caps, anoraks, rubber coats and boots and other kinds of protective clothing were also worn. The seaman illustrated here is wearing a 1940-pattern steel helmet and waterproof foul weather coat. His earphones and speaker are part of the ship's gunnery control equipment. The rubber attachments on his greatcoat skirts were for hitching this equipment to his belt.

Sailors serving on land in naval rifle units had no special uniform as such, so they wore a combination of army and navy clothing and equipment. The large number of losses experienced by the navy at the start of the Russian campaign meant that thousands of sailors were used on land in an effort to slow down the German advance.

At the beginning of the war, the fleet had over 100 vessels, including two battleships and two cruisers.

| | |
|---|---|
| *Date:* | *January 1942* |
| *Unit:* | *Baltic Fleet* |
| *Rank:* | *Seaman* |
| *Theatre:* | *Eastern Front* |
| *Location:* | *Leningrad* |

# *Petty Officer 2nd Class Caspian Flotilla*

**Red Navy petty officers who had attained more than five years' service were entitled to wear the peaked cap with 'square rig'. In cold weather they wore a long single-breasted blue greatcoat which had six yellow buttons, or a short pea-coat which had two rows of six buttons.**

In 1943 naval rating badges were transferred from the sleeves on to the shoulder straps. These consisted of yellow lace stripes, with cyrillic letters attached to the outer ends of the straps to identify the wearer's unit or organisation.

Circular trade badges were worn on the upper sleeves. Trades' devices were embroidered in red and the actual badges, of the same colour as the uniform on which they were intended to be worn, had a red edging. So, for example, boatswains had anchors, helmsmen a steering wheel and gunners had crossed guns. The leather belt carried a brass buckle with the star and hammer and sickle within, superimposed upon an anchor.

This petty officer 2nd Class wears a black and orange guard tally, which was awarded to ships crews for distinguished service. He has a campaign medal attached to his left breast, while around his neck he wears a blue jean collar called a *forminka*. His black bell-bottom trousers were usually worn outside the jumper.

Many Russian ships were old and lacked sophisticated underwater and anti-aircraft equipment. This was rectified to some extent later during the war when kit was made available through lend-lease.

| | |
|---|---|
| **Date:** | *June 1943* |
| **Unit:** | *Caspian Flotilla* |
| **Rank:** | *Petty Officer 2nd Class* |
| **Theatre:** | *Eastern Front* |
| **Location:** | *Black Sea* |

# Petty Officer 2nd Class Black Sea Fleet

Due to extensive Russian losses at the hands of the Germans, not just through loss of ships, but due to ship maintenance problems and ice-bound seas, thousands of sailors had to fight on land during the war. In fact, most of the Baltic Fleet took part in the Defence of Leningrad. However, because the sailors were not trained for this role naval losses were high, which further deprived ships of technicians. Nevertheless, after the first year of the war there was a nucleus of battle-hardened amphibious veterans.

It is estimated that by the end of the war no less than 300,000 men had been employed in 114 assaults. Each naval infantry battalion comprised around 600 sailors. Two battalions were sometimes combined to form a regiment, though usually up to 10 battalions were grouped together to form a brigade. In October 1941 the navy established Independent Naval (Marine) Rifle Brigades, which served at the front and manned coastal artillery.

This petty officer 2nd Class manning a sector of the front wears the uniform of the Red Army, while proudly retaining the striped vest to denote his naval affiliations. On his quilted jacket (*telogreika*) he wears the Medal for the Defence of Sevastopol. The pouch holds a 71-round magazine for the famous PPSh submachine gun, which, instead of the round magazine, is shown here fitted with a curved model.

| | |
|---|---|
| **Date:** | *October 1944* |
| **Unit:** | *Black Sea Fleet* |
| **Rank:** | *Petty Officer 2nd Class* |
| **Theatre:** | *Eastern Front* |
| **Location:** | *Sevastopol* |

# Rear-Admiral Pacific Fleet Red Navy

**This senior officer of the submarine service is wearing the standard uniform of the Red Navy. Officers in the Red Navy were divided into executive and non-executive officers. The former included officers of the Line and of Line Engineering, while the latter included officers serving in all other naval corps or services.**

Line officers wore gold insignia: cap badge, embroideries on the peaked cap's visor, cuff stripes, shoulder straps and buttons. The cap badge, as illustrated here, depicted a foul anchor superimposed on a round, protruding cockade with black centre, surrounded by a laurel wreath, the whole ensigned by a five-pointed red star with hammer and sickle in a white centre.

At the beginning of the war, Russian naval officers wore conventional stripes of lace on the cuffs, but new dress regulations introduced in February 1943 ushered in shoulder straps of a traditional Russian pattern, made of gold or silver lace according to corps, and shorter cuff stripes, as shown here. The shoulder straps were worn by all officers on the dark jacket, tunic and greatcoat, while cuff stripes were worn by officers of the Line and Line Engineering only. The shoulder straps of flag officers were covered with gold or silver lace, with a zig-zag design interwoven. This rear-admiral wears the submariners badge on his right breast.

The Pacific Fleet was based at Vladivostock and Nicolaiev-Komsomolsk, and was instrumental in the occupation of Japanese territory in 1945.

| | |
|---|---|
| *Date:* | *October 1944* |
| *Unit:* | *Pacific Fleet* |
| *Rank:* | *Rear-Admiral* |
| *Theatre:* | *Pacific* |
| *Location:* | *South China Sea* |

# *France*

*Defeatism infused the French forces on the outbreak of war, and though the army had around 1,000,000 men, it was very much a paper tiger. The surprise German attack in 1940 was totally demoralising. It was only later in the war, after being equipped with American equipment and led by De Gaulle, that French forces fought with conviction.*

# *Sergeant Armoured Division French Army*

**In May 1940 the French Army had more than 300 tanks – an impressive figure indeed, and one made more potent by the fact that the quality and firepower of France's tanks was generally superior to that of her German counterparts. However, tactically speaking the French were woefully deficient when it came to armoured formations, and were to suffer when the German panzers smashed west.**

Like most armies prior to World War II, the French had developed special uniforms for tank and armoured car crews, which included a special helmet with neck guard and padded leather front. The earlier versions of this helmet were nothing more than modifications of the standard infantry steel helmet, even retaining the distinctive comb (a feature which was the last thing crews needed while operating in the confined spaces of armoured vehicles). However, in 1935 the final khaki model entered service. In addition, crews were issued with a three-quarter length brown leather coat, plus a blue beret instead of the side cap.

The figure pictured here is a sergeant of motorised troops. He wears the clothing described above, and has his M35 padded helmet tucked under his left arm. As can be seen, the beret sports the tank badge – crossed cannon and a medieval helmet – while his rank badges are worn on the jacket front and his unit markings on his collar. Though these are green, the standard colour was grey.

| | |
|---|---|
| *Date:* | *April 1940* |
| *Unit:* | *Armoured Division* |
| *Rank:* | *Sergeant* |
| *Theatre:* | *Northwest Europe* |
| *Location:* | *Amiens* |

196

# Chasseur Alpin
## 5th Demi-Brigade
## French Army

In mid-April 1940, some 10,000 British and French troops who had been assembled in British ports for possible aid to Finland, were finally embarked. They landed at Namsos and Andalsnes, their mission being to try and take Trondheim and to retain an Allied foothold in Norway (which was then under attack by Germany). A smaller force was also landed at Narvik.

This *chasseur alpin,* or mountain soldier, of the 5th Demi-Brigade was one of those who were put ashore in Norway as part of the Allied Expeditionary Force. He wears the blue *chasseur* beret and waterproof cotton duck anorak, and for additional protection against the cold and wet conditions he has been issued with a sheepskin jacket, which is rolled on top of his rucksack. He carries a pistol in a holster and a 7.5mm MAS 36 carbine.

This private wears gaiters and skis, which were standard issue for French mountain troops, though the skis proved to be of little use during the Norwegian campaign. The French were no different to the armies of other countries when it came to equipping their mountain units; the men were invariably overburdened with kit.

In early June 1940, after succeeding in dislodging the Germans from Narvik even in the face of naval and land superiority, the Allies were then forced to evacuate their troops because of the disasters that had taken place in France. The Germans promptly reoccupied Narvik and completed their conquest of Norway.

| | |
|---|---|
| **Date:** | *April 1940* |
| **Unit:** | *5th Demi-Brigade* |
| **Rank:** | Chasseur Alpin |
| **Theatre:** | *Arctic* |
| **Location:** | *Narvik* |

# *Private First Class 182nd Artillery Regiment*

The traditional horizon blue uniform of World War I gave way to the khaki model in 1935. The khaki tunic (*vareuse*) was single-breasted with a low fall collar and six drab metal buttons in front. Officers' tunics had seven buttons, a breast patch and large side pockets, though all ranks had round cuffs. Standard-issue greatcoats were double-breasted with a large fall collar and two rows of seven buttons in front.

In the French Army there were three kinds of head-dress: the *kepi*, which was worn by all ranks and was made of either blue or khaki cloth; the field cap — *bonnet de police* — made of khaki cloth; and the steel helmet. Arm of service was indicated by the colour of the *kepi* and the collar patches. Thus the figure pictured here has red collar patches, blue piping and unit numbers in blue, which indicates that he is a member of the artillery arm.

This private first class is wearing walking-out dress with a blue-black *kepi*. He wears the khaki tunic, though the army did have a tunic in gaberdine for summer use. By 1938 the old breeches were beginning to be replaced by knickerbockers for dismounted personnel. Note the badge on his upper left arm, which denotes his role as an armourer.

It is a sad fact that the French Army in 1940 was infected with defeatism. This was exacerbated by the Phoney War and the bitter winter of 1939–40. Thus, when the German Army crashed through the Ardennes the French never recovered.

| | |
|---|---|
| *Date:* | *April 1940* |
| *Unit:* | *182nd Artillery Regiment* |
| *Rank:* | *Private First Class* |
| *Theatre:* | *northwest Europe* |
| *Location:* | *Flanders* |

# Major 46th Infantry Regiment

**The rank of French officers was indicated by the insignia that was worn on the sleeves of the tunic, the greatcoat, *kepi* and the forage cap. On the coat and other over-garments, officer rank was indicated by a series of stripes on tabs which were fixed to a coat button. Generals had gold oak leaves embroidered on the *kepi*, while officers of lower levels wore gold and silver lace on the *kepi* to denote rank.**

The major pictured here is wearing the old-style uniform with rank badges on the front of the side cap and cuffs. He is a member of the 46th Infantry Regiment, as shown by the numbers on his collar patches, the khaki colour of the patches, the dark blue piping and the fact that the numbers are in red. Note that each regiment also had a metal badge, which was worn on the right breast pocket. This major, being a field officer, obviously rides a horse, as indicated by the breeches and the boots with the spurs. His medal ribbons are for the *Croix de Guerre* 1914–1918 (in red and green) and the Dardenelles campaign (in white and green).

At the beginning of World War II, as in the Great War 20 years earlier, the main strength of the French Army lay in its infantry arm, which, in turn, relied largely on horse transport. A French infantry division comprised 17,000 men and 500 officers, who were divided between three infantry regiments, two artillery regiments and a reconnaissance group of four squadrons.

| | |
|---|---|
| *Date:* | *May 1940* |
| *Unit:* | *46th Infantry Regiment* |
| *Rank:* | *Major* |
| *Theatre:* | *northwest Europe* |
| *Location:* | *Edan* |

# Private
# Free French Army
# Great Britain

**This Free Frenchman is wearing British battle dress with the distinctive French helmet. The French helmet was first introduced into general service in 1915, and it underwent a number of improvements between the wars. The final version was made of manganese steel and stamped in one piece. Each French arm of service had its own stamped badge which was worn on the front of the helmet, while an unofficial custom was to wear a stamped metal plaque on the peak which bore the name of the wearer and the inscription 'a soldier of the Great War' within two laurel branches.**

Other items of French attire worn by the private pictured here, include his boots and equipment. By the date of this figure, September 1940, the only insignia worn were the nationality title and a strip of red, white and blue ribbon on the shoulder strap, which signified allegiance to the commander of the Free French forces, General de Gaulle. This private's rifle is the French Berthier M07/15, an improvement on the outdated Lebel rifle which was standard issue to French troops in 1940. He also has a French gas mask case.

Those French soldiers who wanted to continue the fight against Nazi Germany (now that it had occupied their home country) were assembled at Olympia in London on 1 July 1940 and formed into the *Légion de Gaulle*, or the Fighting French as they were called by the British.

| | |
|---|---|
| *Date:* | *September 1940* |
| *Unit:* | *Free French Army* |
| *Rank:* | *Private* |
| *Theatre:* | *northwest Europe* |
| *Location:* | *England* |

# Goumier
## *French African Troops*
## *Syria*

With the collapse of the Axis cause in North Africa, Free French officers were able to persuade many Vichy soldiers to join their cause, especially after Germany had occupied Vichy France itself. Vichy soldiers were recruited in such large numbers that the French were able to organise the French Expeditionary Corps, which was deployed to Italy at the end of 1943. At first the corps numbered two divisions, but in the spring of 1944 it was reinforced by a further two divisions.

Free French uniforms were heavily influenced by British and American supplies of clothing. This meant that insignia in French national colours was the only indication as to identity.

However, Free French troops, whether French or from France's colonies, continued to wear their existing uniforms as long as possible, being eventually replaced by either American or British uniforms and hardware. This Moroccan *goumier* serving in the French Expeditionary Corps in Italy is wearing a British steel helmet on top of his turban and a striped *djellabah* over his American combat uniform (the arrangement and colour of the *djellabah* identified the wearer's tribe).

During the Italian campaign the Free French were heavily committed during the battles around Monte Cassino, outflanking German mountain positions and ensuring the Allied victory. After the fall of Rome in May 1944, the French forces were withdrawn from Italy to prepare for the invasion of France.

| | |
|---|---|
| *Date:* | *May 1944* |
| *Unit:* | *French African Troops* |
| *Rank:* | Goumier |
| *Theatre:* | *Mediterranean* |
| *Location:* | *Italy* |

# *Private 2nd Moroccan Division*

**The figure pictured here represents the final uniform worn by Free French troops throughout World War II. The uniform was overwhelmingly American in style, with American khaki wool trousers, and the American winter combat jacket with vertical slit pockets which was favoured by the crews of armoured vehicles. The private pictured here is wearing French M1917 boots with gaiters, while his weapon is the Lee-Enfield .303 rifle, which was manufactured in Great Britain.**

Though American clothing dominated the Free French uniform, individuals continued to wear the French head-dress, such as the steel helmet and the motorised troop helmet, for as long as possible. Even in the American uniform French touches were retained: badges of rank were worn on the head-dress, on the shoulder straps or on a patch on the front of combat clothing.

Military personnel wore a cloth badge on the upper left sleeve which was shaped like the patch worn on the collar of French tunics. The colour of the badge, the chevrons and the regimental number or emblem conformed to the earlier collar patches. However, in order to indicate that they were Free French, the troops in North Africa had three chevrons instead of the usual two.

Free French infantry divisions consisted of three or four infantry regiments with a strong reconnaissance regiment and an artillery regiment, with additional engineers and signals and service troops.

| | |
|---|---|
| *Date:* | *May 1945* |
| *Unit:* | *2nd Moroccan Division* |
| *Rank:* | *Private* |
| *Theatre:* | *northwest Europe* |
| *Location:* | *Germany* |

# Pilot
# Paris Air Region
# French Air Force

This French pilot of a Potez 63/II reconnaissance aircraft is wearing the standard padded chrome leather flying helmet, one-piece overall and Chanole parachute with quick-release harness. On the eve of World War II the French had an impressive number of aircraft: 1200 fighters, 1300 bombers and 800 reconnaissance aircraft. Personnel numbered 110,000 all ranks. However, the air force had been neglected and fielded inferior machines, which were found to be wanting against the Luftwaffe in 1940.

The French Air Force uniform consisted of dark Louise-blue tunic and trousers, with a peaked cap with white cover for summer wear, black beret for everyday and working wear, plus steel helmet as and when required. The peaked cap was blue with a black band, and on the front of the cap above the band was a pair of gold-embroidered wings with the number of the unit for officers, or silver stars for generals, while members of the colonial air force wore an anchor. There was also a standard-issue double-breasted greatcoat which had a fall collar and two rows of six gilt metal buttons, slanting side pockets with flaps, turn-back cuffs, half-belt at the back fastened with two buttons, and gold-embroidered *passants* on the shoulders.

Pilots wore gilt wings ensigned by a five-pointed star, which was usually worn at a 45-degree angle, and pilots of single-seater aircraft wore a double-breasted leather jacket in their aircraft.

| | |
|---|---|
| **Date:** | *April 1940* |
| **Unit:** | *Paris Air Region* |
| **Rank:** | *Pilot* |
| **Theatre:** | *northwest Europe* |
| **Location:** | *France* |

# Sergeant-Major GAO 502 French Air Force

**French Air Force senior NCOs wore the same basic uniform as officers, except that the tunic had a matching cloth belt, five buttons in front, with breast pockets with pleats. Over this was often worn a double-breasted greatcoat with two rows of three gilt metal buttons.**

This figure is Sergeant Duval, an air gunner in the *Groupe Aérienne d'Observation* (GAO) 502, who wears the Louise-blue service dress with badges of rank on the cap and cuffs. All French Air Force NCOs wore 12mm (0.5in) wide chevrons above the cuffs on the blue jacket and stripes of reduced size on the field jacket and on the beret. Chief-sergeants wore three gold chevrons or stripes, regular sergeants had two chevrons, and conscripted sergeants wore only one gold chevron.

Flying personnel wore wings above the right breast pocket of the jacket, as shown here. These wings were called speciality insignia in France and were produced in embroidered and metal versions for blue uniforms and linen uniforms respectively. On the evening dress the wings were replaced by an eagle embroidered in gold. Aerodrome personnel had a cog wheel between the wings, while between the wings of aviation personnel was a five-pointed star. The metal badge on Duval's right breast was worn only by crews of aircraft and airships, while the badge on the left breast pocket flap is a squadron emblem. Medal ribbons are the *Médaille Militaire* (yellow and green), awarded for soldiers who had distinguished themselves in the war, and the *Croix de Guerre* (red and green).

| | |
|---|---|
| *Date:* | *May 1940* |
| *Unit:* | *GAO 502* |
| *Rank:* | *Sergeant-Major* |
| *Theatre:* | *northwest Europe* |
| *Location:* | *France* |

# Petty Officer 2nd Class Atlantic Fleet French Navy

**This petty officer is wearing the summer parade dress: white cap cover and white trousers. His petty officer status is indicated by the officers' uniform and the two yellow diagonal stripes on the sleeve (on the white summer uniform these stripes were often detachable, whereas on the blue tunic they were sewn on).**

On his peaked cap he wears the insignia of petty officers: a foul anchor surrounded by a wreath of two laurel leaves. The gold badge was used by personnel of the *Fleet Equipage*, musicians, firemen, signalmen and harbour personnel, while a red badge was used by musicians, firemen, signalmen and harbour personnel only.

The petty officer 2nd class shown here wears a *fourragère* of the *Croix de Guerre* on his left shoulder, and the badge of a master gunner or machine gunner on his left sleeve. His medal ribbon is the *Medaille d'Orient*, which was awarded to troops who had fought in the French Army of the East during World War I. His rifle, infantry equipment and gaiters were typical of the kit worn by ratings and petty officers with full-dress uniform.

The petty officers' greatcoat followed the same pattern as that of the officers': double-breasted with two rows of five buttons, gold-embroidered *passants*, side pockets with straight flaps and a half-belt at the back fastened with four buttons. The petty officer's walking-out raincoat was the same as that issued to other ratings.

| | |
|---|---|
| **Date:** | *January 1940* |
| **Unit:** | *Atlantic Fleet* |
| **Rank:** | *Petty Officer 2nd Class* |
| **Theatre:** | *Atlantic* |
| **Location:** | *Brest* |

# Lieutenant Mediterranean Fleet French Navy

**The lieutenant illustrated here is wearing the blue service dress of the French Navy. Officers were allowed to wear the blue reefer jacket with cap and white cover, white trousers and white canvas shoes, or they could wear the special white summer jacket. Officers also had a khaki drill uniform for wear in hot climates.**

The peaked cap shown here is blue with black leather peak and chin strap. The badge on the cap is a gold-embroidered open laurel wreath with a foul anchor in the centre. Officers displayed their rank in the form of lace stripes on the cap band, on the cuffs and on the shoulder straps. The embroidered *passants* on this officer's shoulders were originally intended to hold full-dress epaulettes, but they were never actually worn on the reefer jacket.

France did not begin her naval modernisation programme until 1937, though she did succeed in making the French Navy the fourth largest in the world. By the time war broke out on 1 September 1939 the French Navy had mustered 160,000 personnel of all ranks. The Mediterranean Fleet was the strongest, reflecting the agreement with the British to help counter the strength of the Italian Navy. The latter was extremely strong in the Mediterranean, and presented a threat to the important sea routes from France to North Africa and the British routes via the Suez Canal to Gibraltar. It comprised 3 battleships, a seaplane carrier, 10 cruisers, and 48 destroyers, as well as 53 submarines.

| | |
|---|---|
| *Date:* | *May 1940* |
| *Unit:* | *Mediterranean Fleet* |
| *Rank:* | *Lieutenant* |
| *Theatre:* | *Mediterranean* |
| *Location:* | *Toulon* |

# Leading Seaman
# Atlantic Fleet
# French Navy

**The rating pictured here is wearing parade dress: the standard 'square rig' cap with the typical French red pompom, a striped vest and blue collar. In addition to the blue uniform shown here, ratings wore a number of other items of working and foul-weather clothing.**

Mechanics and firemen wore a bright blue one-piece overall and side cap with a red anchor on the left side. French foul-weather clothing was made of black or yellow oilskin, while crews of motor torpedo boats and other fast attack craft were issued with a special outfit consisting of cloth helmet, special lined waterproof jacket with 'plastron' front and two rows of four buttons, and sea boots with wooden soles. For very cold weather ratings were issued with a cloth 'Canadian' coat lined with sheepskin, a grey woollen scarf and sea boots.

Junior quartermasters sported two or three red stripes on the cuffs according to class, while junior ratings wore a special badge on the left breast of the summer vest which depicted a blue anchor surrounded by a blue rectangular frame and with blue stripes at the bottom, which identified their rate class.

This leading seaman carries the legend *Maritime Nationale* on his cap, and his white gaiters were only worn with the parade dress. His weapon is a modified 8mm M92/16 rifle with an M92 knife bayonet attached.

The Atlantic fleet was was based at Brest as an independent force under Vice-Admiral M B Gensoul.

| | |
|---|---|
| *Date:* | *May 1940* |
| *Unit:* | *Atlantic Fleet* |
| *Rank:* | *Leading Seaman* |
| *Theatre:* | *Atlantic* |
| *Location:* | *Brest* |

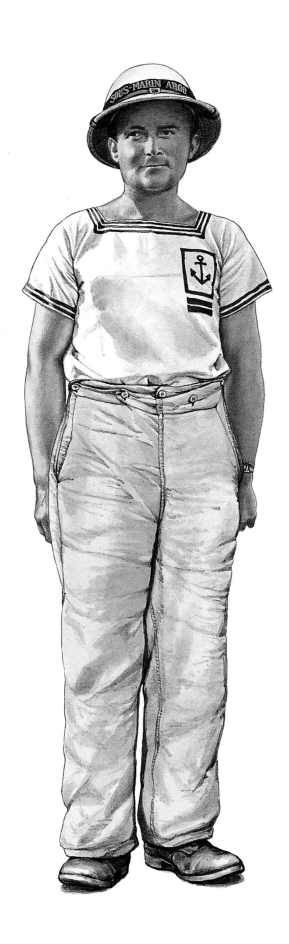

# *Leading Seaman French Fleet French Navy*

**In very hot weather officers and ratings wore a white sun helmet as shown here. A metal version of the cap badge was worn by officers and petty officers, with a yellow metal anchor on the front for ratings, who also wore the cap ribbon illustrated here.**

In 1925 a new tropical uniform was introduced into the French Navy. This consisted of a short-sleeve white cotton shirt with square neck opening. The neck opening and sleeves were edged with two dark blue lines, and on the left breast ratings wore a blue anchor within a rectangular blue-striped border. Underneath the anchor were one to three strips according to rank (seamen and quartermasters wore one to three horizontal blue stripes). The shirt was worn with matching long trousers (though this figure is wearing cotton duck trousers as part of his working rig), white cap cover or helmet and white canvas shoes.

After the fall of France in the summer of 1940, the French Fleet was obliged to keep its ships under Axis control, and to be eventually disarmed by them. The Axis powers, though, were content to leave the French ships in French ports and therefore, in effect, out of the war. However, the Royal Navy's attack on the ports of Mers-el-Kébir and Dakar ensured that the Vichy Fleet remained hostile towards the Allied cause.

On 3 July 1940, the French Fleet at Mers-el-Kébir received a British ultimatum to place itself at the disposal of the British Government. When the French refused the British opened fire, killing 1297 men and destroying three capital ships.

| | |
|---|---|
| *Date:* | *May 1941* |
| *Unit:* | *French Fleet* |
| *Rank:* | *Leading Seaman* |
| *Theatre:* | *Mediterranean* |
| *Location:* | *Marseilles* |

# *British Empire*

*All the main nations of the British Empire sent units to fight against either Germany or Japan — or both. These units fought well, particularly the Australians, New Zealanders, Gurkhas and Indians, being well trained and imbued with British discipline and professionalism. Empire units made crucial contributions in North Africa and the Far East.*

# Private Kimberley Regiment South African Army

**South Africans fought in three theatres in World War II: East Africa, North Africa and Italy. They performed admirably in Africa, though with the fall of Tobruk in June 1942, 9780 South Africans of the 2nd Division – a third of all South Africans in the field – were captured. The 1st South African Division returned home in November 1942, but from April 1944 onwards the 6th South African Division fought in Italy.**

At the beginning of her involvement in the war, South Africa's uniforms were similar to those worn by British soldiers, except for the shape of the sun helmet and the high webbing gaiters. As here, the South African sun helmet had a narrow brim and a khaki puggaree, on which was sometimes worn a metal cap badge and a cloth flash in regimental or corps colours on the right side. (South Africa declared war on Germany on 6 September 1940, though her forces were small: 3350 men of the Permanent Force, 14,631 volunteers of the Active Service Force, and 122,000 citizens enrolled in the Commandos and Defence Rifle Associations.)

This private of the Kimberley Regiment is wearing the 'polo-pattern' helmet with regimental flash on the side as described above. His khaki drill jacket and long trousers were standard issue at the beginning of the war, and his short anklets were a replacement for the long ones which were issued when mobilisation took place in 1940. His webbing equipment is British 1937 pattern, as is the Lee-Enfield .303 SMLE No 1 Mk III bolt-action rifle.

| | |
|---|---|
| *Date:* | *December 1940* |
| *Unit:* | *Kimberley Regiment* |
| *Rank:* | *Private* |
| *Theatre:* | *Mediterranean* |
| *Location:* | *North Africa* |

# Lieutenant Royal South African Air Force

**The Royal South African Air Force was formed in February 1920 as part of the army. Its personnel wore army uniforms with bronzed badges, and South Africans who served with the RAF wore a grey uniform sporting a 'South Africa' flash. Those South Africans who volunteered for service outside the Dominion wore an orange flash on their shoulder straps.**

The fighter pilot pictured here is wearing the distinctive South African sun helmet with South African Air Force cap badge and flash on the side. The rest of his uniform is standard khaki drill, though note the wings on his left breast and the orange flash on the shoulder straps (see above). His shoulder straps also carry his rank insignia. Those South African pilots who were shot down by the enemy and made their way back to friendly lines on foot were awarded a 'winged boot' badge, which they usually wore on the left breast.

The South African Air Force first saw action in Kenya, where its aircraft bombed enemy positions just prior to the outbreak of war. During the Abyssinian campaign South African aircraft accounted for 95 Italian aircraft downed — this was a foretaste of things to come.

During the war in North Africa the South Africans played a major part in the eventual Allied victory, deploying a total of 13 squadrons during the Battle of El Alamein in October 1942, carrying out ground-attack missions and fighter duties.

| | |
|---|---|
| *Date:* | *October 1942* |
| *Unit:* | *Royal South African Air Force* |
| *Rank:* | *Lieutenant* |
| *Theatre:* | *Mediterranean* |
| *Location:* | *North Africa* |

# Private 6th Division Australian Army

**Australian soldiers entered World War II with almost the same uniform as they had sported in the Great War. They wore a shirt-like single-breasted tunic instead of battle dress, which had four bronzed buttons in front, matching shoulder straps and sleeves gathered and fastened at the wrist. The long matching trousers were usually worn with canvas anklets and ankle boots.**

Australian greatcoats were single-breasted with fall collars, five buttons in front, slanting side pockets with flap and turn-back cuffs. Head-dress consisted of wide-brimmed khaki felt slouch or 'wide-awake' hat, as shown here, which was worn on most occasions when the steel helmet was not in use. On formal occasions the brim was folded up on the left and fastened with a bronze Australian badge (as here) or a metal cap badge.

The figure illustrated here is a private of the 2nd Company, 6th Infantry Division. He wears a formation sign on his sleeves which was the same as that worn in World War I, though with a grey frame. His equipment includes 1908-pattern webbing with gas mask and a 1907-pattern sword bayonet. The mess tin was originally introduced at the end of the nineteenth century for dismounted personnel, but was still in use nearly 50 years later.

The 6th Division participated in the Allied offensive of January–February 1941 in North Africa, and was then moved to the Far East when Japan entered the war.

| | |
|---|---|
| **Date:** | *January 1941* |
| **Unit:** | *6th Division* |
| **Rank:** | *Private* |
| **Theatre:** | *Mediterranean* |
| **Location:** | *North Africa* |

# Private
# 9th Division
# Australian Army

**The Australian issue khaki uniform was made of a lighter quality cloth than the British model, making it more suitable for wear in the hot conditions of the desert. That said, it was soon replaced by both British khaki drill and serge uniforms during the North African campaign.**

This Australian private could easily be mistaken for the average Tommy, the only thing betraying his Australian origins being the anklets. On top of his single-breasted greatcoat he wears 1937-pattern webbing with additional ammunition carried in cloth bandoliers. Over his shoulder he carries a Lee-Enfield No 1 Mk III rifle.

The first Australian unit to be raised for service overseas was the 6th Division, the initial infantry establishment of which there were three brigades, each with four battalions. Manpower was not a problem but equipment was: each battalion needed 10 machine-gun carriers, 25-pound field guns, which were needed to replace the 18-pounders and 4.5in howitzers of the field artillery regiments, while the formation of a mechanised reconnaissance regiment required 28 light tanks and 44 machine-gun carriers. The fall of France led to a flood of recruits, which more than fulfilled the Australian Government's requirement of 65,000 men to fill a corps of three divisions – the 6th, 7th and 8th. Indeed, recruitment was discontinued in September 1940, with the manpower for a new division being taken from those men in training and already in Britain.

| | |
|---|---|
| *Date:* | *May 1941* |
| *Unit:* | *9th Division* |
| *Rank:* | *Private* |
| *Theatre:* | *Mediterranean* |
| *Location:* | *Tobruk* |

# Private 7th Division Australian Army

**This soldier of the 7th Australian Division in Syria is wearing British khaki drill uniform with the distinctive 'Digger' slouch hat which sports the Australian general service badge. The canvas anklets just above his boots were unique to Australian troops during the war. His webbing is 1937 pattern and his rifle is the Lee-Enfield .303.**

Australian troops had a reputation for being insubordinate and entirely lacking in any sense of formality. Though there was some truth to this, the courage and tenacity of the Australian fighting man cannot be doubted. When World War II broke out there were only 3000 men plus a staff corps in the entire Australian armed forces. There was, in addition, a Volunteer Militia which numbered 80,000 semi-trained men, but this formation was only committed to the defence of its homeland. When Britain declared war in 1914 the declaration was binding upon the whole Empire, but in 1939 the rest of the Empire was not obliged to follow suit. However, it is to the eternal credit of Australia and New Zealand that they both declared war on Germany on 3 September 1939.

Australia was obviously concerned about the territorial ambitions of Japan, and this at first prevented the despatch of an Australian expeditionary force overseas. However, when intelligence confirmed that Japan would not attack in the Pacific unless the Allies were defeated in Europe, the Australian Government agreed to the raising of a special force of 20,000 men for service at home or abroad.

| | |
|---|---|
| *Date:* | *March 1941* |
| *Unit:* | *7th Division* |
| *Rank:* | *Private* |
| *Theatre:* | *Mediterranean* |
| *Location:* | *Syria* |

# Private 9th Division Australian Army

**The main Australian units which fought in the Mediterranean theatre were the 6th, 7th and 9th Divisions, plus three air force squadrons, one cruiser and some smaller naval craft. The 9th Division played an important part in the defence of Tobruk from February to October 1941, but the price was high: 749 of its men were killed, 1996 wounded and 604 taken prisoner. The division later took part in the Battle of El Alamein, losing a further 1225 dead, 3638 wounded and 946 taken prisoner.**

The figure illustrated here is a private of the 9th Division during the siege of Tobruk. He is wearing a single-breasted tunic with matching long trousers, canvas anklets and ankle boots. Underneath the tunic he wears a leather jerkin lined with thick khaki cloth. This was a World War I British item of clothing, and had proved itself to be extremely practical and popular. Like many Australian soldiers in North Africa this soldier is kitted out with 1937-pattern webbing equipment, steel helmet and a bolt-action Lee-Enfield .303 rifle.

Australian Army badges of rank were the same as those worn in the British Army. Arm-of-service badges as such did not exist, though individual units could be identified by a flash in the arm-of-service colour on the sleeves. The geometric shape of the flash was different for headquarters, divisions, brigades and services.

The 9th Division returned to Australia in February 1943, having performed admirably in the Middle East.

| | |
|---|---|
| *Date:* | *October 1941* |
| *Unit:* | *9th Division* |
| *Rank:* | *Private* |
| *Theatre:* | *Mediterranean* |
| *Location:* | *Tobruk* |

# Leading Seaman
# Task Force 44
# Royal Australian Navy

**The uniform of the Royal Australian Navy, which came into existence as a fleet in 1913, was basically the same as the navy whites worn in the Royal Navy in the Pacific. However, the Australians also had Australian buttons, and hat ribbon sporting 'HMAS', while Australians serving in the Royal Navy wore 'Australia' shoulder flashes.**

The seaman pictured here is wearing a white tropical version of the serge temperate uniform. On his left upper sleeve he wears his badge of rank – an anchor – surmounting a chevron denoting at least three years' good conduct. On his right upper sleeve he wears a non-substantive badge indicating he is a leading torpedo man.

At the beginning of the war the Royal Australian Navy comprised 7 cruisers, 17 destroyers and 74 escort and minesweeping vessels. The main Australian effort from 1941 onwards was in the Pacific, especially in the Battle of the Java Sea. The navy participated in the landings in the Solomons and at Guadalcanal, and took part in the retaking of the Philippines (Task Force 44 was the Anza Squadron) and the Battle of Leyte Gulf. In the Mediterranean the navy assisted the Royal Navy against Axis vessels and provided ships for escort duties. Later in the war the navy assisted the British Pacific Fleet during the Burma campaign.

One of the successes of the Australian Navy was the sinking of the *Bartolomeo Colleoni* by HMAS *Sydney* in the Mediterranean. Unfortunately it was itself sunk soon after by a German raider.

| | |
|---|---|
| **Date:** | *May 1943* |
| **Unit:** | *Task Force 44* |
| **Rank:** | *Leading Seaman* |
| **Theatre:** | *Pacific* |
| **Location:** | *Sydney* |

# Lieutenant Royal Canadian Women's Naval Service

**Like many British Empire units, the Royal Canadian Women's Naval Service wore uniforms identical to the British pattern. The Royal Canadian Navy was formed in 1910, and members wore Royal Navy uniforms but with Canadian buttons and Canadian hat ribbons. Those Canadians who served with the Royal Navy wore 'Canada' shoulder flashes.**

This female lieutenant wears a lightweight uniform which was worn by all ranks in the Royal Canadian Women's Naval Service. Officers wore the three-cornered hat instead of the round sailor's hat, which was worn by those of non-commissioned officer rank. Ratings had black plastic buttons instead of gilt brass. This officer's regulation bag was called a *'pochette'*, and the white lights between the rank distinction lace on the shoulder straps identify this officer as being in the paymaster branch.

In the Canadian Navy, as in the Royal Navy, shoulder straps were worn with greatcoat, watchcoat, white tunic and white mess jacket. All shoulder straps were made of blue cloth, except for those of engineer, medical and accountant officers of flag rank, which were made of the appropriate distinction cloth, with gold lace on top and a leather backing. The straps themselves were 133mm (5.25in) long and 57mm (2.25in) wide and had a button at the top and a leather tongue at the back.

Female recruits fulfilled a number of important roles on shore, thus freeing their male counterparts for active service at sea.

| Date: | June 1943 |
|---|---|
| Unit: | Royal Canadian Women's Naval Service |
| Rank: | Lieutenant |
| Theatre: | northwest Europe |
| Location: | London |

217

# *Private*
# Le Regiment
# de Levis

**The uniforms worn by soldiers in the Canadian Army were basically the same as those worn in the British Army. However, the khaki which was used for Canadian battle dress was of better quality and of a greener shade of khaki than its British counterpart. Badges of rank were identical to those worn in the British Army.**

This private of *Le Regiment de Levis* wears the great-coat which was standard pattern for British Army officers, though with the 'Canada' nationality title attached to it. His Canadian-pattern cap has earflaps and has the regimental cap badge on the front. In addition, there was a winter version of this head-dress which had fur earflaps and was called a Yukon. Though one of the most distinctive items of clothing worn by soldiers in the Canadian Army, nevertheless it fell into disuse.

The Canadians made a significant contribution to the war effort in northwest Europe, taking part in the D-Day landings, the fighting in Normandy and the subsequent campaign into Germany. The 4th Canadian Armoured Division was particularly heavily involved in Normandy, its troops taking part in offensive operations around Caen and then joining the pursuit of the retreating Germans. Canadians fought hard up to the end of the war, the 2nd Canadian Corps being engaged in bitter fighting in northern Holland and Germany until 4 May 1945. In the 11-month campaign since 6 June 1944, the 1st Canadian Army lost 3680 officers and 44,272 men in casualties, of whom 12,579 were killed.

| | |
|---|---|
| *Date:* | *January 1944* |
| *Unit:* | *Le Regiment de Levis* |
| *Rank:* | *Private* |
| *Theatre:* | *northwest Europe* |
| *Location:* | *England* |

# Gunner
# New Zealand Artillery
# New Zealand Army

At the beginning of the war New Zealand troops were still wearing the old-pattern khaki service dress with long matching trousers, short puttees and ankle boots. The most distinctive part of the New Zealand Army uniform was the slouch hat, which was different from the Australian one in that the crown was pointed and indented on four sides, and the brim was never officially folded up. The cap badge was worn in front, and a puggaree in regimental colours was worn around the base of the hat, as shown here.

New Zealand Army officers wore service dress with either the slouch hat or peaked cap. Badges of rank were identical to those of the British, and like other Empire forces the New Zealanders were issued with British equipment.

When they arrived in Egypt, the New Zealanders were issued with British khaki drill uniforms but retained their slouch hats with coloured puggarees, as indicated by this gunner. His equipment is British, including the 1908-pattern webbing and gas mask in the ready position. New Zealanders took part in Wavell's desert offensive in North Africa and the New Zealand Division was formed in Greece in 1941. In the desert war in Africa the New Zealanders proved adept at mobile operations, playing a vital role in the 'Crusader' offensive of 1941 and the engagements of 1942. By the end of the war in North Africa the division had suffered 21,496 casualties out of a total of 43,800 men sent to the Middle East.

| | |
|---|---|
| *Date:* | *December 1940* |
| *Unit:* | *New Zealand Artillery* |
| *Rank:* | *Gunner* |
| *Theatre:* | *Mediterranean* |
| *Location:* | *North Africa* |

# *Private*
# *Royal Gurkha Rifles*
# *Indian Army*

**The Gurkhas were part of the Indian Army, which had an anomalous position in that it was not a colonial force but had a very different situation to that of the Dominion armies. This unique status was reflected in the make-up of Indian brigades, in which one British battalion would serve alongside two Indian battalions.**

The figure illustrated here is a private of the Royal Gurkha Rifles of the Indian Army. His uniform is typical of the dress worn in the Italian campaign. Previously, when in action in the Middle East, Indian troops had worn the same uniform that they had worn in India. Head-dress had consisted of the puggaree, British Mk 1 steel helmet or field service cap. Over the collarless silver grey or cellular khaki shirt was worn a pullover with either khaki drill shorts or long trousers. In Italy in the winter, however, Indian troops were issued with British uniforms in their entirety: battle dress, leather jerkin, woollen gloves and gum boots. Equipment was usually worn underneath the jerkin, with the cloth ammunition bandolier worn over it. Summer wear included beret with badge above the left eye, shirt, shorts, hose tops and anklets and ankle boots.

This Gurkha's weapon is the American Thompson M1928 submachine gun, while attached to his belt is the famous curved Gurkha knife, known as the *kukri*, which was excellent for close-quarter combat.

| | |
|---|---|
| *Date:* | *June 1944* |
| *Unit:* | *Royal Gurkha Rifles* |
| *Rank:* | *Private* |
| *Theatre:* | *Mediterranean* |
| *Location:* | *Italy* |

220

# Sergeant
# 8th Indian Division
# Indian Army

Before World War II the standard Indian Army field service dress consisted of a silver-grey collarless flannel shirt, khaki drill or cellular khaki shirt, or a Mazri grey cotton-type shirt, which was worn by certain units operating on the famous Northwest Frontier. The shirt was usually worn with khaki drill shorts and a khaki woollen pullover if the temperature required it. Footwear usually consisted of knitted woollen socks, woollen hose-tops and short puttees with ankle boots or so-called *chaplis* (a form of sandal normally worn by Frontier Force units).

Modifications to the basic uniform included a khaki serge three-quarter length, single-breasted tunic with a stand collar called a *kurta*, battle dress trousers, webbing anklets and ankle boots. Low supplies of stocks and a system of local purchase meant that the Indian Army experienced great variations in dress, however by 1942 this had become more or less standardised.

The sergeant illustrated here wears a steel helmet covered in sacking, which provides both camouflage and a convenient face cover in the event of a sandstorm. His shirt and shorts are British-pattern khaki drill, though his equipment is a mixture of 1908-pattern webbing and Indian leather. He carries an unusual mixture of weapons: Molotov cocktails in his right hand and the more reliable No 36 hand grenades in his left. (The Molotov cocktail was supposedly effective against armoured vehicles and tanks.)

| | |
|---|---|
| *Date:* | *December 1940* |
| *Unit:* | *8th Indian Division* |
| *Rank:* | *Sergeant* |
| *Theatre:* | *Mediterranean* |
| *Location:* | *North Africa* |

# Corporal 9th Gurkha Rifles Indian Army

**At the start of the war in the Far East in 1941, Indian Army troops not unnaturally wore the same uniform as their compatriots in the Middle East: this comprised puggarees, grey shirts and khaki drill clothing. This attire was also worn by those troops serving in India itself and by those serving along the Indian/Burma border.**

The first item to change was head-dress. The hotchpotch of items, such as the peaked caps and field service caps worn by British officers, the *saffa*, puggaree or slouch hat worn by Gurkhas and Indians, all gave way to the simple beret, though the puggaree was still worn on ceremonial occasions and in action if dyed olive-green.

The figure illustrated here is a corporal of the 9th Gurkha Rifles, 11th Indian Division. He is wearing the khaki drill shirt and shorts (nicknamed 'Bombay Bloomers') with short puttees, 1937-pattern webbing equipment, special web pouches to hold magazines for his Thompson submachine gun, and a web binocular case. His Gurkha affiliations are indicated by the *kukri* in its scabbard and felt hat with rifle-green patch on the puggaree.

The Gurkhas had been a part of the British Army since the nineteenth century, and had served in many theatres since that time. They fought with particular distinction in North Africa, during the Italian campaign, especially at Monte Cassino, and also with the *Chindits* in Burma. They were a welcome addition to any Allied force.

| | |
|---|---|
| ***Date:*** | *December 1941* |
| ***Unit:*** | *9th Gurkha Rifles* |
| ***Rank:*** | *Corporal* |
| ***Theatre:*** | *Pacific* |
| ***Location:*** | *Malaya* |

# Lance-Corporal Royal Gurkha Rifles Indian Army

The Indian Army fought in North Africa against the Axis powers and suffered 15,248 casualties, of whom 1299 were killed, 3738 wounded, 419 posted missing and 9792 made prisoners of war. Following the end of the war in North Africa, the 4th and 9th Indian Divisions were committed to the fighting in Italy, where the men of the 4th Division played a crucial part in the Battle of Monte Cassino, though the division suffered 3000 casualties in the process.

This Gurkha of the 8th Indian Division wears British battle dress, which was the standard uniform for Indian troops by this stage of the war. He has dark rifle-green rank chevrons on his sleeve under the formation sign of the 8th Indian Division. In the Indian Army British and Indian officers holding the King's commission wore British rank badges, while subordinate Indian officers commissioned by the viceroy wore British pips with an additional loop of braid running across the shoulder and under the pip. This figure's webbing equipment is also British, though his Thompson submachine gun is American and the *kukri* hanging at his belt is Gurkha. Aside from the *kukri*, Indian Army soldiers were armed with Indian-pattern bayonets, which had shorter blades than their English counterparts.

The Royal Gurkhas and the Royal Garhwal Rifles of the Indian Army also wore the special double *terai* slouch hat, which was in fact two felt hats one inside the other.

| | |
|---|---|
| *Date:* | *August 1944* |
| *Unit:* | *Royal Gurkha Rifles* |
| *Rank:* | *Lance-Corporal* |
| *Theatre:* | *Mediterranean* |
| *Location:* | *Italy* |

# Subedar-*Major* 20th Burma Rifles Indian Army

In 1942, jungle-green clothing in differing shades began to be issued to troops of the Indian Army. It was worn without insignia when on active service, though a strip of cloth in a regimental colour on the shoulder straps or a coloured lanyard was sometimes worn. Away from the front, formation flashes were worn on the upper sleeves, and a cloth with a regimental designation was embroidered in black. The Indian Army was also the first to try out knitted cardigans in various colours for its troops, such as brown for the Gurkha Rifles.

This *subedar* is wearing the light khaki service dress with Sam Browne belt. His battle dress consists of drill shirt and shorts and 1908-pattern webbing equipment. His infantry officer's sword has a steel hilt, while the scabbard is made of black leather with steel fittings. The two silver badges on his collar are each fashioned in the shape of a peacock. On his shoulder straps he carries his insignia rank: three pips on each shoulder. He wears ammunition boots, with wool puttees around his ankles.

This officer is a Viceroy Commission Officer. As a *subedar*-major he would have been a senior subordinate officer and would advise the British commanding officer in all matters concerning rank and file.

Until 1937, Burma was part of the India Command, but with political separation in 1937, the Burma Rifles were transferred from the Indian Army to Burmese command.

| | |
|---|---|
| *Date:* | *June 1942* |
| *Unit:* | *20th Burma Rifles* |
| *Rank:* | Subedar-*Major* |
| *Theatre:* | *Pacific* |
| *Location:* | *Burma* |

# *Private Royal West African Frontier Force*

The Royal West African Frontier Force was first raised in 1901, and was one of those African colonial units which had performed admirably during World War I. At the beginning of World War II this unit comprised the Nigerian Regiment, the Sierra Leone Battalion, the Gambia Company and the Gold Coast Regiment. The force had fought in the campaign in East Africa, the Nigerians returning to West Africa in August 1941 and those from the Gold Coast returning in October of the same year.

On their return these units were redesignated the 1st and 2nd (West African) Brigade Groups as part of the expansion of West African forces to a strength of three brigade groups in Nigeria, one brigade group in the Gold Coast, and one battalion in both Sierra Leone and the Gambia.

Immediately prior to World War II, the uniform of the Royal West African Frontier Force was upgraded and simplified. The so-called Kilmarnock cap was replaced by the slouch hat, and native sandals were replaced by British ammunition boots. The uniform illustrated on this private is typical of that worn by African soldiers serving in the King's African rifles. The regimental title is worn on a slide on the khaki shoulder straps.

The equipment issued to this soldier is in no way inferior to that issued to many Empire and British troops: 1937-pattern webbing equipment and British Lee-Enfield .303 rifle.

| | |
|---|---|
| *Date:* | *June 1943* |
| *Unit:* | *Royal West African Frontier Force* |
| *Rank:* | *Private* |
| *Theatre:* | *Africa* |
| *Location:* | *Gold Coast* |

# Private Abyssinian Patriot Army

**British operations in East Africa during the early years of the war were a great success, and provided a welcome boost to morale when elsewhere around the globe Allied forces were being pushed back in the face of the Axis onslaught.**

In East Africa two columns of British and Empire troops launched a two-pronged attack against the Italians. The first column of two Indian divisions and native troops advanced from the Sudan on 19 January 1941. The second column of three South African divisions struck north from Kenya five days later. Though the two columns numbered just 70,000 men, and in a three-month campaign they captured 50,000 Italians and conquered the whole of Italian East Africa at the cost of 500 casualties. Their Italian enemies had been beset by supply shortages and low morale, but it was still a fine victory.

A number of Abyssinian troops fought with the British in East Africa, and the private's uniform illustrated here is typical of their attire. Where possible native troops were equipped in the European fashion, though this particular figure has weapons and equipment gleaned from a number of sources. In addition to his ammunition belt and revolver, he also carries a 7.92mm 98K rifle.

Generally speaking, most native troops under British leadership were effective soldiers as they were well trained and well led. Under the Italians, however, native troops were the victims of poor training and inadequate leadership.

| | |
|---|---|
| *Date:* | *February 1941* |
| *Unit:* | *Abyssinian Patriot Army* |
| *Rank:* | *Private* |
| *Theatre:* | *Africa* |
| *Location:* | *Ethiopia* |

# Other Axis Countries

*Tens of thousands of Russians, Romanians, Hungarians, and Spaniards fought on behalf of the Axis during World War II. Sent mainly to the Eastern Front, they were decimated in the fighting in Russia. Those units raised to defend their homelands fought fanatically to keep the Red Army at bay, but it was destined to be a losing battle.*

# *Infantryman Spanish Blue Division*

**The Spanish dictator, Franco, sent a volunteer division of some 18,000 men to fight in the 'crusade against Bolshevism'. The Spanish Blue Division became the 250th Infantry Division on 25 July 1941 and was committed to the war on the Eastern Front. However, after suffering 12,776 casualties the division was subsequently withdrawn from the front in October 1943.**

Spanish volunteers who were fighting for the Germans wore German uniforms, though they retained the blue shirt of the Falangist Party under their field blouses (hence the name Blue Division). On the right sleeve of the field blouse Spaniards wore a badge in the shape of a shield in the national colours, which was also worn on the greatcoat and on the right side of the steel helmet, as can be seen here on this figure's uniform. In addition, the Yoke and Arrows emblem of the Falange and other Falangist insignia were worn in various places on other items of headdress and on the field blouse.

The volunteer private illustrated here wears the standard German field uniform and the matt-grey helmet with rough finish. The field blouse is made from field-grey cloth, and all badges are woven in mouse-grey yarn on a field-grey backing. This volunteer's footwear consists of ankle boots and anklets, and as a section commander he carries an MP40 submachine gun. This weapon was very popular among both Axis and Allied troops (the latter being always on the look-out for captured models).

| | |
|---|---|
| *Date:* | *June 1942* |
| *Unit:* | *Spanish Blue Division* |
| *Rank:* | *Infantryman* |
| *Theatre:* | *Eastern Front* |
| *Location:* | *Ukraine* |

# Sergeant Hungarian Gendarmerie

As part of the Axis, Hungary committed her troops to the war on the Eastern Front. The first detachment to go to Russia was the élite Rapid Corps of 40,000 men and 160 Hungarian and Italian light tanks. The corps fought with the German 17th Army and took part in the Battle of Uman, but at the end of the campaign it had suffered 26,000 casualties and lost 90 per cent of its armour and 1000 other vehicles. It returned to Budapest on 6 December 1941.

The corps left behind a bicycle battalion and four infantry brigades, a total strength of around 63,000 men. Poorly equipped to traverse the vast distances in Russia, only the cavalry element was able to make a significant contribution to the war effort.

The Royal Hungarian Gendarmerie was an élite unit, members of which wore a distinctive black felt hat with cockerel feather plume. However, this feature fell into disuse during the war in Russia and was replaced by the side cap with the same plume on the left side. As this mark was not always recognised by Hungary's allies on the Eastern Front, a German-type metal *gorget* was introduced as a duty badge.

As well as the distinctive cockerel feather, the sergeant also wears a green woollen whistle lanyard. Hungarian rank badges were worn on the collar patches, the background of which was in arm-of-service colour. All members of the Gendarmerie were regular soldiers, and so did not wear triangular badges on the left sleeve, which in other units indicated regular status.

| | |
|---|---|
| *Date:* | *July 1941* |
| *Unit:* | *Hungarian Gendarmerie* |
| *Rank:* | *Sergeant* |
| *Theatre:* | *Eastern Front* |
| *Location:* | *southern Russia* |

229

# *Infantryman Rifle Brigade 2nd Hungarian Army*

**The Royal Hungarian Army first introduced a khaki uniform in 1922. It had a number of unusual features, such as a side cap with high-pointed crown, and special pantaloons which were fastened tightly at the calf with buttons and incorporated a cloth anklet for wear with ankle boots. The personnel of mounted units wore breeches and boots.**

Tunics had the same cut for all ranks, they were single-breasted and had stand-and-fall collar, five buttons in front, and breast and side-pleated patch pockets. Hungarian Army head-dress consisted of the side cap and later a field cap with cloth-covered peak. Troops also wore the German-pattern steel helmet, both the 1915 and 1935 models.

This infantryman is kitted out in winter field service uniform with German-pattern helmet, great-coat, special trousers with integral cloth anklets and ankle boots. His cow-hide pack, rolled blanket and mess tin hark back to Imperial Austria.

By the end of 1942 the 2nd Hungarian Army held part of the German front in Russia, but was subsequently torn apart by the massive Soviet offensive of January 1943. As the Hungarians fled west, they left behind most of their equipment and 147,971 of their comrades. What was left of the 2nd Army was either pulled back to Budapest or served as security troops in the Ukraine.

| | |
|---|---|
| *Date:* | *November 1942* |
| *Unit:* | *rifle brigade* |
| *Rank:* | *Infantryman* |
| *Theatre:* | *Eastern Front* |
| *Location:* | *southern Russia* |

# 2nd Lieutenant 1st Armoured Division Hungarian Army

**The Hungarian 1st Armoured Division was the pride of the Hungarian Army. It comprised 83 Czech LT-38 tanks, 2 Toldi tanks and 22 German Panzer Mk I tanks. However, its crews had little experience and their vehicles were obsolete in comparison with the Russians' T-34 tanks. The inevitable result was that the Hungarians, when confronted with the T-34s, were shot to pieces.**

At the start of the war Hungarian tank crews wore overalls, a double-breasted leather coat and the Italian black leather tank helmet with neck flap. As the war progressed, the uniform changed and crews began to wear khaki overalls with a side cap. The officer pictured here is a 2nd lieutenant. He wears typical armoured crew uniform: a one-piece overall and side cap. The uniform is made of khaki cotton and leather and was worn with another pattern of khaki uniform which closely resembled the special field-grey uniform worn by the crews of German self-propelled guns.

Following the defeat of the 2nd Army, Hungarian soldiers continued to serve under German operational command, however the Russians were nearing Hungary's borders and so the two governments agreed a provisional ceasefire on 15 October 1944. Though the Germans subsequently installed a puppet government in Budapest, this was not enough to avert a Soviet victory. By the end of World War II, a total of 136,000 Hungarian soldiers had been killed in the fighting.

| | |
|---|---|
| *Date:* | *January 1943* |
| *Unit:* | *1st Armoured Division* |
| *Rank:* | *2nd Lieutenant* |
| *Theatre:* | *Eastern Front* |
| *Location:* | *southern Russia* |

# Lieutenant Fighter Squadron Hungarian Air Force

**The Hungarian Air Force was a branch of the army, and so its personnel wore khaki uniforms which differed only in certain detail from those worn in the rest of the army. This junior officer is wearing the khaki service dress underneath a German sheepskin flying jacket.**

The air force greatcoat was double-breasted with a large fall-collar and two rows of six buttons. The peaked cap was khaki with brown leather peak, gold piping around the bottom of the band for officers, and twisted gold chin cord. Winter flying suits were made of black or brown leather with zip-fasteners, pack-type parachute and goggles, while in summer pilots wore shirt-sleeve order and canvas flying helmet, or a one-piece beige canvas flying suit. This officer is wearing the khaki field cap with the air force cap badge on the side.

Hungarian Air Force rank was indicated on the shoulder straps, on the tunic for all ranks, on the shoulder straps for officers, on the cuffs for other ranks and also on the greatcoat. In addition, flying officers and NCOs wore rectangular patches in the same colours, which bore the same rank distinction as on the shoulder straps, on both cuffs of the flying suit and the jacket. All officers had gold buttons and badges, NCOs had silver and other ranks bronze. Junior officers had one inverted medium-gold lace chevron above one to three medium-gold lace stripes on the shoulder straps and cuff patches, which were piped in gold.

| | |
|---|---|
| *Date:* | *May 1943* |
| *Unit:* | *fighter squadron* |
| *Rank:* | *Lieutenant* |
| *Theatre:* | *Eastern Front* |
| *Location:* | *southern Russia* |

# Major
# Cavalry Division
# Bulgarian Army

**Bulgaria was forced into the Axis camp by a combination of territorial ambitions, her common experience with Germany in World War I and a fear of Soviet intentions in the Balkans. Germany was very successful in the Balkans, and as a result she awarded Bulgaria with Greek Macedonia. However, Bulgaria was then forced to enter into a four-year campaign against partisans in the area. A coup in September 1944 meant that Bulgaria joined the Russians.**

Despite the introduction of a number of German features on the uniform, such as collar patches, Bulgarian Army uniforms were heavily influenced by Tsarist Russia. This officer wears wartime service dress with greatcoat, which for general officers had scarlet lapels and scarlet piping around the collar, cuffs, down the front and on the half-belt, and pocket flaps at the back. The tunic worn under the greatcoat had either a stand-and-fall collar or an open collar worn with shirt and tie. The arm-of-service of this particular officer, as indicated by the piping, is that of the cavalry.

Bulgarian Army badges of rank appeared in the form of Russian shoulder boards, but the Bulgarian versions were much narrower. The greatcoat worn by this officer has two rows of gilt buttons, and he displays his rank on the shoulder boards: one pip and two stripes. He is wearing marching boots and puttees instead of the riding boots that were usually worn by officers.

| | |
|---|---|
| **Date:** | *June 1943* |
| **Unit:** | *cavalry division* |
| **Rank:** | *Major* |
| **Theatre:** | *Balkans* |
| **Location:** | *Macedonia* |

# Seaman
# *Lake Ladoga Flotilla*
# *Finnish Navy*

**In the Finnish Navy both officers and petty officers wore an open double-breasted blue jacket with two rows of four or five buttons, open left breast pocket, and side pockets with straight flaps. The jacket was worn with white shirt, black tie, matching long trousers and black shoes.**

Finnish ratings, as illustrated here, wore the standard 'square rig', over the top of which this seaman wears protective clothing: a fleece-lined beige foul-weather suit with attached hood, patch breast and side pockets with flap, tab and button on the cuffs and matching trousers. The exception was the Finnish coastal artillery, members of which wore obsolete grey Model-1922 uniforms with dark grey cuffs and collar.

Head-dress in the Finnish Navy consisted of a blue cap with long tally, as worn here, on which appeared the name of the vessel or the installation, in gold letters. Officers wore a dark blue peaked cap with blue or white top and gold-embroidered cap badge. There was also a blue side cap with light blue piping, black leather chin strap, and a circular cockade in the national colours.

With regard to rank insignia, Finnish naval officers sported rank distinction lace on the cuffs, on the greatcoat and on the white tunic shoulder straps. Other ranks sported chevrons on the upper left sleeve. The colour of the lights between the rank distinction lace served to identify the branch or corps of the officers.

| | |
|---|---|
| *Date:* | *September 1939* |
| *Unit:* | *Lake Ladoga Flotilla* |
| *Rank:* | *Seaman* |
| *Theatre:* | *Lake Ladoga* |
| *Location:* | *Baltic* |

# *Marshal Mannerheim Finnish Army*

Finland had one of the smallest armies in Europe at the beginning of World War II, with only nine divisions in total. The divisions in turn lacked vehicles, communications equipment, anti-tank guns and automatic weapons. The army relied on a small regular cadre, which in turn relied on an annual intake of conscripts to complete its numbers. A conscript would serve for up to 18 months, after which time he would pass into the reserve until the age of 26, when finally he passed into the militia.

Finland was divided into nine Military Districts, each of which was required to field a division, plus depots, installations and general facilities to enable the army to mobilise more effectively.

At the head of the Finnish army was Marshal Mannerheim, who is illustrated here. He was the only person in the armed forces to hold the rank of marshal, and so his uniform was in many respects a one-off. The badges on his shoulder straps are the Finnish lion in silver, and above them is the regimental badge of Mannerheim's old regiment, the *Uusimaa* Dragoons. Note that the Marshal does not wear rank badges on his collar, but if he had, such badges would have consisted of crossed batons and three lions in gold on a silver background.

Suspended from his neck Mannerheim wears the Mannerheim Cross of the Cross of Liberty, an award for outstanding bravery and merit in wartime. On his left sleeve he sports a Civil Guard badge.

| | |
|---|---|
| *Date:* | *September 1939* |
| *Unit:* | *Finnish Army* |
| *Rank:* | *Marshal* |
| *Theatre:* | *Eastern Front* |
| *Location:* | *Helsinki* |

# Captain 2nd Division Finnish Army

**The uniform of the Finnish Army was modernised in 1936, with a dark-grey uniform replacing the old light-grey one. The Model-1936 tunic was single-breasted with matching shoulder straps, stand-and-fall collar and six buttons in front. As can be seen here, the pleated breast-patch pockets had a flap and button, as did the side pockets.**

All ranks in the army wore matching breeches (generals with red and general staff officers with crimson *lampassen*) and black leather boots. In winter soldiers wore the double-breasted greatcoat with two rows of six buttons, slash side pockets with flap, fall collar and turn-back cuffs. This officer wears breeches padded with leather.

In cold weather soldiers of the Finnish Army wore the winter field cap, which had a matching peak and flap that fastened in front with two buttons, while above the buttons other ranks wore the Finnish blue and white cockade while officers sported a gilt metal lion. The summer head-dress consisted of a side cap with a brown leather chin strap and cockade for other ranks and a gold lion for officers. In action troops wore the steel helmet, which at first was the German 1915-Model but was then replaced by the 1935-Model.

As well as the rank stars pinned directly on to his tunic collar, this captain also wears a knife at his waist. This was used for tasks such as skinning animals and was a vital part of his survival equipment (because of the environment in which they operated, Finnish troops received survival training).

| | |
|---|---|
| *Date:* | *January 1943* |
| *Unit:* | *2nd Division* |
| *Rank:* | *Captain* |
| *Theatre:* | *Eastern Front* |
| *Location:* | *around Leningrad* |

# *Private*
# *IV Corps*
# *Finnish Army*

**This Finnish soldier is wearing the standard field cap and lightweight tunic/shirt which he has outside his trousers, after the Russian style. By this stage of the war the German influence over the Finnish uniform had grown stronger, which led to more standardisation.**

The Finnish style of rank distinction was found on collar patches and by the rank distinction lace on the greatcoat cuffs. On the raincoat and other types of winter clothing rank distinction lace appeared on a patch which was buttoned on to the cuffs. Other ranks sported chevrons on the shoulder straps. Arm-of-service was indicated by the colour of the collar patches and the yellow metal badges worn on the shoulder straps. Until 1917 Finland had been a part of the Russian Empire, and this was reflected in the metal badge worn on the left breast pocket.

Winter clothing was never a problem for the Fins, who had sizeable quantities of sheepskin caps and coats, snow camouflage clothing and other kinds of warm weather wear, including felt boots. In addition, after their success in the Winter War the Fins used winter clothing from captured Russians.

The Fins attacked the Soviet Union in 1941, but after they had regained the territories lost in the 'Winter War' they went on the defensive, engaging in very little fighting until 1944.

| | |
|---|---|
| *Date:* | *March 1944* |
| *Unit:* | *IV Corps* |
| *Rank:* | *Private* |
| *Theatre:* | *Eastern Front* |
| *Location:* | *Lake Ladoga* |

# Lieutenant Infantry Division Finnish Army

**The figure illustrated here is a lieutenant of the Finnish Army. He is wearing a field uniform which differs in a number of respects from the standard Finnish Army service dress uniform. For example, his tunic is shorter, the breast pocket is fastened by an ordinary button and the overall quality of the uniform is inferior to the standard issue. His headwear is the old 1915-pattern German helmet, which by 1944 had been largely replaced by the 1935-pattern model.**

Over his shoulder this officer carries a map case, and tucked into his left boot is a spoon. His weapon is the excellent Russian PPD 1940G submachine gun, a robust weapon which was easy to maintain in the field.

In Word War II the Finnish Army was basically an infantry organisation. Though severely lacking in support services, the quality of its officers and men more than compensated for this deficiency. Having said that, the Fins fought much more effectively when defending their homeland than they did as part of Nazi Germany's 'crusade against Bolshevism'.

An average Finnish infantry division consisted of three infantry regiments and one field artillery regiment plus a few support troops. By May 1944 the Finnish Army had 270,000 troops, 1900 artillery pieces and 800 tanks in the field. This was a large umber, but there were deficiencies in two key areas: inadequate anti-tank guns and too few aircraft to protect ground forces.

| | |
|---|---|
| *Date:* | *May 1944* |
| *Unit:* | *infantry division* |
| *Rank:* | *Lieutenant* |
| *Theatre:* | *Eastern Front* |
| *Location:* | *Karelia* |

# *Lieutenant 2nd* Calarasci *Regiment*

In 1931 the Romanian Army adopted a British-style service dress for its officers, having changed the colour of the general field uniform from horizon-blue to khaki in 1916. The tunic was single-breasted with stand-and-fall collar, matching pointed shoulder straps and cuffs, and a fly front. The breast pockets had a pleat, flap and button, while side pockets had a flap and button only. Cuffs were gathered and fastened tightly around the waist with two buttons. The tunic was worn with matching pantaloons, puttees and leather ankle boots.

Romanian Army officers also wore the closed tunic in action, while officers' service dress tunic was worn open with four gilt buttons in front, pleated breast-patch pockets with flap and button, and large side pockets. The cuffs were pointed with two buttons at the back. The tunic was worn with white or khaki shirt and khaki tie, long khaki trousers or light khaki breeches and black leather lace-up field boots. The greatcoat was double-breasted with large collar, turn-back cuffs and side pockets with straight flaps.

This cavalry officer is wearing standard officers' service dress with rank badges on the shoulder straps, the arm-of-service colour appearing on the collar patches and cap band. He has special cavalry pattern buttons on the shoulder straps and boots. Above his left breast pocket he wears the Romanian medal ribbon, with the ribbon of the German Iron Cross 2nd Class by his Sam Browne belt.

| Date: | *July 1942* |
|---|---|
| Unit: | *2nd* Calarasci *Regiment* |
| Rank: | *Lieutenant* |
| Theatre: | *Eastern Front* |
| Location: | *southern Russia* |

# *Private Infantry Division Romanian Army*

**Romanian mountain troops wore a green beret and tank crews a black one, while the standard army steel helmet, as shown here, was the Dutch M1928 manufactured under licence both with and without the Romanian coat of arms on the front (this helmet sports the coat of arms).**

The uniform of this private is of the standard pattern. In the summer, soldiers wore a lightweight tunic which became bleached almost white by the sun. The tunic was worn with khaki cloth pantaloons with puttees or long trousers with ankle boots and leather anklets. In the summer, Romanian troops fighting in Russia were adequately clothed, but in the bitter Russian winter they suffered badly because of the lack of proper winter clothing. Generally, the average soldier would be issued with just a lambswool cap, short unlined greatcoat, unpadded trousers and short lace-up boots.

The equipment of this soldier is a clear indication of the German influence over the Romanian Army, with his mixture of Romanian and German equipment and his Mauser M1924 rifle.

This private is a member of an infantry division, the latter forming the bulk of the Romanian Army during the war. A typical infantry division comprised three infantry regiments, one field artillery regiment and a reconnaissance battalion. In 1940 there were 21 infantry divisions in the army, plus 3 infantry brigades, 4 mountain infantry brigades and a guards infantry brigade.

| | |
|---|---|
| *Date:* | *July 1942* |
| *Unit:* | *infantry division* |
| *Rank:* | *Private* |
| *Theatre:* | *Eastern Front* |
| *Location:* | *Odessa* |

240

# Private
# Infantry Division
# Romanian Army

In August 1944, the massive Soviet offensive in southern Russia had left the German 6th Army totally shattered. This latter force had been grouped with the 3rd Romanian Army to form Group *Dumitrescu*, and Group *Wöhler* comprised the German 8th Army and Romanian 4th Army. The total collapse of the front meant that Romania was forced to abandon Hitler and to seek an accommodation with Russia.

A change of regime was enough to secure the alliance with the Soviet Union, and on 31 August 1944 the Red Army occupied Bucharest. At first Romanian soldiers were automatically taken prisoner by the Russian Army, but eventually two Romanian armies, numbering more than 28 divisions and 540,000 men, joined the Soviet Army during operations in the Danube area. However, the fighting on behalf of the Russians cost the Romanians an additional 170,000 soldiers killed, wounded and missing (previously, while fighting for the Germans the Romanians had already lost more than 250,000 killed, wounded and missing).

The private illustrated here wears the uniform that is typical of the dress worn by Romanian soldiers fighting alongside the Red Army during the final months of the war. He wears a peaked cap and has a rolled greatcoat over his shoulder. The German influence is still in evidence: he carries a metal ammunition box with an offset handle (to enable two boxes to be carried in one hand) and a Mauser rifle.

| | |
|---|---|
| *Date:* | *March 1945* |
| *Unit:* | *infantry division* |
| *Rank:* | *Private* |
| *Theatre:* | *Eastern Front* |
| *Location:* | *Austria* |

# Rating Danube Flotilla Romanian Navy

**Romanian Navy ratings wore a blue and white striped shirt, a blue jumper which was worn outside the trousers, blue jean collar edged with three white stripes, plus a black scarf. The hat was a German-pattern model with '*Marina Regala*' in yellow on the ribbon, which was worn without the long ribbon hanging at the back.**

This rating wears the standard navy greatcoat, which was double-breasted with two rows of four gilt metal buttons (officers wore rank distinction lace on the greatcoat cuffs).

Naval officers wore the traditional blue service dress, while their white tunic was single-breasted with stand collar and blue shoulder straps, five gilt metal buttons, patch breast and side pockets with straight flap and button. The tunic was worn along with a white cap cover, white trousers and white canvas shoes. Petty officers wore a single-breasted blue tunic with stand collar and five gilt metal buttons, slash left-breast pocket, and side pockets with straight flaps, matching long trousers and black shoes. The peaked cap was blue with a black peak and chin strap and yellow metal anchor badge.

Rank was indicated by one to three red tape stripes under the trade or speciality badge on the left upper sleeve for ratings, while officers wore combinations of gold lace rings on the cuffs and shoulder straps.

The Danube Flotilla was the first part of the navy to see action, against the Russians. When German naval forces arrived on the Danube the Romanian ships operated under German control.

| | |
|---|---|
| **Date:** | *June 1941* |
| **Unit:** | *Danube Flotilla* |
| **Rank:** | *Rating* |
| **Theatre:** | *Eastern Front* |
| **Location:** | *Black Sea* |

# Trumpeter Vichy French Colonial Infantry

**France standardised the uniforms of her African and colonial troops on the Metropolitan pattern, while at the same time retaining certain distinct national features of her own. (France at the beginning of the war boasted a substantial number of overseas territories, such as Algeria, Tunisia, Morocco, Syria and Lebanon.)**

With the defeat of France followed by the Armistice in 1940, there was a demilitarisation of Tunisia and a general reduction in the number of French colonial troops. Vichy France was allowed 55,000 men in Morocco and 50,000 in Algeria, while the Army of the Levant in Syria was reduced from 100,000 to just under 40,000 soldiers.

Though the Army of the Levant had been more than halved, this force nevertheless posed a potential threat to Allied interests in the Middle East, as it was situated adjacent to the strategically vulnerable British oil and supply lines. As a result, Vichy Syria was invaded by a composite Allied force on 8 June 1941, the Vichy troops putting up a spirited resistance, despite the added tragedy of having to fight fellow Frenchmen.

The Vichy soldier, viewed here from the back, is typical of the infantry troops who made up the bulk of Vichy forces in the Middle East. His 2-litre (3.5-pint) water bottle and pack forms part of the 1935-pattern equipment, though the coat hanger and haversack certainly did not. His bugle, hanging by his side, has a red, white and blue tasselled cord.

| | |
|---|---|
| *Date:* | *June 1941* |
| *Unit:* | *Vichy French Colonial Infantry* |
| *Rank:* | *Trumpeter* |
| *Theatre:* | *Mediterranean* |
| *Location:* | *Syria* |

# *Private* *Vichy French* *Moroccan* Spahis

**In Syria the Vichy commander, General Dentz, had a contingent of African troops. These were divided into battalions: six Algerian, three Tunisian, three Senegalese and one Moroccan rifle battalion. In addition, there was a formation of North African cavalry consisting of the 4th Tunisian, 1st Moroccan and the 8th Algerian *Spahis* – a total of 7000 men. The Moroccans were reckoned to be among the best of the colonial troops.**

This Moroccan *Spahi* wears the standard French steel helmet with the crescent emblem worn by all Mohammedan troops. His collar patches bear his regimental number, while buttoned to the front of his *djellabah* is the rank badge of a *soldat de premiére classe*. Attached to his special leather equipment is an 1892 knife bayonet.

The fighting in Syria came to an end on 11 July 1941, the Vichy forces losing a total of 6000 men, 1000 of whom had been killed. In addition, 37,736 soldiers were taken prisoner, 5668 of whom joined the ranks of the Free French while the rest were transported to France. This was a poor response and indicates the lukewarm support for De Gaulle and his Free French at this stage of the war.

This resistance contrasts with the reaction of Vichy French forces in North Africa, who hardly resisted the Anglo-American 'Torch' landings. The defeat of the Axis in North Africa resulted in the German invasion of unoccupied France and the *de facto* end of the Vichy Army in Africa and the Middle East.

| | |
|---|---|
| *Date:* | *July 1941* |
| *Unit:* | *Vichy French Moroccan* Spahis |
| *Rank:* | *Private* |
| *Theatre:* | *Mediterranean* |
| *Location:* | *Syria* |

# Colonel Vichy French Colonial Infantry

**Before World War II French colonial officers wore a light khaki working uniform, while white undress uniform consisted of sun helmet, tunic and trousers. Lower ranks serving in colonial forces had both a khaki drill uniform with shirt or tunic with stand collar, shorts or pantaloons, or alternatively a khaki cloth uniform made up of a double-breasted khaki tunic, pantaloons and greatcoat.**

Both uniforms were usually worn with ankle boots and long khaki puttees. European military personnel wore either the sun helmet, *kepi*, beret or side cap for head-dress, while indigenous troops on active duty wore a red fez (*chechia*) with khaki cover. It was standard practice for troops to wear the steel helmet in action: this usually sported a circular stamped-metal badge bearing numerous devices.

This officer from Madagascar wears traditional tropical dress with sun helmet. On the front of the helmet can be seen the gilt metal anchor – the emblem of French colonial forces. Badges of rank were worn in the same manner on both temperate and tropical uniforms, though during the war it was more common to see officers wearing rank badge on their shoulder straps, as here. Other ranks wore their badges on a tab which was fixed to the front of their tunic, shirt or special clothing. Arm-of-service was usually identified by the coloured *kepi* or by the colour or combination of colours on the collar patches. Regimental numbers were carried on the front of the *kepi* or on the collar patch.

| | |
|---|---|
| **Date:** | *July 1942* |
| **Unit:** | *Vichy French Colonial Infantry* |
| **Rank:** | *Colonel* |
| **Theatre:** | *Africa* |
| **Location:** | *Madagascar* |

# *Private French Volunteer Legion*

**In the autumn of 1941, 2452 French volunteers crossed over into the Soviet Union to fight on Germany's behalf against the threat of 'Bolshevism'. The so-called *Légion Volontaire Française* spent its time fighting partisans in the rear areas, while in June 1943 the unit's two independent battalions were united to fight against partisans in the Ukraine. The legion was officially disbanded on 1 September 1944.**

French volunteers who served with the German Army wore German uniforms but were allowed to wear the national colours of their tricolour on their right sleeves and on the right side of their steel helmets. The recruits wore a mixture of German and French decorations. The private illustrated here is a good example, with his German field uniform and French medals (from left to right, these are: the Military Medal for distinguished service by non-commissioned officers, the Combatants' Cross for those called up in 1940, and the Colonial Medal with bars for two campaigns).

This private is wearing the 1935-pattern steel helmet on the left side of which can be seen the French tricolour in the form of a shield-shaped badge, also on the right sleeve of his greatcoat. His weapon is the German Kar 98k bolt-action rifle, though he holds it in the French manner.

Frenchmen also fought in the Waffen-SS, and some 20,000 volunteers were to answer the call to join the 'crusade against Bolshevism'.

| | |
|---|---|
| *Date:* | *June 1943* |
| *Unit:* | *French Volunteer Legion* |
| *Rank:* | *Private* |
| *Theatre:* | *Eastern Front* |
| *Location:* | *Ukraine* |

# Captain
# Croat Air Force
# Legion

**Croatia was able to raise substantial forces during World War II in order to fight for the Axis powers. These forces were a mixture of regular and paramilitary units, and by the end of 1941 there was a total of 114,000 soldiers under arms, with a further 38,000 soldiers in territorial units.**

The Croat Air Force flew machines which came from the former Yugoslav Air Force or which had been supplied by Italy. In October 1941, a Croatian Air Force Legion was formed, made up of one fighter squadron of Messerschmitt Bf 109s and one bomber squadron.

Officers in the Croat Air Force wore the grey-blue service dress of the former Yugoslav Air Force, but with new insignia. Croatian versions of Luftwaffe rank badges were worn on the collar patches and the shoulder straps, however on the latter the German star was replaced by a metal trefoil. Rank badges could not be worn on the sleeve by other ranks – they were required to wear white metal trefoils on grey cloth shoulder straps.

This captain of the Croat Air Force is dressed in grey-blue with Croatian cap badges, and Luftwaffe-type shoulder straps. The top cap badge bears the letters 'NDH', standing for *Nezavisna Drzava Hrvatska*, or Independent State of Croatia. The Croatian Air Force Legion fought on the Eastern Front in German uniforms but with Croat badges. On the right sleeve of the tunic and greatcoat they wore the winged badge of the Croatian Air Force.

| | |
|---|---|
| *Date:* | *June 1942* |
| *Unit:* | *Croat Air Force Legion* |
| *Rank:* | *Captain* |
| *Theatre:* | *Eastern Front* |
| *Location:* | *Russia* |

247

# Sergeant Infantry Division Slovak Army

**In March 1939 Hitler summoned the leaders of the Slovak populist party to Berlin and told them that unless they broke away from Czechoslovakia he would allow the Hungarians to invade their country. Thus, Slovakia was bullied by Hitler into joining the Axis cause. Nevertheless, Slovakia was still able to commit substantial numbers of troops to the attack on Russia. This commitment totalled 40,393 men, 1346 officers, 2011 vehicles and 695 lorries in July 1941. In Russia, the Slovaks suffered heavy casualties and were subsequently withdrawn from the front in 1943 to carry out security duties.**

Slovakian troops who were fighting on the Eastern Front continued to wear the khaki uniforms of the former Czechoslovak Army, but with rank badges on the collar patches instead of on the shoulder straps. The sergeant pictured here is wearing the old Czech uniform, but with the special helmet markings of the Slovak Light Division. As can be seen, he wears his rank badges on his collar patches, which also bear his arm-of-service colour. His weapon is the Czech version of the German Mauser, designated VZ (short rifle) 24.

As well as infantry units (consisting of two infantry divisions and divisional troops), the Slovak Army was able to commit a partially motorised light brigade, which included a battalion of Czech light tanks. In addition, a small Slovak air detachment fought in Russia.

| | |
|---|---|
| *Date:* | *January 1943* |
| *Unit:* | *Infantry Division* |
| *Rank:* | *Sergeant* |
| *Theatre:* | *Eastern Front* |
| *Location:* | *Russia* |

# Other Allied Countries

*It is often forgotten that thousands of servicemen from the Low Countries, the Balkans, Poland, Norway and China fought in World War II. Many carried on fighting after their homelands had been overrun by the Axis. Carrying their national flags on their uniforms in the form of patches or flashes, they fought with a determination admired by all sides.*

# *Colonel 7th Mounted Rifles Polish Army*

During World War I, the Poles had fought on both sides, so after the country was founded in November 1918 the Polish Army was formed from numerous units which returned to Poland wearing different uniforms: a mixture of Austrian, German and French designs, though there were examples of Russian and even Italian military attire. The first dress regulations were issued in 1919, but in the 1930s new regulations resulted in the uniforms worn by Polish military personnel at the beginning of World War I.

Officers wore evening dress which consisted of a 1936-Model khaki tunic and dark trousers with double lateral stripes and piping within. A special silk evening belt was also worn with this uniform. The garrison or walking-out uniform was made of khaki material and consisted of tunic and breeches or long trousers. The field uniform was very similar, but without any patches or badges, though rank insignia was retained on the shoulder straps. The summer tunic was made of a light khaki dress linen.

This commanding officer of the 7th *Wielkopolski* Mounted Rifles wears the standard officers' khaki service dress with traditional flat-topped, square-shaped *czapka*. His regiment is identified by the colour of the cap band and the pennant-shaped collar patches. On his left-breast pocket he sports the regimental badge of the 7th Mounted Rifles and above that the badge of his former regiment, the 1st Mounted Rifles. The medal is the *Virtuti Militari*, an award for gallantry.

| | |
|---|---|
| *Date:* | *September 1939* |
| *Unit:* | *7th Mounted Rifles* |
| *Rank:* | *Colonel* |
| *Theatre:* | *Eastern Front* |
| *Location:* | *Poland* |

# Tank Crewman Armoured Corps Polish Army

In the Polish Army tank crews were attired very much like their French counterparts, with double-breasted black leather jacket, black beret and a khaki-painted French motorised troop helmet. This 'tankie' wears a one-piece khaki overall under the leather jacket. The distinctive insignia of Polish armoured troops – the orange and black triangular collar patches – can be clearly seen. This insignia was also worn on the greatcoat, which was single-breasted with fall collar, six buttons in front, turn-back cuffs with tab and two buttons, and plain pointed shoulder straps.

Polish rank badges were worn on the head-dress and on the shoulder straps. General officers were identified by the zigzag embroidery on the cap band, collar patches, shoulder straps and cuffs, and by dark blue stripes on the breeches and long trousers. As shown here, arm-of-service and regimental colours appeared on the cap band and collar patches, either in the shape of lane pennants for cavalry and armoured units, or shaped like the collar points in the French manner for all other units.

On the outbreak of war the Polish Army was pathetically weak in armoured forces, having only 340 light tanks and 700 tankettes. Worse, the Polish High Command had no idea how to use even these meagre forces in a modern armoured campaign. The result was annihilation, with only 53 Renault R-35 light tanks managing to escape to Romania.

| | |
|---|---|
| *Date:* | *September 1939* |
| *Unit:* | *Armoured Corps* |
| *Rank:* | *Tank crewman* |
| *Theatre:* | *Eastern Front* |
| *Location:* | *Poland* |

# Sergeant Polish Army in Russia

**In September 1939, Russia invaded eastern Poland and imprisoned thousands of Poles in labour and prisoner-of-war camps, as part of a secret agreement with the Germans. Nevertheless, when the German attack on the Soviet Union began in June 1941, the Russians allowed the formation of a fighting force, composed of those same imprisoned Poles, within the USSR's borders.**

At first these soldiers wore the clothing they had worn in the prison camps: tattered old Polish uniforms or just plain civilian clothing. However, by agreement with the exiled Polish Government in London and the Russian authorities, the British subsequently supplied large quantities of British Army clothing to the Poles. This attire was worn with Red Army equipment, hence the rather curious-looking NCO illustrated here.

This figure is, in fact, a Polish cavalryman who is in the process of being transferred to the Middle East. He wears a British steel helmet which sports the Polish eagle, battle dress top, leather equipment, cavalry breeches, puttees and boots and a Russian Tokarev 7.62mm M1940 rifle. He carries his NCO rank – a chevron – on his shoulder straps.

In April 1943 the Polish Government in exile and the Soviet Union severed relations, and so Russia began recruiting Polish units which would fight with the Red Army and would serve its own interests. As a result, these units wore Red Army uniforms and carried Russian weapons and equipment.

| | |
|---|---|
| *Date:* | *November 1941* |
| *Unit:* | *Polish Army in Russia* |
| *Rank:* | *Sergeant* |
| *Theatre:* | *Eastern Front* |
| *Location:* | *southern Russia* |

# Private
# II Polish Corps
# Polish Army

**Those Poles who were released by Stalin to fight for the British first made their way from Russia to Iraq, where they were formed into II Polish Corps (this unit also included a small number of Poles who were in the Middle East at the beginning of the war). The corps moved to Italy in late 1943, a force of 50,000 men which was attached to the 8th Army. It took part in the actions around Monte Cassino in May 1944, and fought in Italy right up to the end of the war.**

Polish troops in Italy generally wore British uniforms. Their national uniforms, if they had any at all, were reserved for wear on special occasions. This private is wearing uniform which was originally developed for British mountain troops engaged on missions such as the raid on the German Heavy Water plant at Telemark in Norway.

During the campaign in Italy this dress was usually issued for winter wear. Over the light snowsuit can be seen special commando equipment made of canvas, which was designed to be jettisoned quickly in water. His armament includes two No 36 grenades and a .303 Lee-Enfield rifle.

Though the Poles were issued with British uniforms, rations, equipment and weapons, wherever possible they wore their national insignia, for example the national eagle on their head-dress. Though their armies had been beaten by the Germans, it was a matter of intense national pride to the Poles that they remind the enemy they were not defeated.

| | |
|---|---|
| *Date:* | *October 1944* |
| *Unit:* | *II Polish Corps* |
| *Rank:* | *Private* |
| *Theatre:* | *Mediterranean* |
| *Location:* | *Italy* |

# Captain Bomber Brigade Polish Air Force

**Up until 1936 Polish Air Force personnel wore army uniforms with yellow patches and cap bands, with white metal or cloth wings on the upper left sleeve of the tunic and greatcoat. In 1936, though, a new 'steel blue' or grey uniform was introduced.**

This captain is wearing the 1936-pattern service dress with rank badges on the front of the cap and on the shoulder straps. On his peaked cap he sports the air force version of the Polish eagle, while on his left breast he wears the Pilot Observer (combat) badge, which was issued in 1928 for aviators with dual qualifications.

Generals wore silver-embroidered Polish eagles on the ends of the collar on both sides, with silver-embroidered zigzags around both cuffs, and black *lampassen* on trousers and breeches. Staff officers had the Polish eagle in white metal on the collar, and reserve officers had the letters 'SPR' within a wreath.

Polish Air Force greatcoats were grey and double-breasted with two rows of three white metal buttons, matching shoulder straps, turn-back cuffs and half-belt fastened at the back with two buttons. There was also a black leather double-breasted coat with black cloth collar and shoulder straps.

Other ranks in the air force wore a grey tunic which was single-breasted with stand-and-fall collar, matching shoulder straps, seven white metal buttons in front, breast and side patch pockets with straight flap and button, and straight cuffs fastened at the back with one button.

| | |
|---|---|
| *Date:* | *September 1939* |
| *Unit:* | *bomber brigade* |
| *Rank:* | *Captain* |
| *Theatre:* | *Eastern Front* |
| *Location:* | *Poland* |

# Lieutenant
# Fighter Squadron
# Polish Air Force

**This is the Polish flying uniform worn by crews of enclosed aircraft during summer months. It is a one-piece suit made of undyed linen. The scarf around this lieutenant's neck is his own, it provided protection against chaffing from the rough overall cloth. His headwear is the standard leather flying helmet and goggles.**

Rank insignia for junior officers comprised one to three five-pointed stars on the shoulder straps, on the front of the cap and on the left front of the beret. On the upper left sleeve of the flying suit, as can be seen here, was worn a circular black cloth badge edged with silver braid, with one to three five-pointed silver stars in the centre. On the peaked cap was a row of silver braid.

Polish flying personnel also wore a white or gilt metal diving eagle suspended from a small chain above the left breast pocket. The various categories in the Polish Air Force wore a distinguishing letter in white or gilt metal in the centre of the wreath held in the eagle's beak. Squadron badges were worn on the left breast pocket, or painted on the front of the life-jacket.

At the beginning of the war the Polish Air Force comprised a total of 433 aircraft, which were divided between 59 fighters, 154 bombers, 84 observation aircraft and 36 liaison machines. However, when war came the air force was completely overwhelmed by the quality and quantity of the Luftwaffe. In addition, the attack caught many units unawares and their aircraft were destroyed before they had even taken off.

| | |
|---|---|
| *Date:* | *September 1939* |
| *Unit:* | *fighter squadron* |
| *Rank:* | *Lieutenant* |
| *Theatre:* | *Eastern Front* |
| *Location:* | *Poland* |

# *Captain*
# *No 302 Squadron*
# *Polish Air Force*

**From December 1939 Polish military personnel began to serve with the British Royal Air Force Volunteer Reserve, and in August 1940 an independent Polish Air Force was established in England. It was originally intended that all foreign personnel serving in the RAF would belong to the Volunteer Reserve and wear British uniforms with national shoulder flashes.**

The establishment of the Polish Air Force, though, meant that the Poles wore their own cap badges, their Polish Air Force rank in the form of collar patches, while their acting RAF rank was worn in the standard British manner. To conform to RAF practice, all Polish Air Force badges were changed from silver to gold, though the other ranks' cap eagle remained in white metal. Officers' cap badges, originally embroidered in silver, were manufactured with silver eagle and gold-feathered wings and shield. The 'Poland' shoulder flash, seen here on this captain, was embroidered in gold for officers or light blue for other ranks on a grey or dark blue background.

This Polish Air Force captain holds a rank equivalent to RAF flight lieutenant, and wears RAF officers' service dress, upon which he wears the badge for No 302 Squadron, the ribbon for the *Virtuti Militari* award and above that the Polish pilot's badge. He wears the new-style Polish Air Force cap badge on the front of his peaked cap, and the non-regulation brown scarf around his neck, which was traditionally worn by members of No 302 Squadron.

| | |
|---|---|
| *Date:* | *June 1940* |
| *Unit:* | *No 302 Squadron* |
| *Rank:* | *Captain* |
| *Theatre:* | *northwest Europe* |
| *Location:* | *England* |

# *Able Seaman*
# *Marynarka Wojenna*
# *Polish Navy*

**Ratings and officers wore uniforms similar to those worn in other navies. The standard naval greatcoat was double-breasted with two rows of four gilt buttons. In warm weather officers and petty officers wore a white cap cover, single-breasted white tunic with stand collar, four buttons, matching long white trousers and white canvas shoes.**

This rating is wearing the traditional naval 'square rig'. In the summer or in the tropics ratings wore a white uniform, and during the war they also wore British naval tropical dress. Polish working dress included a white American-pattern hat, and white denim jumper and trousers. Petty officers wore a blue single-breasted tunic with stand collar, patch pockets and five buttons in front.

Rank in the Polish Navy was indicated by lace on the cuffs and shoulder straps for officers, warrant officers and petty officers, and on the upper sleeve for other ratings. Officers also wore gold braid on the peaked cap according to rank group, with five-pointed stars on the chin strap indicating exact rank. Ratings' rank was indicated by one or two diagonal gold lace stripes edged in red on the upper left sleeve, as shown on this figure, while petty officers had three diagonal gold lace stripes edged in red on the upper left sleeve.

Trade and speciality badges were worn on the upper left sleeve in yellow for petty officers and red for seamen. This rating sports the badge of a radio technician.

| | |
|---|---|
| *Date:* | *September 1939* |
| *Unit:* | Marynarka Wojenna |
| *Rank:* | *Able Seaman* |
| *Theatre:* | *Eastern Front* |
| *Location:* | *Poland* |

# *Colonel*
# *1st Infantry Regiment*
# *Belgian Army*

**At the beginning of World War II the uniforms of the Belgian Army presented a curious contrast. On the one hand, the soldiers wore dress which was almost identical to the French uniform, while the officers wore English-style service dress.**

The Belgian khaki tunic was single-breasted with stand-and-fall collar, five gilt metal buttons in front and plain pointed shoulder straps, to which the unit number was fixed. Breast-patch pockets had pleats, flaps and buttons, while the side pockets had flap and button only. As can be seen here, the officer's tunic had long skirts and large patch pockets, and was worn with white or light khaki shirt and khaki tie. Unmounted personnel wore matching pantaloons with black ankle boots and front-lacing gaiters, while cyclists and mounted personnel had high leggings. Officers wore either beige cord breeches and brown riding boots or long khaki trousers and brown shoes.

This colonel of the 1st Infantry Regiment is wearing standard service dress, which is very similar to that worn by British officers during this period. The Belgian greatcoat was double-breasted with fall collar and two rows of five buttons in front and side pockets with flap and button.

Belgian head-dress included a khaki peaked cap with matching peak, as here, which sported a crown in the wearer's arm-of-service colour (and the red collar patches with blue piping). Officers had gold chin cords, warrant officers silver, and other ranks a brown leather chin strap.

| | |
|---|---|
| *Date:* | *April 1940* |
| *Unit:* | *1st Infantry Regiment* |
| *Rank:* | *Colonel* |
| *Theatre:* | *northwest Europe* |
| *Location:* | *Belgium* |

# Sergeant Infantry Division Belgian Army

**Belgian rank distinctions appeared on the peaked cap, side cap, the collar patches and shoulder straps. Other ranks wore their rank badges on the cuffs. The rank of the NCO shown here can be identified by the diagonal bar on his sleeve.**

His steel helmet is the French model, with a stamped Belgian lion's head on the front, or a regimental number and a crown in paint. Rifle troops wore a bright green beret with a boar's head cap badge and a black leather coat, similar in cut to the tunic, or a short single-breasted version of the greatcoat. They also used high leather leggings. Belgian motorised troops had a special leather-covered helmet with the lion's head in front, and a short brown leather coat. Tank troops wore the French mechanised troops' helmet and a short black leather coat.

This sergeant wears infantry arm-of-service colours on his collar patches, while the infantry is also indicated by the crown on his shoulder straps. On his left sleeve he wears his regimental number, though this was often removed for security reasons. On his left breast he wears a spray of flowers to commemorate Labour Day, 1 May 1940. His weapon is the excellent 7.65mm Mauser M1889, a bolt-action weapon which was a copy of the German model.

The Belgian Army faced the full fury of the German *Blitzkrieg*, and was defeated by the panzer columns. Within two weeks the Belgian armed forces had been shattered, and on 28 May 1940 the last units surrendered, the total cost being 23,350 killed and wounded.

| | |
|---|---|
| **Date:** | *1 May 1940* |
| **Unit:** | *infantry division* |
| **Rank:** | *Sergeant* |
| **Theatre:** | *northwest Europe* |
| **Location:** | *Belgium* |

# Major 1st Regiment Belgian Air Force

**An English-style grey uniform was introduced for flying personnel in 1929, as shown here on this major of the Belgian Air Force. Ground personnel wore the same khaki uniforms as members of the army, though they wore distinctive collar patches: sky blue with scarlet piping.**

As can be seen here, the grey uniform included long trousers and riding boots, and all officers had a black cap band with the Aviator's badge at the front, sided in the case of generals by a vertical gold bar on each side. Senior officers had gold piping at the top of the cap band, and all wore the tricoloured Belgian cockade on the front of the peaked cap. A similar but larger winged badge was worn on the left sleeve, and during the war on the left breast above the ribbons. This badge, embroidered in gold for officers and in silver for other ranks on a dark blue or black background, depicted the Royal Cypher of the reigning monarch, sided by wings. NCOs and other ranks of the ground personnel wore a special badge – a propeller on a disc – on the left side of the forage cap and on both shoulder straps, in the latter's case above the regimental number.

Belgian personnel who were serving with the British Royal Air Force wore RAF uniform with the 'Belgium' shoulder flash in light blue on a dark blue or grey background.

The Belgian Air Force was in a sorry state when the Germans attacked in 1940; only 180 of the 234 aircraft were operational – and most of these were obsolete.

| | |
|---|---|
| *Date:* | *May 1940* |
| *Unit:* | *1st Regiment* |
| *Rank:* | *Major* |
| *Theatre:* | *northwest Europe* |
| *Location:* | *Belgium* |

# Colonel Chinese Nationalist Army

**Chinese Army uniforms underwent several changes between 1937 and 1945, though both the Nationalist and Communist armies were to suffer severe shortages of clothing and equipment, so that uniformity was never achieved and great regional differences were to remain throughout the war.**

After World War I, the Chinese Army had adopted a German-style grey-green uniform, but during the war with Japan two distinct colours were worn in the field. In the summer, different shades of khaki cotton were worn, while in the winter uniforms were made of a bright blue cotton. As shown here on this figure, the single-breasted tunic had a stand-and-fall collar and five buttons in front. Breast and side patch pockets had both flap and button, while long or short trousers were worn with tightly bound puttees, which were worn right up to the knee, with canvas or leather boots or sandals.

The colonel pictured here is wearing a khaki peaked cap of the Nationalist Army, while his collar patches sport the red arm-of-service colour of the infantry and the three triangles denote his rank of colonel. In general, rank was indicated on the collar in the form of detachable patches made of cloth, plastic or metal.

This officer's footwear of brown leather ankle boots and knee-length leggings, notwithstanding that stated above, is European in origin, reflecting the German influence over the Chinese Army in the 1920s and early 1930s.

| | |
|---|---|
| **Date:** | *June 1942* |
| **Unit:** | *Chinese Nationalist Army* |
| **Rank:** | *Colonel* |
| **Theatre:** | *Pacific* |
| **Location:** | *China* |

261

# 1st Lieutenant Chinese Nationalist Air Force

**The Chinese Nationalist Air Force only became an independent arm of the services in the mid-1930s, and even then it had to rely heavily on the United States for the supply of aircraft, equipment and for training. Chinese air force personnel wore army uniforms, that is, khaki, though with a different headdress.**

The 1st lieutenant illustrated here is wearing the khaki peaked cap, which had a light khaki band, a black leather peak and a chin strap. The cap badge consisted of gold-embroidered wings with the enamel 'white sun and blue sky' badge in the centre. There was also a khaki side cap with brass winged propeller or the 'white sun and blue sky' on the left front.

In the summer months officers wore a white cap cover and white cotton version of the khaki service dress. For everyday wear in hot weather officers had light khaki shirt and shorts. Other ranks wore army uniforms, while ground crew sported various types of overalls. Flying uniform was mostly American, though the Chinese did make use of the kits from captured Japanese.

Rank badges were worn on the cuffs until 1940, when they were moved to the shoulder. At first badges were embroidered, but due to manufacturing problems they began to be made in metal and even plastic. As a junior officer, this 1st Lieutenant wears a gilt metal winged bird above two metal stripes on the cuffs (these would later be transferred to the shoulder straps).

| | |
|---|---|
| *Date:* | *September 1939* |
| *Unit:* | *Chinese Nationalist Air Force* |
| *Rank:* | *1st Lieutenant* |
| *Theatre:* | *Pacific* |
| *Location:* | *China* |

# Pilot American Volunteer Group

In the 1930s the Chinese Air Force was composed largely of foreign volunteers from America and Italy. Most of the air force's aircraft were destroyed by the Japanese in 1937, and so the Chinese issued an appeal for more foreign assistance. At first a force of British, American and Dutch pilots came forward to help, but this unit had been destroyed by 1938. The Russians took over, but their assistance was not enough to cover the vastness of China.

In early 1939, following the Japanese air raids on Chungking, the Chinese issued fresh appeals for assistance. The American Volunteer Group answered the call. In June 1941 the Group consisted of 100 pilots and 150 mechanics, and in July it was given 269 fighters and 66 bombers. Once it had arrived in China, though, the Group soon began to suffer from a lack of spare parts and from the inefficiency of Chinese ground crews. As a result, when the China-America Task Force was formed following America's entry into the war, only a handful of Group pilots actually enlisted.

The pilot illustrated here is wearing a mixture of Chinese and American kit. The zip-fronted flying jacket is American, though with a Nationalist emblem on the breast. The inset patch shown here was sewn on to the back of the jacket and it instructed any Chinese person to safeguard the pilot after a crash or parachute landing. In his holster this pilot carries an American Model 1911 pistol.

| | |
|---|---|
| *Date:* | *June 1941* |
| *Unit:* | *American Volunteer Group* |
| *Rank:* | *Pilot* |
| *Theatre:* | *Pacific* |
| *Location:* | *China* |

# Guerrilla Chinese Communist Forces

**Communist guerrillas under the leadership of Mao Tse-tung were Japan's main opponents in northern China. In fact, Mao's forces were ragtag and woefully lacking in equipment. However, the organisation and cohesion was very strong, with Communist Party members 'planted' at even the lowest levels to ensure total loyalty to the cause. The basic squad of 10 to 16 men, for example, was composed of three small teams, and each team leader was often a party member. In April 1945 Mao claimed he had 910,000 regular troops, together with around 2.5 million operational guerrillas.**

Chinese communist troops wore the same khaki uniforms as the Nationalists, and even sported the 'white sun and blue sky' emblem when the two groups were united against the Japanese. Once the civil war broke out again, however, the communists began to replace the army field cap with the round peaked cloth cap or the so-called 'Mao cap', on the front of which was sometimes worn a five-pointed red star.

This guerrilla wears a primitive *bandolier* made from cotton or canvas, in which he stores his small-arms ammunition for his Chinese-made rifle. Over the shoulder of his blue jacket he carries two stick-type grenades. This guerrilla does not wear the red five-pointed star on the front of his cap, illustrating the level of diversity regarding uniforms found within the Chinese communist forces.

| | |
|---|---|
| *Date:* | *April 1944* |
| *Unit:* | *Chinese Communist Forces* |
| *Rank:* | *Guerrilla* |
| *Theatre:* | *Pacific* |
| *Location:* | *China* |

# Senior Sergeant Artillery Arm Yugoslav Army

**The uniform of the Yugoslav Army closely followed the Serbian pattern, which was originally fashioned from a mixture of Austro-Hungarian and Imperial Russian designs. By the outbreak of war in 1939 the army displayed a distinct lack of standardisation, with at least three different models of steel helmet in use and different-coloured uniforms. Officers, for example, wore field-grey, whereas other ranks wore World War I Serbian light grey dress or a khaki brown.**

The standard Yugoslav Army tunic was single-breasted with a stand collar, fly front, matching shoulder straps with square ends, slanting breast and side slash pockets with Austrian-pattern flaps, and turn-back cuffs. As can be seen from this figure, the tunic was worn with matching pantaloons, puttees and ankle boots. The greatcoat was double-breasted with fall collar and two rows of six buttons converging towards the waist, turn-back cuffs and side pockets with straight flaps.

The senior sergeant illustrated here is a member of the artillery arm, as indicated by the black arm-of-service colour on his shoulder straps and collar. He does not wear Russian-style shoulder straps worn by the officer corps, but he does wear an officers' belt, a habit copied from the French. NCOs also had the metal cypher of King Peter over the national cockade on the cap front (at the end of March 1941 a group of officers had overthrown the Regent Prince Paul and declared Crown Prince Peter as the new king).

| | |
|---|---|
| *Date:* | *March 1941* |
| *Unit:* | *artillery arm* |
| *Rank:* | *Senior Sergeant* |
| *Theatre:* | *Balkans* |
| *Location:* | *Yugoslavia* |

# *Private Infantry Division Yugoslav Army*

**The soldier illustrated here is wearing the World War I vintage Serbian uniform, which was in the process of being replaced by the new single-breasted tunic. He has a distinctly French look about him, aided by the fact that his helmet is the French Adrian model with the Yugoslav coat of arms on the front. His weapon is the Yugoslav 7.9mm M1924 rifle (which was the Czech ZB made under licence in Yugoslavia).**

This uniform was not particularly comfortable or practical. A more useful dress was worn by Yugoslav mountain troops, which included a loosely cut tunic and long baggy trousers gathered at the ankle. Crews of armoured fighting vehicles wore the French helmet for motorised troops and a brown leather double-breasted jacket.

In general in the Yugoslav Army, arm-of-service was indicted by the colour of the collar, piping, and stripe and underlay of the shoulder straps, as well as by the badge on the shoulder straps, greatcoat collar patches, and trouser piping for officers. Other ranks sported coloured collar patches on the tunic and greatcoat, while NCOs wore coloured shoulder straps or shoulder strap piping. The private pictured here wears a dark red arm-of-service colour, which indicated his status of infantryman. Infantry did not wear badges on their collar patches or shoulder straps, although mountain infantry wore a triangular badge which depicted a mountain landscape framed by skis and ski poles.

| | |
|---|---|
| *Date:* | *April 1941* |
| *Unit:* | *infantry division* |
| *Rank:* | *Private* |
| *Theatre:* | *Balkans* |
| *Location:* | *Yugoslavia* |

# Captain
# Infantry Regiment
# Yugoslav Army

This officer is wearing the standard service dress of the Royal Yugoslav Army. In general, officers' uniform was superior in quality to that worn by other ranks. The rank badges took the form of Imperial Russian shoulder boards, while on the front of the side cap was worn an oval enamel cockade in the national colours, over the top of which was superimposed the gilt metal cypher of King Peter I. Officers also wore a stiff *kepi* with black leather peak and chin strap and an oval cockade in white, blue and red with the royal cypher in gilt metal in the centre.

The turn-back cuffs on the officers' uniform were piped in the wearer's arm-of-service colour, and the stand collar and matching breeches also carried this colour. The shoulder boards of the captain illustrated here not only indicate his arm of service – in this case the infantry – but also his rank and regimental number.

A Yugoslav infantry division consisted of a headquarters, two to four infantry regiments, one to two artillery regiments or an independent artillery battalion and technical troops. Each infantry regiment had around 2400 men, supported by 168 machine guns and 4 infantry guns.

The Yugoslav Army was not only rather antiquated, it was also strung out along a rather lengthy border. When the German invasion came on 6 April 1941, it was cut to pieces and all resistance ended 11 days later.

| | |
|---|---|
| *Date:* | *April 1941* |
| *Unit:* | *infantry regiment* |
| *Rank:* | *Captain* |
| *Theatre:* | *Balkans* |
| *Location:* | *Yugoslavia* |

# Partisan Yugoslav People's Liberation Army

At first the mainly Serb partisans under the command of Tito made little impression on the German occupiers. But by May 1944 Tito's so-called 'Liberation Army' had grown to 500,000 men, supplied from the pre-war Yugoslav Army and Allied air drops. By the beginning of January 1945 Tito had cleared Yugoslavia of most Axis troops and collaborators, though his forces carried out their own programme of repression and brutality immediately after the war.

Tito's partisans wore whatever they could get their hands on, and were not above taking equipment and clothing from their German or Italian occupiers. Until November 1942, an improvised system of rank badges prevailed, the badges consisting of stars, bars and chevrons cut from red cloth, which were worn on the upper left sleeve. In May 1943 the definitive rank system was introduced, consisting of white badges for other ranks and yellow for officers.

By the latter stages of the war, and with British assistance, Tito's partisans had become well-equipped. The soldier pictured here is wearing a mixture of clothing, including German shirt, Yugoslav Army cap, British khaki drill trousers and British anklets and ammunition boots. Tied to his belt is a British battle dress top, while slung over his shoulder is a German MG 43 machine gun with lots of ammunition. The grenades are British. Note the red five-pointed star on the front of his cap, which was a standard communist designation.

| | |
|---|---|
| *Date:* | *1945* |
| *Unit:* | *Yugoslav People's Liberation Army* |
| *Rank:* | *Partisan* |
| *Theatre:* | *Balkans* |
| *Location:* | *Yugoslavia* |

268

# Captain
# Fighter Flight
# Yugoslav Air Force

Like many European air forces, the Royal Yugoslav Air Force had a grey-blue uniform, which was introduced in 1938. The uniform consisted of a peaked cap, side cap and open tunic with patch pockets which was either worn with long matching trousers and black shoes, or matching breeches and black high boots. Summer wear consisted of a cap with a white cover and a white version of the service dress tunic.

The air force greatcoat was double-breasted with two rows of four gilt metal buttons, slanting side pockets with flap, and turn-back cuffs piped in black. Other ranks wore essentially the same uniform as officers, though of a type made from coarser cloth with white metal buttons (sergeants had yellow buttons). Officers of the Anti-Aircraft Artillery Corps wore air force uniform but with black cloth tunic collar, and just above the black piped turn-back cuffs they wore gold-embroidered crossed cannon barrels ensigned by a winged bird.

The captain shown here wears the standard officers' service dress, with rank badges worn on the shoulder and cuffs: three narrow gold lace stripes on the cuffs, and gold lace shoulder straps on a dark blue base with one dark blue stripe down the centre and three four-pointed silver stars. Note the eagle just above the cuff stripes, which indicate that he is flying personnel, and the qualified pilot's badge on the right breast. The decoration is the Yugoslav Order of the White Eagle.

| | |
|---|---|
| *Date:* | *April 1941* |
| *Unit:* | *fighter flight* |
| *Rank:* | *Captain* |
| *Theatre:* | *Balkans* |
| *Location:* | *Yugoslavia* |

# *General Minister of Defence Czechoslovak Army*

**The Czech Army introduced a khaki uniform in 1920. The tunic was single-breasted with stand-and-fall collar and fly front with concealed buttons. The patch pockets had a flap with concealed button, and the shoulder straps were made of the same material as the tunic.**

This is General Sergej Ingr, Czech Minister of Defence-in-Exile in England. A Czech Army camp in England was first established at Cholmondeley Castle near Chester, where the units were organised into battalions of motorised infantry. Following further training the units were moved to new bases, from where they gave assistance to bombed cities.

The Czech Army was assisted by the French, and thus the Czechs came to England wearing French uniforms. These uniforms continued to be worn until they could be replaced by British versions.

Here, General Ingr is wearing a French tunic with a Czech peaked cap which sports a Czech embroidered peak. His rank of general is indicated by the shoulder straps and lime leaf emblem on the collar patches. The three cuff stars indicate that he is a divisional commander.

For a short period in Britain the Czechs wore British battle dress uniforms with French helmets. On the British uniforms the Czechs retained their cap badges and rank insignia on the shoulder straps, while wearing a 'Czechoslovakia' title on the upper left sleeve. Officers wore their Officer's Academy graduation badge on their right breasts, as here.

| | |
|---|---|
| *Date:* | *November 1940* |
| *Unit:* | *Ministry of Defence* |
| *Rank:* | *General* |
| *Theatre:* | *northwest Europe* |
| *Location:* | *England* |

# Lance-Sergeant 1st Infantry Regiment Czechoslovak Army

Following the Munich Agreement in 1938, numbers of Czech military personnel started to leave their homeland. A small number went to Poland – 1000 soldiers and 150 airmen who formed the nucleus of a Czech Army – but after Poland was conquered by the Germans the Czechs were forced to leave. Following this, some Czechs went to the Soviet Union, while others went to France.

When the Czechs arrived in France, the French at first insisted that they serve in the French Foreign Legion. However, following France's entry into the war this obligation was cancelled. Instead, the Czechs were formed into the 1st Czech Division, composed of the 1st and 2nd Infantry Regiments.

Naturally enough, the equipment and weapons with which the 1st Czech Division was supplied were French, however they turned out to be obsolete. Both regiments fought during the Battle of France, trying to halt the advance of the 16th Panzer Division. However, they had their flanks turned and were forced to fight a lengthy rearguard action.

Czechs serving in France wore French Army uniforms with Czech rank badges on their shoulder straps. As in Britain, Graduates of the Officer's Academy wore their graduation badges on their right breast pockets. This sergeant of the 1st Infantry Regiment is wearing the new pattern French tunic and pantaloons. On his head he wears the distinctive French steel helmet, while in his holster he carries a French 8mm M1892 revolver.

| | |
|---|---|
| *Date:* | *May 1940* |
| *Unit:* | *1st Infantry Regiment* |
| *Rank:* | *Lance-Sergeant* |
| *Theatre:* | *northwest Europe* |
| *Location:* | *France* |

# Staff Captain Czechoslovak Air Force

**After Germany had annexed Czechoslovakia, Czech air personnel made their way to France, where they served as part of the French Air Force. The Czechs therefore wore French uniform, though with Czech cap badges, badges of rank, and pilot's and observer's badges.**

On his peaked cap this officer wears a gold metal cap badge depicting the Czech lion superimposed on a square diamond-shaped base, with or without crossed swords for combatants and non-combatant personnel respectively. The cap had gold twisted chin strap cords, while generals wore additional gold embroidery on the visor.

On the shoulder straps of this French Louise-blue uniform this Czech staff captain wears his rank insignia. Badges of rank were also placed on the shoulder straps of other ranks, but generals had special embroidered straps and wore their rank stars on the sleeves, above the cuffs.

There were four senior and four junior officers in the air force. The former were identified by a gold-embroidered stripe all around the loose sides of their shoulder straps and wore from one to four gold-embroidered five-pointed stars, as here. Junior officers had plain straps with piping and from one to four three-pointed stars.

This officer wears the Czech pilots' badge on his left breast pocket and the French aircraft pilots' badge with aviation wings above it on his right breast. The medal ribbon is for the *Croix de Guerre*.

| | |
|---|---|
| **Date:** | *May 1940* |
| **Unit:** | *Czechoslovak Air Force* |
| **Rank:** | *Staff Captain* |
| **Theatre:** | *northwest Europe* |
| **Location:** | *France* |

# Private
# Jutland Division
# Danish Army

Germany invaded Denmark in 1940 on the pretext that by doing so she was preventing Britain from attacking her! Hitler wanted the takeover to be as 'peaceful' as possible, so casualties were minimal: 12 airmen, 11 soldiers and 3 frontier guards were killed. The Danes were allowed to retain a certain amount of autonomy, though their armed forces were reduced to 3300 men. These consisted of the Royal Life Guards, trained conscripts and conscripts required for repair and maintenance work.

Even if the Danes had wanted to put up resistance it was doubtful if they could have, for their armed forces were in a poor overall state. For example, a khaki field uniform was introduced in 1923, but for economic reasons it was still in store in 1940, and so when the German invasion came the rank and file were still wearing obsolete black greatcoats and light grey trousers. Officers and NCOs, who normally provided their own uniforms, were in a better position and wore khaki.

This private is wearing the 1915-pattern wool uniform, which was totally obsolete by 1940. Note the trousers turned over the boots – a characteristic feature of Danish uniform. On his back this soldier carries a haversack, below which is a 1926-pattern gas mask. Also on his belt is an entrenching tool with a knife bayonet attached. His head-dress is the Danish-pattern M1923 steel helmet, while his weapon is a Danish M1889 8mm rifle, the ammunition for which is carried in pouches on his belt.

| | |
|---|---|
| **Date:** | *January 1940* |
| **Unit:** | *Jutland Division* |
| **Rank:** | *Private* |
| **Theatre:** | *Baltic* |
| **Location:** | *Denmark* |

# Warrant Officer 7th Infantry Regiment Danish Army

**The Danish Army Model 1923 uniform consisted of a single-breasted tunic with stand-and-fall collar and six brass buttons in front. The pleated breast patch pockets had a flap and button, while the side patch pockets were plain. Generals were also entitled to wear an open tunic with shirt and tie, while soldiers wore long matching trousers, which were rolled up over the calf-length brown leather lace-up boots.**

This soldier wears the aged 1864 black greatcoat, which was double-breasted with two rows of six buttons in front, stand-and-fall collar and turn-back cuffs. His headwear is the distinctive Danish steel helmet, while tucked into his Sam Browne belt he carries a khaki field cap, which carries the national cockade on the front. Other headgear included the peaked cap, which was made of khaki cloth with brown leather peak and chin strap (generals had gold braid). On the front was the army emblem surmounted by a red and white national cockade.

Rank was indicated by the number, width and colour of the lace and braid on the side cap, and the shoulder straps. Corporals wore yellow lace chevrons on the sleeves. When it came to identifying arm-of-service, certain categories of commissioned ranks wore gilt metal badges on the tunic collar, while other ranks wore an enamelled badge above the right breast pocket. The rank of this soldier can be identified by the two gold rosettes on his brown silk shoulder straps.

| | |
|---|---|
| *Date:* | *February 1940* |
| *Unit:* | *7th Infantry Regiment* |
| *Rank:* | *Warrant Officer* |
| *Theatre:* | *Baltic* |
| *Location:* | *Denmark* |

# 1st Lieutenant Reconnaissance Unit Danish Air Force

**The Danish Air Force came into being in the 1920s as part of the Danish Army, and because of this its air force personnel also wore army uniforms. The officer pictured here wears the M1923-pattern khaki uniform with closed-collar tunic, though an open-collar tunic was also worn.**

Gold-embroidered wings for pilots and observers were worn on the right breast, while flying clothing and equipment of British manufacture was used by both the Danish Army and by Denmark's naval air services. On the peaked cap, as shown here, officers wore the national cockade and below that the officers' badge. This officer's rank is denoted by the gold star on the collar and the two five-pointed stars (of a 1st lieutenant) on the grey silk shoulder straps. His boots are tucked into the standard-pattern highly polished boots.

Following the German invasion of Denmark, a number of air force personnel managed to escape to England, where they served in the Royal Air Force or in Norwegian units operating from England. They were identified by the 'Denmark' shoulder flash, embroidered in light blue on grey-blue for officers and light blue on dark blue, or black, for airmen, though this insignia was not officially introduced until 1944.

Another group of Danish airmen escaped to Sweden, where they formed an air force group as part of the Danish Brigade and wore Swedish flying equipment and clothing.

| | |
|---|---|
| *Date:* | *January 1940* |
| *Unit:* | *Reconnaissance Unit* |
| *Rank:* | *1st Lieutenant* |
| *Theatre:* | *Baltic* |
| *Location:* | *Denmark* |

# Private Evzones *Greek Army*

**This private is a member of the *Evzones*, the crack infantry of the Greek Army. Originally formed as light infantry during the Greek War of Independence at the beginning of the nineteenth century, the *Evzones* were highlanders who became part of the regular army in 1833. In 1940 they served in light regiments and in the Royal Guard.**

The uniform worn by the *Evzones* was very distinctive, and consisted of a white-sleeved shirt, waistcoat, pleated kilt (*Fustenella*) and a red-tasselled cap. They wore shoes with woollen pompons as shown here. In wartime, of course, their dress was somewhat more practical.

The *Evzones* illustrated here is wearing the Greek steel helmet over his side cap and a coarse compressed goat-fleece cape over his service dress. Instead of the typical pantaloons and puttees this private wears tight pantaloons, stockings and footwear, which were military versions of the native dress of the Greek mountain inhabitants.

A standard Greek infantry division consisted of three infantry regiments (each regiment had around 58 officers and 1100 men), a regiment of divisional artillery and support units. The mountain divisions played an important part in the military inventory given the geography of Greece. They were organised along similar lines as the infantry divisions, though with rather less artillery. A mountain division had around 12,000 men.

| | |
|---|---|
| **Date:** | *February 1940* |
| **Unit:** | Evzones |
| **Rank:** | *Private* |
| **Theatre:** | *Balkans* |
| **Location:** | *Greece* |

# Lieutenant-Colonel
# II Corps
# Greek Army

The Greek Army adopted an olive-green khaki uniform in 1912, which, by the outbreak of World War II, incorporated many British features, especially the officers' uniform, as shown here. Indeed, the service dress worn by this officer is almost identical to the British model, with metal rank badges on the shoulder straps (field officers wore a silver crown and one to three six-pointed gilt metal stars on the shoulder straps, and three rows of narrow and one of medium drab lace on the *kepi*).

His tunic is single-breasted with a stand-and-fall collar and five buttons in front. The pleated breast and plain side pockets have buttoning flaps, and the shoulder straps are made of the same cloth as the tunic and bear the cypher of his infantry regiment or unit number. The standard greatcoat was single-breasted with five buttons in front and a large fall collar and side pockets with flaps, while the officers' version was double-breasted with six buttons in front, fall collar and turn-back cuffs.

An alternative officers' tunic had a closed collar, but this was in the process of being phased out by the time the war started. Soldiers wore matching pantaloons with puttees and ankle boots, while officers wore breeches and riding boots, or leather leggings. Arm-of-service colours appeared on the pointed collar patches thus: red for infantry, black for artillery, green for cavalry, crimson for engineers and crimson velvet for medical personnel.

| | |
|---|---|
| *Date:* | *March 1940* |
| *Unit:* | *II Corps* |
| *Rank:* | *Lieutenant-Colonel* |
| *Theatre:* | *Balkans* |
| *Location:* | *Greece* |

# *Lieutenant Artillery Regiment Greek Army*

In the Greek Army officers wore either the *kepi* or khaki peaked cap with matching peak (embroidered in gold for generals), and all ranks were issued with a side cap. On the front of the *kepi*, peaked cap or side cap, as can be seen here, was the black, light blue and white circular Greek cockade surmounted by a silver crown. In combat, all ranks wore a steel helmet, and the British-model steel helmet was in the process of being replaced by the new Greek model.

The *kepi* worn by this particular officer is the pre-war model with rank distinction lace. His other rank insignia is worn on the shoulder straps, while his arm-of-service colour indicates that he is a member of the artillery. Because he is a mounted officer, this lieutenant wears riding breeches and boots, along with a Sam Browne belt. He also carries binoculars and a map case over his shoulder.

The Greek Army was deficient in weapons and motor transport, but nevertheless it repulsed the Italian invaders in October 1940 – to the surprise of the whole world. The Greeks also put up a spirited performance against the Germans in April 1941, but the *Wehrmacht* was the best in the world and Greece's British and Commonwealth allies were quickly in full retreat. Soon after, the Greek forces in eastern Macedonia were forced to capitulate, and on 20 April the Greek *Epirus* Army surrendered. Two days later the Allies were forced to begin their evacuation of Greece.

| | |
|---|---|
| **Date:** | *October 1940* |
| **Unit:** | *artillery regiment* |
| **Rank:** | *Lieutenant* |
| **Theatre:** | *Balkans* |
| **Location:** | *Greece* |

# Wing Commander Fighter Squadron Greek Air Force

**Greek Air Force officers wore an open single-breasted grey tunic with four gilt metal buttons in front, pleated patch-breast and patch side pockets with three-pointed flap and button. The tunic was worn with a white or grey shirt and black tie, matching long trousers, and black leather shoes.**

The peaked cap was grey with a black mohair band, black leather peak and chin strap, and embroidered eagle. On active service Greek Air Force officers preferred to wear breeches and high boots (in hot weather they wore a khaki drill uniform). The air force side cap and greatcoat were, like the rest of the Greek uniform, modelled on the British Royal Air Force pattern.

Other ranks wore a grey-blue version of the khaki uniform with side cap, single-breasted tunic, pantaloons, puttees and ankle boots. NCOs and warrant officers sported rank insignia which consisted of differing numbers of yellow lace chevrons. Junior officers wore differing numbers of blue lace rings, while senior officers also wore the rings with one row of gold-embroidered oak leaves on the cap peak. Note the diamond-shaped 'curl' on the upper row of this wing commander's cuff rings. In addition, he wears embroidered wings on his left breast above his medal ribbons.

The Greek Air Force was extremely small, with just 250 officers and 3000 men, though many of the pilots had been trained in England and fought well against the Axis.

| Date: | March 1941 |
|---|---|
| Unit: | fighter squadron |
| Rank: | Wing Commander |
| Theatre: | Balkans |
| Location: | Greece |

# Able Seaman
# Aegean
# Greek Navy

**The uniform of the Greek Navy closely resembled that of the Royal Navy. Officers wore the peaked cap with or without white cover and a gold-embroidered cap badge on the front. The blue 'reefer' jacket had rank distinction lace on the cuffs and was worn with long trousers and black leather shoes. Summer wear for officers comprised a white tunic with stand collar, with white trousers and standard-issue white canvas shoes.**

Ratings wore the dress that is illustrated here, while the tropical version comprised a white uniform. This able seaman's leggings are the same pattern as that of those worn in the Royal Navy, though the waistbelt and leather ammunition pouches are Greek Army issue.

This rating carries his rank distinction on the sleeve: one red chevron. Petty officers wore one narrow, one wide, one narrow and one wide, and two wide gold lace chevrons on the upper sleeves. Officers wore rank distinction lace on the cuffs and on the shoulder straps of the greatcoat and white tunic. As in the Royal Navy, officers served either in the line, reserve or volunteer reserve and wore the same distinctive pattern of lace rings and curls as their British counterparts.

In the Greek Navy the various branches or corps wore different colours between the lace on the cuffs and shoulder straps, while trade and specialist badges were worn on the sleeves. This able seaman wears the torpedo speciality badge below his chevron.

| | |
|---|---|
| *Date:* | *April 1941* |
| *Unit:* | *Greek Navy* |
| *Rank:* | *Able Seaman* |
| *Theatre:* | *Mediterranean* |
| *Location:* | *Greece* |

# Lieutenant-Colonel Cyclist Regiment Dutch Army

**In 1912 the Dutch Army began receiving a new grey-green field uniform. This officer wears the new uniform with the side cap which was introduced in 1937 to replace the *kepi*. Badges of rank are worn on the collar – two stars and a bar for the lieutenant-colonel pictured here – while his arm-of-service is indicated by the blue (infantry) piping and the bicycle wheel on the collar.**

This officer's tunic is single-breasted with stand collar and round cuffs piped in his arm-of-service colour, plus seven bronze buttons down the front. The tunic that had been worn prior to the war sported two slash breast pockets with pointed flaps and buttons, which were set low on the chest. The later tunic was a looser pattern with pleated patch-breast and side pockets with pointed flaps and small buttons. The shoulder straps are made of matching cloth and are finished in a roll to stop equipment from slipping off the shoulders.

Dismounted personnel wore matching pantaloons, puttees and black ankle boots, while mounted other ranks and officers had breeches reinforced with black leather, and black riding boots. As can be seen here, the outside seam of the breeches for officers was piped in the wearer's arm-of-service colour, with the exception of cavalry, horse artillery and police troops.

On their head-dress army personnel wore an oval orange cockade joined to a small button by a white or yellow (officers gold or silver) braid loop.

| | |
|---|---|
| *Date:* | *April 1940* |
| *Unit:* | *cyclist regiment* |
| *Rank:* | *Lieutenant-Colonel* |
| *Theatre:* | *northwest Europe* |
| *Location:* | *Holland* |

# 2nd Lieutenant Fighter Squadron Dutch Air Force

**The Dutch Air Force was part of the Dutch Army and so its members wore army uniform with light blue piping. Officers wore gold-embroidered rotary engine and propeller badges on both sides of the collar, while other ranks wore the same badge in bronze metal. Pilots wore gilt metal wings above the left-breast pocket of the tunic, and in the same position on the greatcoat.**

The junior officer shown here – a 2nd lieutenant – is wearing a privately purchased uniform made out of whipcord, in contrast to the coarse and darker cloth of the standard-issue uniform. His head-dress consists of the grey-green *kepi*, which had become obsolete by 1940. The colour of the piping and the badge on the collar identify him as an airman, while the metal 'wings' on his left breast indicate that he is a qualified pilot.

Fighter pilots wore a leather flying helmet and a three-quarter length double-breasted leather coat, which was of French manufacture, with rank badges on the collar.

In June 1940 a unit of the Dutch Naval Air Service became No 320 (Dutch) Squadron RAF. Its members wore RAF uniforms with the Dutch lion in gilt metal for officers and bronze metal for other ranks on the left front of the side cap, with a *Nederland* shoulder flash on the sleeves.

In 1940 the Dutch Air Force had 139 operational aircraft, some obsolete. Nearly all of them were mostly all destroyed on the ground.

| | |
|---|---|
| *Date:* | *May 1940* |
| *Unit:* | *fighter squadron* |
| *Rank:* | *2nd Lieutenant* |
| *Theatre:* | *northwest Europe* |
| *Location:* | *Holland* |

# *Leading Seaman Dutch Navy Rotterdam*

**This leading seaman wears the standard naval 'square rig', along with a cap tally bearing the legend 'Royal Navy' in Gothic lettering. He carries infantry equipment and a 6.5mm M1895 rifle.**

Officers wore the standard 'reefer' jacket and matching trousers. They did not have a greatcoat as such, but instead wore a double-breasted frock coat with *passants* and two rows of six buttons, and rank distinction lace on the cuffs. Ratings were issued with a double-breasted pea-coat, which was worn with the blue jean collar outside.

In the summer officers wore a white cap cover, white jumper with blue jean collar, white trousers and black leather shoes. The white jumper was worn outside the white trousers, but the blue jumper was worn inside, along with a black leather waistbelt with a brass buckle.

Tropical wear for ratings included either a white sun helmet or a straw panama hat with cap tally, a short-sleeved shirt with blue jean edging around the neck opening and sleeves, a white belt with brass buckle, white shorts and socks and black leather shoes.

Officers and warrant personnel wore rank distinction lace on the cuffs and on the shoulder straps of the white tunic. Ratings wore cuff rank badges, while senior petty officers wore their rank badges on the cuffs of the blue uniform.

The Dutch Navy played a limited role in the war, especially once defeat became certain.

| | |
|---|---|
| **Date:** | *May 1940* |
| **Unit:** | *Dutch Navy* |
| **Rank:** | *Leading Seaman* |
| **Theatre:** | *northwest Europe* |
| **Location:** | *Holland* |

# Lieutenant Infantry Division Norwegian Army

**The lieutenant shown here is wearing the grey-green service uniform which was introduced in 1912. The tunic is single-breasted with stand-and-fall collar, fly front, breast and side pockets with flaps, round cuffs and no shoulder straps.**

The Norwegians also had a winter tunic which was of a looser fit to enable thick underclothing to be worn. The patch pockets were sewn on the outside. The summer version of the tunic was made of light-weight cotton drill with side pockets only. In addition, the Norwegian Army was also issued with a cotton duck anorak.

Trousers were made of the same material as the tunic, and were usually worn tucked into thick woollen socks and ankle boots. Head-dress was a stiff grey-green *kepi* with black leather peak and chin strap. On the front was a circular cockade in the national colours – white, blue and red – which was joined by a black and silver (black and gold for generals) loop to a red-enamelled button charged with a gilt metal rampant lion. The other ranks' button was white metal. However, the most common head-dress was a soft field cap with matching peak and ear flaps, which fastened at the side of the cap with a small button, and a cloth cockade.

Rank was indicated by the number of rows and the colour of the lace or braid on the *kepi*, the lace and the number of stars on the tunic collar and greatcoat shoulder straps, and also by the lace on the cuffs of NCOs.

| | |
|---|---|
| **Date:** | *April 1940* |
| **Unit:** | *infantry division* |
| **Rank:** | *Lieutenant* |
| **Theatre:** | *Arctic* |
| **Location:** | *Norway* |

# Lieutenant No 331 Squadron Norwegian Air Force

**The Norwegian Air Force was part of the army, and so its members wore army uniforms with light green piping. In the spring of 1940 plans were put in motion for the reorganisation of the army and naval air services, but the Germans invaded and Norway's plans came to nothing.**

Many Norwegians escaped to Britain after Norway fell to Germany, where they served in the RAF. In 1941, the Norwegian Air Force became a separate arm from the RAF, with its own grey uniform, but with its rank badges based on the British pattern. The officer illustrated here wears the new grey uniform introduced for the combined Royal Norwegian Air Force. Note the nationality title on his upper left sleeve (the Norwegian flag was worn on the upper right sleeve).

As a junior officer the lieutenant here wears two five-pointed white metals stars on the ends of his collar (on the greatcoat the stars were worn on the shoulder straps). Senior officers wore silver lace on the front and bottom edge of the tunic and battle dress blouse, along with one to three five-pointed white metal or silver-embroidered stars. The greatcoat shoulder straps were edged with silver lace and had one to three stars, as did the junior officers' version. Silver chin cords were also worn on the peaked cap. Generals wore wide lace on the front and bottom edges of the tunic and battle dress blouse collar, and one to three five-pointed white metal or silver-embroidered stars.

| | |
|---|---|
| **Date:** | *September 1941* |
| **Unit:** | *No 331 Squadron* |
| **Rank:** | *Lieutenant* |
| **Theatre:** | *northwest Europe* |
| **Location:** | *England* |

# Seaman Armoured Cruiser Norwegian Navy

**The uniform in service in the Norwegian Navy in World War II was based on dress regulations issued in October 1907. Officers and petty officers wore a standard 'reefer' jacket with matching trousers, together with double-breasted greatcoat, blue peaked cap with black leather peak and chin strap, and gold-embroidered cap badge for petty officers, officers and flag officers.**

Ratings wore a white shirt with neck opening edged in mid-blue jean, blue jumper with blue jean collar edged with three white stripes, and a black scarf. Trousers were made of matching material. In summer they wore a white version of the blue uniform, and in winter they sported a blue pea-coat with the blue jean collar on the outside. Ratings' hats were blue with a blue pompom on top, and black ribbon with 'Royal Norwegian Navy' in Norwegian, in yellow or gold lettering. Above the ribbon on the front was a circular metal cockade in the national colours of red, white and blue.

Rank insignia was indicated by the pattern of cap badge for admirals, officers, chief petty officers, quartermasters, cadets and petty officers. Ratings wore a crowned red foul anchor, or crowned red foul anchor above one or two diagonal red lace stripes on the upper left sleeve. Officers in certain branches could be identified by the shape of the 'curl' on the rank distinction lace, or the absence of a 'curl', and the colour of the 'lights' between the rank distinction lace.

| | |
|---|---|
| **Date:** | *April 1940* |
| **Unit:** | *Norwegian Navy* |
| **Rank:** | *Lieutenant* |
| **Theatre:** | *Baltic* |
| **Location:** | *Norway* |

# Index

# Index